Uncle John's
PRESENTS

THE
ULTIMATE
CHALLENGE
Trivia
Quiz

Uncle John's PRESENTS

THE ULTIMATE CHALLENGE
Trivia Quiz

The Bathroom Reader's Institute
Ashland, Oregon, and San Diego, California

**Uncle John's Presents
The Ultimate Challenge Trivia Quiz**

"Bathroom Reader," "Portable Press," and
"Bathroom Readers' Institute" are registered trademarks
of Baker & Taylor, Inc. All rights reserved.

For information, write The Bathroom Readers' Institute
10350 Barnes Canyon Road, Suite 100, San Diego, CA 92121
e-mail: unclejohn@btol.com

ISBN 13: 978-1-59223-826-2
ISBN 10: 1-59223-826-2

Library of Congress Cataloging-in-Publication Data

Uncle John presents the ultimate challenge trivia quiz.
p. cm.
ISBN 978-1-59223-826-2 (pbk.)
1. Questions and answers. I. Title: Ultimate challenge trivia quiz.
AG195.U53 2007
031.02--dc22

2007031906

First printing: October 2007
Second printing: April 2008

08 09 10 11   10 9 8 7 6 5 4 3 2

CONTENTS

The WC

Americana

Sports

ix

The Arts

Science

Pop Culture

"If we wonder often, the gift of knowledge will come."

—**Arapaho proverb**

THANK YOU!

*The Bathroom Readers' Institute sincerely thanks the
following people whose writing, editing, advice,
and assistance made this book possible.*

Gordon Javna

Stephanie Spadaccini

JoAnn Padgett

Dan Mansfield

Melinda Allman

Brian Boone

Amy Miller

Jay Newman

Julia Papps

Thom Little

Jennifer Payne

Katie Jones

Jahnna Beecham

Sydney Stanley

Lorraine Bodger

Michelle Sedgwick

Megan Boone

David Calder

Myles Callum

Cynthia Francisco

Malcolm Hillgartner

Richard Willis

Maggie McLaughlin

Monica Maestas

Lea Markson

Lisa Meyers

Marc Tyler Nobleman

Karen Malchow

Brendan Quigley

Rachel McCall

Mike Spaur

Judy Plapinger

Susan Steiner

Michael Feldman

Bonnie Vandewater

Merv Griffin

Angela Kern

Art Fleming

Michael Brunsfeld

Jack Barry

"There is much pleasure to be gained from useless knowledge."

—Bertrand Russell

INTRODUCTION

So you want to be a trivia champion? You're in good company. Uncle John has been a trivia collector since he was a little kid, and he loves to share his collection with . . . well, everyone he meets. (He doesn't call it trivia, though; he calls it "important information that not everyone knows" . . . or "uncommon knowledge," for short.)

Uncle John is also a sucker for nostalgia, so many of the answers and questions on these pages are designed to make you smile. We've included nostalgic movies (*Butch Cassidy and the Sundance Kid*), songs ("Yesterday"), TV shows (*Friends*), and pastimes (baseball, hide-and-seek). Sometimes, the answer will get stuck on the tip of your tongue: Who was that masked man? And other times, it will fly out of your mouth: Batman! But no matter the question or answer, you'll be able to test yourself, your family, and your friends to see who in your group is the ultimate trivia champion.

Get Ready to Play!

The rules of this book are simple: There are no rules. You can quiz your friends, your family, or even your teacher (don't forget to let them quiz you, too). You can even quiz yourself. The only rule (OK, so there is one rule) is just to have fun. To wet your whistle, here are a few teasers:

- Of locusts, earthquakes, or darkness, which is not one of the 10 plagues in the book of Exodus?
- Within 10 miles per hour, what is the speed of the average male golfer's driving swing?
- What Muppet's signature phrase was "Wocka, wocka, wocka"?
- Name one of the three Native American tribes that fought Custer's troops at the Battle of the Little Bighorn.
- Of Quito, Arequipa, or Montevideo, which is not a capital of a South American city?

Now, if you want to know the answers, you better start reading!

As always, go with the flow . . .

—Uncle John and the BRI Staff

WHERE'S THE REMOTE?

*Some of Uncle John's favorite TV shows are set
in these U.S. cities.*

1. *The Drew Carey Show* is set in Drew Carey's Ohio hometown. Name that city.

2. Both *Happy Days* and the spin-off *Laverne & Shirley* are set in the Midwest's "Brew City." Where is that?

3. There's *CSI: Miami* and *CSI: New York*, but in what sin city is the original *CSI: Crime Scene Investigation* set?

4. For 20 seasons, *Gunsmoke* told the stories of the inhabitants of what onetime Wild West town in Kansas?

5. *Homicide: Life on the Street* was a gritty look at inner-city life and crime that was executive-produced by Barry Levinson (think director of *Diner*) in what East Coast city?

6. Murphy Brown, played by Candice Bergen, is the star reporter of the fictional TV news magazine *FYI* in what real city?

7. The sitcom *Wings*, featuring future *Monk* star Tony Shalhoub, was set mostly at a small airport in what island town along the Eastern seaboard?

8. The action in the sitcom *Alice* centers on Mel's Diner, which was located in what Southwestern city?

9. *Bonanza*, the weekly saga of a family in the post–Civil War era, was set on a ranch on the outskirts of what Nevada town?

10. Hapless women's shoe salesman Al, lazy housewife Peg, and the rest of the Bundy clan from *Married . . . with Children* all live in which city?

Answers on page 319.

A QUIZ ABOUT NOTHING

Have you been watching Seinfeld *reruns—and do you hope to for the rest of your life? If so, this quiz is for you.*

1. On which NBC show did Jerry agree to wear the "puffy shirt" for an interview with Bryant Gumbel?

2. What name did George tell his fiancée Susan that he wanted to give to their first child, as a tribute to Mickey Mantle?

3. What seemingly harmless objects, bought by George, caused Susan's untimely death?

4. What is the name of the holiday invented by George's father Frank as an alternative to Christmas?

5. After being banned from the Soup Nazi's shop, who discovered his secret recipes hidden in an old armoire?

6. What was Kramer's first name?

7. What was the subject of Kramer's coffee-table book?

8. What was so unusual about the "space pen" that Jack Klompus gave to Jerry down in Florida?

9. What actor was purported to be the former owner of the used Chrysler LeBaron that George bought?

10. What was notable about the baby that the gang goes to see in the Hamptons?

11. Elaine became the president of the J. Peterman Corporation after the founder flipped out and hid away in which country?

12. Library investigator Lt. Bookman accused Jerry of failing to return which book by Norman Mailer 20 years ago?

Answers on page 319.

THE FACTORY FACTOR

Factories can provide some interesting settings for movies and television.

1. The 1980 Best Picture *Norma Rae* also brought a Best Actress award for Sally Field. What kind of factory did she work in?

2. A German businessman owns a factory and staffs it with Jews in order to protect them from the Germans in what 1993 winner of seven Oscars, including Best Picture and Best Director?

3. Johnny Depp is Willy in what 2005 movie based on a 1964 Roald Dahl book?

4. The dramatic end scenes of this 1984 sci-fi action thriller—starring Arnold Schwarzenegger, Linda Hamilton, and Michael Biehn—take place in an automated factory. What's the movie?

5. *Blue Collar* was a 1978 comedy with Zeke, Jerry, and Smokey (Richard Pryor, Harvey Keitel, and Yaphet Kotto) as workers in what kind of factory?

6. Charlie Chaplin's Little Tramp stars in *Modern Times*, a 1936 film about surviving in the industrialized world. What's his job?

7. Michael Keaton, Gedde Watanabe, and George Wendt are in the cast of this 1986 culture-shock comedy about a Japanese company that buys an American auto plant. What's the movie?

8. In the 2007 thriller *Mr. Brooks*, Kevin Costner is a pillar of the community (and serial killer on the side) who owns a factory. What do they make?

9. In the beginning of *8 Mile*, the semiautobiographical film starring Eminem, where does the main character, Jimmy, work?

10. In Charles Bronson's *Death Wish 4*, the final sequel in this series, there's a factory that doubles as a drug lab. What kind of factory is it?

Answers on page 319.

YOU CAN QUOTE ME

Can you identify these movie lines and the characters who said them?

1. "A boy's best friend is his mother." Who said it, and in what movie?

2. "Not bad for a little furball," says Han Solo about a daring Ewok exploit—in what film?

3. "I must be crazy to be in a loony bin like this." What's the film, and who's talking?

4. When Adrian asks him why he fights, a boxer says, "'Cause I can't sing or dance." What's the film?

5. "I'm sixteen years old and I don't need a governess," says Liesl in this movie.

6. "Listen, you hear it? . . . *Carpe*—hear it?—*Carpe, carpe diem*, seize the day boys, make your lives extraordinary," says John Keating (played by Robin Williams) in what film?

7. "If there's anything in the world I hate, it's leeches. Filthy little devils," says Charlie Allnut. Who plays him, and in what movie?

8. Marshal Will Kane says, "Seems like all everybody and his brother wants is to get me out of town." What's the film, and who plays Kane?

9. "There are two kinds of people in this world: those who stand up and face the music, and those who run for cover. Cover's better." Al Pacino gets that line in what movie?

10. "Preview of coming attractions," says Grace Kelly to James Stewart, as she pulls her negligee out of an overnight bag. What's the Alfred Hitchcock movie?

Answers on page 319.

POPCORN PLEASURES

Movies for foodies.

1. Sandra Oh learned how to ride a motorcycle for her part in what 2004 film about a road trip through California's wine country?

2. Ang Lee directed what 1994 film about the love lives of a Chinese chef and his three grown daughters?

3. A woman just out of prison goes to work as a waitress in Gilead, Maine, in what 1996 movie that had Ellen Burstyn and Marcia Gay Harden in the cast?

4. Charlton Heston is a cop investigating a mysterious food in what futuristic 1973 film?

5. "Leave the gun. Take the cannolis." This is a line from what 1972 Oscar winner?

6. Juliette Binoche and Johnny Depp star in what "sweet" romantic comedy set in a small French village?

7. Villagers in Denmark are treated to a loving, lavish banquet by a housemaid who turns out to be a world-class chef in what 1987 film?

8. One of the sexiest eating scenes ever was a highlight of this bawdy 1963 comedy based on a Henry Fielding novel. What was the movie?

9. Bob Hoskins plays a catering manager who studies tapes of a TV chef in this 1999 film that was called "complex, horrifying, one of the thrillers of the decade." What was the movie?

10. A Puerto Rican girl and her family come up with a bizarre plan to attract business to their Spanish restaurant in Harlem in what 2000 movie?

Answers on page 320.

ALPHABET SOUP

WTSF? That stands for "What's That Stand For"?

1. *C.P.O. Sharkey*, a 1976–78 comedy, starred insult comic Don Rickles as the title character. What does C.P.O. stand for?

2. On *Friends*, one of Chandler Bing's jobs as a data processing executive involves checking out his ANUS and WENUS. What do those stand for?

3. There were numerous references on *The West Wing* to POTUS. What's that?

4. The title character on *ALF* is named Gordon Shumway. ALF is his nickname. What does it stand for?

5. The popular series *JAG* ran for ten seasons and is still seen in syndication around the world. What does JAG stand for?

6. "Who shot J. R.?" was the big question for *Dallas* fans in 1980. What do J. R. Ewing Jr.'s initials stand for?

7. A revolting smell left in Jerry Seinfeld's car by a parking valet led George Costanza to come up with the acronym B.B.O. What does that mean?

8. Ninotchka, the Widow, Susie Spirit, and Debbie Debutante were just a few of the performers on *GLOW*. What's GLOW?

9. What does the "S" stand for in M*A*S*H?

10. Mr. T played B. A. Baracus on *The A-Team*. What does "B. A." stand for?

11. Peter Graves, Barbara Bain, Greg Morris, and company worked for the IMF. What does that stand for?

PRIMETIME PHOBIAS

What are these TV characters so afraid of?

1. On an episode of *Friends*, it was revealed that Monica was afraid of what "dressed as humans"?

2. On *Happy Days*, we learned that Richie Cunningham's sister, Joanie, was afraid of "the bogeyman." Who played Joanie?

3. Jerry Seinfeld had a germ phobia. On one episode, he couldn't bring himself to kiss his girlfriend, Jenna, after discovering that what had fallen into the toilet?

4. On *Cheers*, Sam Malone played a recovering alcoholic. He was afraid of falling off the wagon so he carried what for good luck, and to remind him to stay sober?

5. On *Frasier*, if you wanted to get psychiatrists Frasier or Niles Crane to do something he didn't want to do, you needed only to quote a certain person. Who was it?

6. On *The A-Team*, what was B. A. Baracus (played by Mr. T) afraid of?

7. On *The X-Files*, agent Dana Scully had a childhood fear of this.

8. Another character who shares Agent Scully's fear is an attorney on *Boston Legal*. Which one?

9. What cable TV character has a fear of practically everything—heights, the dark, crowds, germs, milk, cracks in sidewalks, crooked paintings, etc.?

10. Woody Boyd (Woody Harrelson) on *Cheers* had a strange fear of what sport?

Answers on page 320.

TELENOVELS

Test your knowledge about these small-screen page turners.

1. The Professor was just beginning work on his next book, *Fun with Ferns*, when the S.S. *Minnow* set sail on this show.

2. What private eye in this series lived in Robin Masters' Oahu mansion while writing *How to Be a World Class Private Investigator*?

3. A certain sitcom palomino worked on a memoir called *Love and the Single Horse, or The True Adventures of a Palomino Playboy*. What show was he on?

4. Valene Ewing was writing a novel called *Capricorn Crude* on what series?

5. A collection of puns and riddles sent by kids to a talk-show hostess known as "the Queen of Nice" was compiled into a book titled *Kids Are Punny*. What was the talk show?

6. Court bailiff Bull Shannon wrote a book called *Puff the Flesh-Eating Dragon*, described as "Mother Goose Meets the Terminator," on what series?

7. On what show does Morticia write an updated fairy tale called *Cinderella, the Teenage Delinquent*?

8. The autobiography/cookbook titled *Are You Hungry, Dear?* was written by Doris Roberts, who was starred in what sitcom?

9. The Cigarette-Smoking Man tries to write Tom Clancy-esque spy novels on what series?

10. *The Encyclopedia of Voodoo* is an ancient black-arts text used on what sitcom?

11. Speaking of occult texts, on what series could you find *The Book of Shadows*, a mystical book of secrets and spells?

Answers on page 320.

TV "CAT"ALOG

These cool cats found homes on the tube.

1. What Nickelodeon show set in "Toecheese, Illinois," featured a fat, dumb cat and a neurotic Chihuahua?

2. What's the name of the TV cartoon cat who lives with the Nutmeg family, has a feline girlfriend named Sonja, and likes to torment Spike, the neighborhood bulldog?

3. What orange cartoon cat lives with Jon Arbuckle and has a feline friend named Fluffy?

4. What's the name of the cat that inspired a hit song by Phoebe Buffay on *Friends*?

5. Gimmel, a silver Persian cat, is the corporate mascot of what pet food company?

6. Kit, a gray Siamese, is transformed into a human named Katrina on what series?

7. On *The Addams Family*, Gomez and Morticia had a pet named Kitty Cat. What kind of feline was it?

8. On *ALF*, what was the name of the family's pet cat that ALF would have liked to . . . well, have for dinner?

9. Scratchy the Cat appears on *The Krusty the Clown Show*, a show-within-a-show on what cartoon series?

10. What was the name of the Saturday-morning cartoon series that starred a lisping, wisecracking purple cat whose motto was "It never hurts to help"?

11. *Friends* again: Phoebe thinks a stray cat is the reincarnated soul of her mother. What's the cat's name?

Answers on page 321.

TV and Movies

TV OPENERS

We'll give you the opening line; you name the TV show.

1. "Once upon a time, there were three little girls who went to the police academy."

2. "In the criminal justice system, the people are represented by two separate yet equally important groups."

3. "What you are about to see is not a news broadcast."

4. "There are pretenders among us. Geniuses with the ability to become anyone they want to be."

5. "You got big dreams? You want fame? Well, fame costs. And right here is where you start paying—in sweat."

6. "In time of the ancient gods, warlords, and kings, a land in turmoil cried out for a hero."

7. "She is a protector of the jungle, a force of nature, and one with the animals."

8. "My name is Sydney Bristow. Seven years ago I was recruited by a secret branch of the CIA called SD-6."

9. "What you are about to see is real. The litigants on the screen are not actors. They are genuine citizens who, having filed their claims in a real small claims court, have been persuaded to drop their suits there and have them settled here, in this forum . . . "

10. "Gentlemen, you are about to enter the most fascinating field of medical science. The world of forensic medicine."

11. "Following in his father's footsteps as a naval aviator, Lieutenant Commander Harmon Rabb Junior suffered a crash while landing his *Tomcat* on a storm-tossed carrier at sea."

Answers on page 321.

OLD WINE IN NEW BOTTLES

Modern updates of classics in movies and literature.

1. This 1995 chick flick starred Alicia Silverstone in an updated version of Jane Austen's *Emma*. What's the movie?

2. Bill Murray is a curmudgeonly TV exec in what 1988 movie based on *A Christmas Carol*?

3. Julia Stiles is headstrong and ill-tempered in *10 Things I Hate About You*, a modern version of what Shakespearean play?

4. Ethan Hawke and Robert De Niro are in the cast of 1998's *Great Expectations*. What blonde actress plays Estella in the movie?

5. Charles Dickens's *Oliver Twist* got a facelift in a contemporary 1996 gay version called what?

6. *West Side Story* is based on what Shakespearean play?

7. Joely Richardson starred in a 1998 film called *Under Heaven* in theaters and *In the Shadows* on video. It was based on the novel *The Wings of the Dove*. Who is the author?

8. *Congo* was a modern version of an earlier story, *King Solomon's Mines*, about a search for treasure in Africa. Who wrote *Congo*?

9. *East of Eden*, John Steinbeck's story of brother against brother, is based on what two characters in the book of Genesis?

10. *King Kong, The Hunchback of Notre Dame*, and *The Phantom of the Opera* are all based on what old fable?

11. *Once Upon a Mattress*, a 1959 Broadway musical starring Carol Burnett, was a modern version of what Hans Christian Andersen fairy tale?

Answers on page 321.

CULTURE CLASH

East meets West, city folk meet country folk, and a story unfolds.

1. A big-city cop hides out in Pennsylvania Dutch country to protect a young Amish boy in what 1985 thriller?

2. Richard Chamberlain starred in what 1980 miniseries set in feudal Japan, based on a James Clavell novel?

3. Debra Winger, John Malkovich, and Campbell Scott starred in what 1990 Bernardo Bertolucci film set in North Africa?

4. Burt Reynolds, Jon Voight, Ned Beatty, and Ronny Cox are in the cast of this movie about a river-rafting trip that turns into a nightmare. What was the film?

5. The subtitle of this 1988 movie was "The Story of Dian Fossey." What was the main title?

6. An American dam engineer in Brazil spends years searching for his son, who he believes was kidnapped by a rain-forest tribe. What's the film?

7. Robin Williams is a Russian musician who decides to defect to America—while he's at a perfume counter in Bloomingdale's. What was this bittersweet 1984 comedy?

8. It won seven Academy Awards in 1963, including Best Picture and Best Director, yet this nearly four-hour film had no women in speaking roles. What was the movie?

9. Denzel Washington and Sarita Choudhury star in a story about an Indian girl from Uganda who falls in love with an African American man who cleans carpets. What's the 1991 film?

10. A British woman accuses a young Indian doctor of rape during a visit to the Malabar Caverns in what 1984 David Lean film based on an E. M. Forster novel?

Answers on page 321.

HOME SWEET HOME

Real and fictional houses in movies and television.

1. After striking "black gold, Texas tea" on their Ozark homestead, this family moved to a luxurious 32-room, 14-bath mansion at 518 Crestview Drive in Beverly Hills. What was the sitcom?

2. Sue Ellen, Bobby, Pam, Miss Ellie, and Jock all lived on this sprawling homestead. What was it called, and what was the series?

3. This family, including children Bud and Kelly, and a dog named Buck, lives at 9764 Jeopardy Lane in Chicago. Whose house is it?

4. On what show do mother and daughter Lorelai and Rory live in the quirky Connecticut town of Stars Hollow?

5. Who lives at 742 Evergreen Terrace in fictional Springfield?

6. Who lived in the 50-foot-long mobile home located at 2354 Pacific Coast Highway in the Paradise Cove Trailer Colony (later given as 29 Cove Road in Malibu)?

7. This long-running 1980s series was set in a "Tuscan Valley" winery that was actually the Napa Valley, north of San Francisco. The real-life Spring Mountain Winery sat in for the fictional one.

8. The white Victorian home owned by the mysterious Mr. Roarke was actually a California registered landmark known as the Queen Anne Cottage in Arcadia, California. What was the series?

9. It's supposed to be a foreign country, but the location for this medical drama was actually Malibu Creek State Park in California. The officers' living quarters were nicknamed "the Swamp."

10. The Sugarbaker sisters operated their interior decorating firm out of their home at 1521 Sycamore Street in Atlanta, but the exterior shots were actually taken in Little Rock, Arkansas, a few blocks from the Governor's Mansion. What was the series?

TV and Movies

IT'S ALIVE!

Can you name these classic horror films?

1. Matthew Broderick and Jean Reno track this mutant lizard through the streets of Manhattan in which 1998 movie remake?

2. Set inside a space freighter, which film pits six unarmed men and one woman against a monster whose blood has an extremely low pH level?

3. What giant prehistoric bird, disturbed from its slumber by H-bomb tests, gave this 1956 movie its name?

4. John Hammond tried to build an "amusement park" on a Central American island in which 1993 movie based on a book by Michael Crichton?

5. What 1976 remake of a 1933 classic about a huge beast who goes ape on Broadway featured the screen debut of Jessica Lange?

6. Steve McQueen's first starring role was in this 1958 low-budget film about a gelatinous alien brought to Earth in a meteorite?

7. *Gunsmoke* star James Arness played an eight-foot alien terrorizing an Arctic research team in which 1951 sci-fi classic?

8. What 2000 Vin Diesel film is about a planet filled with nasty flying predators that only come out at night?

9. Which 1990 movie with Kevin Bacon and Fred Ward battling giant worms in the desert featured as many laughs as thrills and spawned a spate of sequels?

10. Ants the size of Hummers wreak havoc in a small Southwestern town in which 1954 movie?

11. A 40-foot snake swallows Jon Voight whole in which 1997 movie with Ice Cube and Owen Wilson?

Answers on page 322.

COLORFUL CHARACTERS

The correct answer contains a color.

1. What TV journalist did Candice Bergen play on CBS from 1988 to 1998?

2. Superman's alter ego, Clark Kent, worked as a reporter at the *Daily Planet*. Who was his boss?

3. Will Ferrell plays which San Diego news anchorman in a 2004 Hollywood comedy also starring Christina Applegate?

4. The only child of Rhett and Scarlett in *Gone With the Wind* is known by what alliterative nickname?

5. What is the name of the Lone Ranger's horse?

6. Brooke Shields and Christopher Atkins were shipwreck survivors in this 1980 film.

7. Appearing for the first time in 1940, which comic book superhero possessed a ring that gave him a wide variety of powers?

8. Which cartoon sailor's girlfriend has a mother named Nana, a father named Cole, a brother named Castor, and a sister named Diesel?

9. He rode a horse named Thunder, and the kid in the classic movie *A Christmas Story* longed for a BB gun named after what movie cowboy of the 1940s and 1950s?

10. This dashing hero rescued prisoners from the guillotine during the French Reign of Terror. His name comes from the small red flower he used to sign his messages. Who was he?

11. What is the first name of George "Kingfish" Stevens's wife on the early radio and TV show *Amos n' Andy*?

Answers on page 322.

B-LIST ACTORS

These actors and actresses could have starred on the A-Team!

1. What movie legend played a wife abuser, a superhero's disembodied father, a mutineer, and a soldier gone AWOL on the silver screen?

2. Who was the only major cast member in the movie *Speed* to reappear in the sequel *Speed 2: Cruise Control* three years later?

3. Warren Beatty married his costar of the 1991 film *Bugsy*. Who was she?

4. Which chain-smoking actor holds the top spot on the American Film Institute's list of best American male stars?

5. Who was rumored to have lost her role on the most popular sitcom of the 1980s after a torrid sex scene with Mickey Rourke hit the big screen?

6. This Oscar also-ran is second only to fellow Brit Peter O'Toole for most nominations for Best Actor (seven) without winning. His stage *Hamlet* in 1962 is considered one of the best of all time.

7. Which actress was best known for her role in *Goodfellas* until her appearance as Dr. Jennifer Melfi in *The Sopranos*?

8. Although he won an Academy Award for *Marty*, which actor is best known for his TV sitcom role as a bumbling PT-boat captain?

9. Which veteran character actor was unforgettable in Mel Brooks' *Young Frankenstein* but is best known today for playing Frank Barone on TV's *Everybody Loves Raymond*?

10. Which actor who appeared in blockbusters such as *A Few Good Men* and *JFK* made his 1978 screen debut as Chip Diller in *National Lampoon's Animal House*?

Answers on page 322.

THE FUGITIVES

And some runaways, too.

1. Warren Beatty and Faye Dunaway starred as a real-life bank-robbing couple in what 1967 movie?

2. Harrison Ford was Dr. Richard Kimble in what 1993 movie based on a TV series of the same name?

3. Sailor and Lula are a couple on the run from the mob in what 1990 film starring Nicolas Cage and Laura Dern?

4. Richard Dreyfuss is a former Berkeley activist-turned-private detective searching for a fellow ex-radical who's now a fugitive. What's the 1978 film?

5. What 1974 movie about a married couple on the run was the first feature film by Steven Spielberg?

6. Two women start out in a 1966 Thunderbird for a fishing trip in the mountains but soon find themselves outlaw heroines after one of them shoots a rapist. What's this 1991 road movie?

7. The Hole in the Wall Gang and "Raindrops Keep Falling on My Head" are just two of the memorable features of what 1969 Western about two irresistible outlaws?

8. A runaway heiress boards a bus and meets an out-of-work reporter in what 1934 movie that was the first to win Academy Awards in all five major categories?

9. After being relocated by the government, three aboriginal girls go on a 1,500-mile trek across the Australian Outback in what 2002 film?

10. Sheltered and bored, a princess escapes her guardians and falls in love with an American newspaperman in Rome. What's this 1953 movie that introduced Audrey Hepburn to American audiences?

Answers on page 323.

WHO ARE YOU?

Mistaken identity in pop culture.

1. What star of *Shoulder Arms* once placed third in a look-alike contest for people who supposedly looked like him.

2. In this 1979 British comedy, a baby is born in a stable a close to the one where Jesus is born and is, of course, mistaken for the Messiah.

3. The U.S. president falls into a coma while having an affair with an aide, and a look-alike is put in his place, in what 1993 comedy?

4. A simple-minded gardener is considered a mysterious sage when his utterances—derived mostly from his TV viewing—are regarded as profound wisdom. What's the movie?

5. In the 1964 movie *Good Neighbor Sam*, a married advertising man agrees to pose as a friend's husband so she can collect a multimillion-dollar inheritance. Who played Sam?

6. Mistaken for a government agent, a Madison Avenue advertising exec is pursued across America in what 1959 comic thriller by Alfred Hitchcock?

7. In season six of this popular HBO series, the main character dreams he's mistaken for a conservative, law-abiding citizen named Kevin Finnerty. What's the HBO series?

8. A funeral is held for Harry Lime, but later when the police dig up his grave, they find that Joseph Harbin has been buried in his place. In what 1949 British film noir would you find Harry Lime?

9. Mistaken for a millionaire, Jeff Bridges plays "the Dude," a stoner and slacker who loves bowling in what 1998 comedy?

10. After she witnesses a murder, a lounge singer goes into hiding as a nun in what 1992 comedy starring Whoopi Goldberg?

Answers on page 323.

DON'T MIND IF I DO

Television has produced its share of tipplers and boozers.

1. Marcia Cross's character, Bree, has a drinking problem but won't admit it—on what TV series?

2. On *Reba*, one of the characters is a recovering alcoholic, and then it turns out that Reba's character is as well. Who's the other character, whose drinking problem started in her teens?

3. White House Chief of Staff Leo McGarry on *The West Wing* is such a strong personality, you wouldn't think he had problems, but he's a recovering alcoholic and drug abuser with a failing marriage. Who played McGarry?

4. On *The Simpsons*, this belching boozer hangs out at Moe's Tavern and once drank beer that had spilled into a butt-laden ashtray. Ewww! Who is this guy, voiced by Dan Castellaneta?

5. On *The Andy Griffith Show*, Mayberry's town drunk would often lock himself up in the town jail when he wanted to sleep off a binge. Who was this character?

6. Daniel J. Travanti played a good police captain with a drinking problem on *Hill Street Blues*. What was his character's name?

7. On *Dallas*, this alcoholic was married to the devious and always-scheming J. R. Ewing. What was her name?

8. Also on *Cheers*, who played the portly accountant Norm Peterson?

9. Recovering alcoholic Murphy Brown (Candice Bergen) once stayed at what famed rehab spot?

10. Bailey Salinger on *Party of Five* is a recovering alcoholic who later gets a job in a bar—maybe not the best idea. Who played Bailey Salinger?

Answers on page 323.

"SCHWING!"

Get your padooka into the lingo quiz-schizzle.

1. "May the Good Fairy sprinkle stardust on your bippy," said Dick, on what series that gave us "You bet your bippy"?

2. "Squawkin' like a two-pound chicken layin' a three-pound egg" was an example of the hillbilly lingo you could hear on what long-running rural comedy?

3. If they're talking about butt-munches, 'nads, and "firing your squirt gun," you must be watching what MTV cartoon show?

4. In 1994, what tall talk-show host invented a new swear word, "krunk," so that the networks wouldn't know whether to censor it or not. Example: "What the krunk do you want?"

5. Way back in the 1950s, the first host of *The Tonight Show* (then a New York local show) could often be heard screaming "Schmock, schmock!" Who was this zany character?

6. "1, 2, 3, 4, 5, 6, 7, 8, Schlemeel, schlemazel, Hasenpfeffer Incorporated!" On what *Happy Days* spinoff could you hear those lyrics?

7. The American Dialect Society named "truthiness" as its 2005 Word of the Year. What political satirist is credited with popularizing the word?

8. "Party on!" "Excellent!" and "Schwing!" are three of the many catchphrases that emanated from what popular recurring sketch on *Saturday Night Live*?

9. "Patience is a virgin" is a typical malapropism of Balki Bartokomous, a character on what 1986–93 sitcom?

10. Slavic immigrants Latka Gravas and his wife Simka had their own language on *Taxi*, with words like "Plumitz" (the dance performed at the end of a marriage ceremony) and "Yak-Da-veh!" ("Kiss my ass!"). Who played Latka?

SOUNDS, SMELLS, & LOOKS LIKE TEEN SPIRIT

*Remember these movies featuring raging hormones
and lots of driving around in cars? See if you do.*

1. Amber Tamblyn played teenage Joan Girardi in what TV series?

2. Rachel McAdams plays 17-year-old Allie Hamilton in what 2004 movie version of a Nicholas Sparks novel?

3. Acting since age four, she's been in such films as *Purple People Eater*, *Patriot Games*, *American Beauty*, and *Ghost World*. Who is she?

4. Wolfman Jack played himself in this 1973 film, and there was a pretty girl credited as "Blonde in T-Bird." Name the film and the blonde?

5. What beauty starred in *My Father the Hero*, *Roswell*, *Knocked Up*, and now is a major player on *Grey's Anatomy*?

6. Matt Damon had one line in his debut film, which also starred Annabeth Gish, Lili Taylor, and Julia Roberts. What's the movie?

7. What film had early appearances by several actors who would later become stars, including Sean Penn, Eric Stoltz, Jennifer Jason Leigh, Nicolas Cage, Anthony Edwards, and Forest Whitaker?

8. At 18, Mia Sara was a teenager when she made this film, but her cast-mates—Matthew Broderick, Jennifer Grey, Alan Ruck, and Charlie Sheen—were in their twenties and playing high school students.

9. "I gave her my heart and she gave me a pen," says Lloyd Dobler (John Cusack) after his breakup with Diane Court (Ione Skye). What was the 1989 film?

10. Christian Slater made his film debut in a movie with another (un-related) Slater—Helen. She plays a 17-year-old girl who becomes a kind of outlaw-martyr and teen icon in what 1985 movie?

Answers on page 324.

WILD AND CRAZY FLICKS

Educate yourself about the films of Steve Martin.

1. Neal Page (Martin) heads home for the holidays and the trip goes horribly wrong after he meets up with Del Griffith (John Candy) in which 1987 John Hughes film?

2. What movie features Martin as "poor black child" Navin R. Johnson who made millions with his invention, the "Opt-Grab"?

3. What 1950s television sitcom character—a hedonistic but likable G.I.—did Martin bring to the big screen in 1996?

4. Martin teams up with Chevy Chase and Martin Short in this comedy about three out-of-work silent screen stars traveling to Mexico to save the day.

5. Martin plays wacky weatherman Harris K. Telemacher in what 1991 parody of the Southern California lifestyle?

6. Martin and Michael Caine play two Riviera con men out to fleece a rich American woman in what 1988 comedy?

7. What film starring Martin and Goldie Hawn is a remake of a 1970 comedy, scripted by Neil Simon and starring Jack Lemmon and Sandy Dennis?

8. Lily Tomlin's character dies and is reincarnated as the right half of her lawyer's (Martin's) body in what 1984 slapstick spoof?

9. Martin, a con man/evangelist, and Debra Winger, his partner in crime, both find love (but not with each other) in this 1992 film set in a small farm town.

10. Martin's first appearance on the big screen was in a 1978 "filmization" of what Beatles album released 11 years previously?

Answers on page 324.

"BLACK" & "WHITE" MOVIES

These colorful adjectives appear in each answer.

1. "She mates and she kills" is the tagline for what 1987 movie starring Debra Winger and Theresa Russell?

2. What 1991 family film, based on a Jack London novel, tells the story of a young Yukon gold miner and the dog he saves from its cruel owner?

3. Burt Reynolds is a moonshiner going after a bad cop who murdered his brother in this 1973 flick.

4. An Arab terrorist group plots to steal the Goodyear blimp, fill it with explosives, and set it off during the Super Bowl in what 1977 thriller?

5. In 1979, the Disney Studios tried their hands at sci-fi with this film about a huge collapsed star's immense gravitational pull.

6. What classic 1949 gangster film ends with James Cagney shouting "Made it, Ma! Top of the world!" before a burning oil tank explodes?

7. Wesley Snipes and Woody Harrelson are two basketball hustlers in this 1992 film.

8. What 2001 movie re-creates the events of October 1993, when two U.S. Army helicopters crash-landed in Mogadishu, Somalia?

9. Two FBI agents (played by Marlon and Shawn Wayans) go undercover as women to find an heiress and her kidnappers in this 2004 movie.

10. A six-year-old quarterhorse is the star of this 1994 movie, based on Anna Sewell's classic children's story.

Answers on page 324.

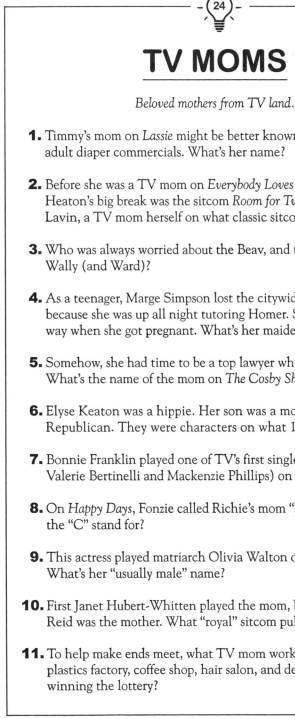

TV MOMS

Beloved mothers from TV land.

1. Timmy's mom on *Lassie* might be better known these days for her adult diaper commercials. What's her name?

2. Before she was a TV mom on *Everybody Loves Raymond*, Patricia Heaton's big break was the sitcom *Room for Two*, costarring Linda Lavin, a TV mom herself on what classic sitcom?

3. Who was always worried about the Beav, and to a lesser extent, Wally (and Ward)?

4. As a teenager, Marge Simpson lost the citywide debate tournament because she was up all night tutoring Homer. She married him anyway when she got pregnant. What's her maiden name?

5. Somehow, she had time to be a top lawyer while raising five kids. What's the name of the mom on *The Cosby Show*?

6. Elyse Keaton was a hippie. Her son was a money-obsessed Republican. They were characters on what 1980s show?

7. Bonnie Franklin played one of TV's first single moms (raising Valerie Bertinelli and Mackenzie Phillips) on what 1970s show?

8. On *Happy Days*, Fonzie called Richie's mom "Mrs. C." What does the "C" stand for?

9. This actress played matriarch Olivia Walton on *The Waltons*. What's her "usually male" name?

10. First Janet Hubert-Whitten played the mom, but then Daphne Reid was the mother. What "royal" sitcom pulled off the switch?

11. To help make ends meet, what TV mom worked variously at a plastics factory, coffee shop, hair salon, and deli before ultimately winning the lottery?

YOU LOOKIN' AT ME?

Then do the quiz about famous film lines.

1. Which movie features Ray Liotta narrating the line, "As far back as I can remember, I always wanted to be a gangster"?

2. In which classic film is Colin Clive screaming the phrase, "It's alive! It's alive!" at the top of his lungs?

3. Jeff Goldblum makes his point when he states, "If the Pirates of the Caribbean breaks down, the pirates don't eat the tourists," in which 1993 thriller?

4. R. Lee Ermey informs Vincent D'Onofrio, "You're so ugly, you could be a modern art masterpiece," in which 1987 Vietnam War movie?

5. "Joey, you like movies about gladiators?" is a query made by Peter Graves in which groundbreaking 1980 comedy?

6. Speaking of instructions, Faye Dunaway's memorable quote, "No wire hangers, ever!" appears in this 1981 docudrama.

7. Tom Hanks comes down hard on one of his players with "There's no crying in baseball!" in which 1992 film?

8. On the phone, Johnny Depp explains to a movie producer, "Worst movie you ever saw? Well, my next one will be better," in which 1994 dramatic comedy?

9. A gun-wielding Nicolas Cage calmly tells the cashier, "I'll be taking these Huggies and, uh, whatever cash you got," in this black comedy.

10. In this 1944 drama, Lauren Bacall tells Humphrey Bogart, "You know how to whistle, don't you, Steve? You just put your lips together and blow."

Answers on page 325.

TV and Movies

HOLLYWOOD SHORTS

No, not boxers . . . film titles of four characters or less.

1. Will Ferrell plays a misfit from the North Pole who travels to New York in search of his father in this 2003 holiday movie.

2. The title character discovers that it isn't easy being green in this 2003 Ang Lee film with Nick Nolte, Jennifer Connelly, and Sam Elliott.

3. Which 1991 big-budget version of a J. M. Barrie fantasy had small roles filled by big names like Gwyneth Paltrow, Jimmy Buffett, Carrie Fisher, George Lucas, Glenn Close, and David Crosby?

4. What 1988 Tom Hanks movie begins with a 13-year-old making a wish to a mechanical carnival fortune-teller?

5. Brad is Achilles, Orlando is Paris, and Diane Kruger is Helen in which 2004 epic battle flick?

6. Bad boy Xander Cage is given the choice of going to jail or working for the NSA in which 2002 testosterone-intensive action movie starring Vin Diesel?

7. What 1995 cop drama is famous for pairing two Hollywood heavyweights, Pacino and De Niro, in the same film?

8. Known as the "Father of the Summer Blockbuster Movies," which 1975 film stars "Bruce," a big mechanism nicknamed after Steven Spielberg's lawyer?

9. The Battle of Thermopylae in 480 BC, as envisioned by comic creator Frank Miller, came to the big screen in 2007 in this bloody epic film.

10. This 2000 film, which spawned two successful sequels, centers on a private school for gifted, genetically impaired individuals who may or may not be dangerous to others.

Answers on page 325.

HOMER ALONE

A Simpsons *quiz just about Homer.*

1. What is the name of Homer's favorite bar?

2. Where did Homer acquire the family dog, Santa's Little Helper?

3. What article of clothing does Homer wear to work that causes him to be committed to the New Bedlam Rest Home?

4. *Mr. Smith Goes to Washington* is rewritten into a bloody action flick by Homer and which Hollywood heavyweight?

5. What type of magic device does Homer use to create thousands of Homer clones?

6. Homer has only 24 hours to live after being poisoned by what exotic food?

7. Who comes to Springfield to buy Homer's fledgling Internet company called CompuGlobal-HyperMegaNet?

8. What radical medicine does Dr. Hibbert prescribe for Homer after he's attacked by a flock of crows?

9. Homer J. Simpson learns his middle name when he visits the commune where his mother once lived. What is his middle name?

10. On what street in Springfield is Homer's house located?

11. What is the name of the seafood restaurant Homer almost puts out of business on its all-you-can-eat night?

12. What is the first name of Homer's father?

13. What's Homer's favorite brand of beer?

Answers on page 325.

JINGLES ALL THE WAY

Classic advertising jingles and slogans that you just can't forget.

1. The spokeswoman for this margarine warned, "It's not nice to fool Mother Nature."

2. Which laundry detergent's big pitch was its ability to get rid of "ring around the collar"?

3. What gasoline brand boasted, "You can trust your car to the man who wears the star"?

4. What is the last word in the classic jingle "You'll wonder where the yellow went when you brush your teeth with" what?

5. Which beer was supposedly better than the others because it came "From the land of sky-blue waters"?

6. This pet food jingle begins, "My dog's faster than your dog. My dog's bigger than yours."

7. What beer once was said to be "the one beer to have when you're having more than one"?

8. Which coffee's jingle promotes it as "that heavenly coffee" and claims "better coffee a millionaire's money can't buy"?

9. "A little dab'll do ya" served as which product's catchphrase for decades?

10. A kid exclaims, "Look, Ma, no cavities!" in this toothpaste's long-running commercial?

11. Which gasoline brand told consumers to "put a tiger in your tank"?

12. "It takes a licking and keeps on ticking" is the boast of what product?

Answers on page 325.

MARVELOUS MUPPETS

It's time to get things started and see how much you know about the Muppets.

1. Originally, Jim Henson provided this Muppet's voice—a character he created in 1955 from the cloth of his mother's old coat.

2. On the animated *The Muppet Babies*, this former TV star of the 1950s and '60s—and one of America's favorite moms—was the voice of the babies' nanny. (Bonus: Name her old show.)

3. In *The Muppet Movie* (1979), Kermit and friends must evade and outsmart disreputable Doc Hopper, who wants Kermit as the new spokesman for his Frog Leg restaurant chain. Name the Oscar-nominated actor who played Doc.

4. Jim Henson gave two explanations for the origin of "Muppet": one, it was just a word he liked the sound of; two, it was what two words combined?

5. Legendary stars—including Johnny Cash, Lena Horne, Julie Andrews, and Gene Kelly—regularly appeared as guests on this 30-minute television program, which ran from 1976 to 1981.

6. As a high school senior, Jim Henson got his start in entertainment by performing on a local television show in what city?

7. What Muppet's signature phrase was "Wocka, wocka, wocka"?

8. These crabby critics, named after two famous New York City hotels, considered it "like a kind of torture to have to watch" *The Muppet Show*. Can you name them?

9. This English-born actor who voiced many Muppet characters also provided the voice for Yoda in the Star Wars movies.

10. This famous facility on Los Angeles's La Brea Avenue has dreamed up "creatures" for many movies, including *The Dark Crystal*, *Labyrinth*, and *Babe*. What's its name?

Answers on page 326.

WHAT'S MY LINE?

Occupations of movie and TV characters.

1. What does Melinda Gordon (Jennifer Love Hewitt) do on *Ghost Whisperer* when she's not whispering to ghosts?

2. On *Bones*, Dr. Temperance Brennan (Emily Deschanel) has a main job and a highly lucrative avocation. What are they?

3. On *Sex and the City*, what job did Carrie Bradshaw (Sarah Jessica Parker) have?

4. Before she was a crime scene investigator, Catherine Willows (Marg Helgenberger) of *CSI* supported herself through college with what kind of job?

5. Name one of three possible ways Tony Soprano (James Gandolfini) could have described his business.

6. On the last season of *I Love Lucy*, the Ricardos and the Mertzes go into business together in Connecticut. What was their line of work?

7. On this series, because of his exceptional intelligence, Jarod (Michael T. Weiss) could assume whatever identity he needed—doctor, accountant, bounty hunter, bartender, chili cook, anatomy professor. What was the series?

8. On *Doogie Howser, M.D.*, Doogie (Neil Patrick Harris) has been a doctor since he was how old?

9. Comedian Garry Shandling played a neurotic talk-show host on this HBO series that started in 1992.

10. On *The Jeff Foxworthy Show*, what was Jeff's occupation?

11. In the successful 1981–86 series *The Fall Guy*, Lee Majors played Colt Seavers, a what who moonlighted as a what?

Answers on page 326.

CULT FAVORITES

Movies and TV series considered "cult favorites."

1. "She gets kidnapped. He gets killed. But it all ends up okay." This is a the promo line for what 1987 film starring Robin Wright Penn?

2. Kyle MacLachlan and Mädchen Amick were among the cast of this 1990–91 series in which an FBI agent investigates the murder of a young girl. What was the series?

3. Some other names considered for this series were *Owl-Stretching Time, A Toad Elevating Moment,* and *A Horse, a Bucket and a Spoon.* What was the series?

4. The keyboardist's philosophy was "Have a good time, all the time," in what 1984 "rockumentary"?

5. Richard Dreyfuss, Harrison Ford, Cindy Williams, Ron Howard, and Suzanne Somers went on to even bigger careers after appearing in what 1973 film?

6. The presence of Uma Thurman, Natalie Portman, and Mira Sorvino give a hint to the title of this 1996 film. What was it?

7. Rocketed into space by a mad scientist, a janitor and his two robots are forced to watch unbearably bad movies in what series?

8. Just 17 episodes were enough to make this British series a cult favorite. (The protagonist is known only as "Number Six.")

9. Seven actors played the main character in this series that ran for 26 years. It's been described as "the adventures of an eccentric renegade time-traveling alien and his companions." What's the show?

10. Twelve-year-old Mathilda wants to learn how to be a "cleaner," like her reluctant guardian Leon, in what 1994 Luc Besson film?

Answers on page 326.

CREATURE FEATURES

Name the creepy characters in this quiz.

1. Frankenstein movies have their source in the 1818 novel *Frankenstein; or, The Modern Prometheus.* Who was the author?

2. What 1990 movie about deadly spiders starred John Goodman and Jeff Daniels?

3. One of the world's most recognized movie characters is the Japanese monster, Godzilla. What type of creature is he?

4. A small Nevada town fights subterranean worm-creatures dubbed "Graboids" in what 1990 monster comedy?

5. Bill Pullman and Bridget Fonda starred in the 1999 horror film *Lake Placid.* What was the scary creature in this feature?

6. What's the setting for Alfred Hitchcock's 1963 horror thriller *The Birds*?

7. A 1954 sci-fi/horror film, considered a classic of the '50s, features a scaly, amphibious monster called the "Gill Man." What was the movie?

8. The "Yowie" of Australian folklore is a large, unidentified hominid analogous to what creatures alleged to exist in other parts of the world?

9. Who played the part of Ann Darrow in the 2005 remake of *King Kong*?

10. Jennifer Lopez, Ice Cube, and Jon Voight starred in what 1997 creature feature?

11. Tim Burton directed a 1984 horror-movie parody with a cast that included Shelley Duvall, Daniel Stern, and 13-year-old Sofia Coppola. What was the film?

Answers on page 327.

ARE WE HAVING FUN YET?

Sitcom potpourri.

1. What *Happy Days* character had the motto " Live fast, love hard, and don't let anyone else use your comb"?

2. After an interview in which Mary Richards answered questions forthrightly, Mr. Grant told her, "You have spunk." Then, after a beat, he added, "I hate spunk!" Who played Mr. Grant?

3. Dating dos and don'ts: On what sitcom did the group decide that "We should do this again" means "You will never see me naked" and "I think we should see other people" means "Ha, ha, I already am"?

4. What character on *The Mary Tyler Moore Show* revealed his mantra as "A little song, a little dance, a little seltzer down your pants"?

5. What sitcom offered these candidates for the four worst words in the English language: "We have to talk" and "Whose bra is this?"

6. On *Perfect Strangers*, Balki was known to talk about "America—and of the free and home of the whopper" or say "Stop it! This is a man of the loincloth!" when referring to a priest. Who played Balki?

7. In 1992, the phrase "Me want cookie!" made its debut in the classic reference book *Bartlett's Familiar Quotations*. Who said it, and on what show?

8. What sitcom character's dream was to have his own personal executive washroom with a mighty Ferguson toilet "for a man's flush"?

9. Ling Woo is a successful attorney at Cash/Fish & Associates who also designs clothing, and owns a mud-wrestling club and an escort service. Who played Ling Woo and on what series?

10. This gossipy roller skating cutie was one of the best-loved characters on the 1980s *Facts of Life*.

COOL CATS

This puzzler is purr-posefully and cat-egorically all about cats.

1. Who was the early comic-strip cat whose love, Ignatz the Mouse, always pelted him with bricks?

2. What is the name of the slacker cat who hates nearly everything, including spiders, diets, Mondays, and Februaries?

3. The musical *Cats* is based on the book *Old Possum's Book of Practical Cats* by what expatriate American poet?

4. What's the name of the cat who is famous not only for his vanishing act but also his grin?

5. A meowing kitten—a parody of the MGM lion—was the symbol of whose TV production company during the 1970s and 1980s?

6. Who is the "spokescat" for Nine Lives pet food?

7. What cat is known for sputtering "Sufferin' succotash!" when he was thwarted by his pint-sized nemesis, a yellow bird?

8. The Cat in the Hat's standard uniform was a red-and-white hat, a red bow tie, and what other item of clothing?

9. Which cartoonist, whose stylized cats decorate everything from clocks to coffee mugs, got his big break in *Playboy* magazine in the 1960s?

10. Who is the much-despised feline companion of the Hogwarts school caretaker Argus Filch, in the Harry Potter series?

11. Before he was adopted by the Clintons, this First Cat started out life as a stray. What was his name?

12. A Texas feline named CopyCat, born in 2001, was famous for being the first what?

Answers on page 327.

O.K. ANIMALS

Every answer is an animal whose name begins with "O" or "K."

1. What is the only marsupial that's native to North America?

2. *San Francisco Chronicle*'s executive editor and Sharon Stone's ex made headlines when he was bitten by what animal at a zoo?

3. And you thought this marine mammal was a nice guy. If we told you that his family includes weasels and polecats, would you know who we're talking about?

4. What wild, spotted cat did Salvador Dalí keep as an exotic pet?

5. In Edgar Allen Poe's 1841 short story "The Murders in the Rue Morgue," the murderer turns out to be what kind of animal?

6. What cute, tree-hugging Australian eats nothing but eucalyptus leaves and has fingerprints that resemble human ones?

7. What mostly nocturnal birds of prey can turn their heads 135 degrees in either direction?

8. Arms are the proper name for what we (incorrectly) call tentacles for what creature?

9. Name this largest living species of bird, some of which have weighed in at nearly 350 pounds.

10. The call of what Australian bird is regularly described as sounding like human laughter?

11. Snakes are the ironic food of choice for this largest venomous land snake.

12. Sometimes called long-horned grasshoppers due to their long, slender shape, they get their name from the way their song sounds.

Answers on page 328.

ANIMALS AT LARGE

Fictional creatures bigger than their real-life counterparts.

1. It used to be assumed that he was an oversized canary, but what *Sesame Street* character claims that he's a "golden condor"?

2. What hookah-smoking insect was huge compared to Alice when she was shrunk to only three inches tall in *Alice's Adventures in Wonderland*?

3. This colossal crimson children's book character and star of his own PBS show was the runt of the litter when he first went to live with Emily Elizabeth. What is his name?

4. In the 2001 film *Donnie Darko*, the character Frank wears a costume resembling a grotesque, human-sized what?

5. In the 1949 film and 1998 remake *Mighty Joe Young*, the title animal is a large what?

6. What legendary bird of prey did Marco Polo describe as large enough to grip an elephant in its talons?

7. What large Looney Tunes rooster with a Southern accent was among the many characters voiced by Mel Blanc?

8. In the opening themes to multiple cartoon series of the 1960s and 1970s, underwater superhero Aquaman was shown riding a super-sized what?

9. In the 1954 movie *Them!*, what kind of gigantic mutant insects were the result of nuclear testing in New Mexico?

10. What's the punchline to the joke that asks, "What did the 500-pound canary say?"

11. In the 1941 film *Dumbo*, what kind of birds help teach the title elephant to fly using his especially large ears?

Answers on page 328.

Animals

DON'T GO NEAR THE WATER!

Beware these underwater creatures.

1. In Haiti, scientist Wade Davis found that the poisonous pufferfish was an ingredient in Vodou (commonly known as voodoo) powder that can allegedly transform a person into a what?

2. Chomp! The piranha is a freshwater fish found in the rivers of what continent?

3. Australia's Steve Irwin, "the Crocodile Hunter," died during the filming of a documentary titled *Ocean's Deadliest* after being stung by what sea creature?

4. What voracious predatory fish shares its name with a coupe manufactured by Plymouth from 1964 to 1974?

5. The animated feature film that was widely announced with the title *Sharkslayer* was ultimately released under what name?

6. Besides humans, what is the only other animal known to have preyed on great white sharks?

7. What American state is the only place in the world that alligators and crocodiles can be found together?

8. True or false: A sea snake's venom is more toxic than the venom of a land snake.

9. If it looks like a jellyfish and swims like a jellyfish, it might be an underwater colony of these creatures that's also know as a bluebottle.

10. Based on a real-life incident, the dramatic 1778 painting *Watson and the Shark* depicts an attack that took place in the harbor of what Caribbean city?

Answers on page 328.

Animals

GREAT APES

What's so great about the great apes?

1. Which U.S. president costarred with a chimp in the comic flick *Bedtime for Bonzo*?

2. What did Enos the chimp do in 1961 as a "dress rehearsal" for what John Glenn did less than three months later?

3. Already famous for communicating in sign language, what gorilla participated in the first interspecies online chat?

4. After studying chimpanzees for more than 40 years, who was dubbed Dame Commander of the British Empire in 2004?

5. What redhead of the ape family is named for the Malaysian words for "man of the woods"?

6. Lesser apes like gibbons travel the jungle by "brachiation." What is it?

7. What gorilla researcher was murdered in Rwanda on December 24, 1985?

8. In a famous series of children's books, who brought Curious George out of Africa and into the big city?

9. He was Tarzan's pal all through the flicks of the 1930s. In 2007, he celebrated his 75th birthday. Who is the world's oldest known chimp?

10. Who made international headlines at the Jersey Zoo when he aided a five-year-old boy who fell into the gorilla cage?

11. What movie beast prompted character Carl Denham to say, "Oh no, it wasn't the airplanes. It was beauty killed the beast?"

12. What musical trio—three gorillas dressed in overcoats and derby hats—was the brainchild of Ernie Kovacs?

Answers on page 328.

DOG DISH

Name that breed.

1. Toy, miniature, or standard—what cuddly breed, originally from France, are smart and make excellent watchdogs?

2. As its name infers, which breed of retriever originated along the Maryland coast?

3. What two breeds sired the mixed breed known as a Cockeranian?

4. They snore, they drool, and they look something like Winston Churchill, which is fitting because they're England's national dog. What are they?

5. Which breed of dog—named for the valley in Yorkshire, England, where it was first bred—is the largest member of the terrier family?

6. One of the oldest hound breeds, which dog has the keenest sense of smell of any domestic animal?

7. What breed of hunting dog, the most popular of the setters, was the subject of a 1962 Disney boy-and-his-dog flick *Big Red*?

8. Which dog breed, named after a medieval hospice in the Swiss Alps, boasts a member named Barry who saved 40 lives between 1800 and 1810?

9. Which compactly built dog, part bulldog with a screw tail, takes its name from the Massachusetts city where it was first developed?

10. What Tibetan breed, some of which are said to house the soul of the Dalai Lama, has its country's capital city in its name?

11. Which breed of fast, aerodynamic hound appears on tombs of Egyptian pharaohs and is even mentioned in the Bible?

Answers on page 329.

FOR THE BIRDS

You'll find a bird in every answer.

1. In Coleridge's *The Rime of the Ancient Mariner*, what symbol of a heavy burden does the Mariner have to wear around his neck?

2. Which wild beverage brand is sold in varieties called "Rare Breed," "Russell's Reserve," and "Kentucky Spirit"?

3. Their origins are unrelated, but what game bird bears the same name as a word, first recorded by Rudyard Kipling, that means to grumble or complain?

4. Who was given the title, "Clown Prince of the Harlem Globetrotters," and participated in more than 7,500 consecutive performances between 1954 and 1976?

5. With a history that stretches back to the 17th century, they're typically pendulum driven and strike the hours using small bellows and pipes. What are they?

6. What ballet by Igor Stravinsky is named for a bird found in the mythology of China, Egypt, Greece, Persia, and Russia?

7. Which Beatles song, originally on their *White Album*, has the refrain, "You were only waiting for this moment to arise"?

8. What brand of chocolate was first created in a small confectioner's shop on the South Side of Chicago in 1955 as an ice cream coating?

9. Astronaut Michael Collins called it "the weirdest looking contraption [he had] ever seen in the sky"—but it worked. Name the lunar module that landed on the moon on July 20, 1969.

10. Who wrote the popular four-part satiric novel about trips to such places as Brobdingnag, Glubbdubdrib, and the Country of the Houyhnhnms?

Answers on page 329.

GOOD MOUSEKEEPING

How well do you know these murine stars of page and screen?

1. What's the name of Sylvester's not-so-mousey behaving adversary in the Looney Tunes cartoons?

2. This New York–based protagonist of E. B. White's first children's story has appeared in a book, an animated TV series, and three movies. What's his name?

3. Two-time Academy Award winner Ub Iwerks was the first animator to bring Mickey Mouse to life. Who originally provided the iconic character's voice?

4. What cat-and-mouse duo were created by the animation team of Hanna-Barbera . . . and which one is the mouse?

5. What Depression-era John Steinbeck novella takes its title from a line in the famous Robert Burns poem "To a Mouse"?

6. What's the title of the 1966 Daniel Keyes Nebula-award-winning science fiction novel about a laboratory mouse in an intelligence-boosting experiment? (Hint: It later became a movie called *Charley* starring Cliff Robertson.)

7. This courageous, rapier-wielding mouse appears in three of *The Chronicles of Narnia* books.

8. He's a secret agent in a British cartoon series, wears a black eye-patch, and has a hamster sidekick. Who is he?

9. What's the name of the mouse in *The Simpsons* cartoon-within-a-cartoon?

10. Can you remember the fragrant first name of the Great Mouse Detective from the 1986 Disney film?

THIS LITTLE PIGGY

How well do you know the following swine?

1. Kermit the Frog is subjected to kisses and karate chops from this blush-colored pig.

2. In the nursery rhyme "To Market, to Market," what's the reason for going to the market?

3. In *Winnie-the-Pooh*, who lives in a "very grand house in the middle of a beech tree"?

4. A supermarket chain in Southern states has a mascot that looks a lot like Porky Pig. What's the name of the chain?

5. Speaking of Porky Pig, what's his girlfriend's name?

6. Who's the mascot of Springfield A&M in *The Simpsons*?

7. In George Orwell's *Animal Farm*, a common farm pig eventually becomes a dictator. What's the pig's name?

8. A giant boar terrorizes the outback in a 1984 Australian film. What's the name of the film?

9. What's the full name of the pig in the 1965–71 sitcom *Green Acres*?

10. In a film that won an Oscar for visual effects, what's the name of the pig who wants to be a sheep dog?

11. What's the name of the pig featured in novels and stories by P. G. Wodehouse?

12. E. B. White's bestselling story *Charlotte's Web* features a pig who's saved twice—first by a girl, then by a spider. What's the pig's name?

Answers on page 329.

IT TAKES ALL KINDS

Do you know what makes these critters not only wild, but wacky too?

1. The olive baboon always knows when his lady love is fertile because her bottom turns what color?

2. What decorative bird gives an unromantic ear-splitting scream just to let the ladies know he is there?

3. Who has a nasty habit of vomiting up dead creatures to keep his enemies away?

4. On July 5, 1996, Dolly came into the world as a cute little lamb. What made her birth so unique and amazing?

5. What bird livens up meals by eating with its head upside down?

6. Don't pick a fight with the rude Sonoran coral snake—if it thinks you're the enemy, that popping sound you hear will be what?

7. He may be small, but this Australian animal mates for up to 12 hours a day with as many females as possible.

8. What creatures have taste sensors on their feet so that they can take a taste of something just by standing on it?

9. Sloths do what for 18 hours a day (and manage to do it in trees besides)?

10. What tiny champ can jump 200 times the length of its own body—which would be equal to a 1,200-foot jump by a 6-foot man?

11. Snakes don't close their eyes to go to sleep because they don't have what?

12. This animal is plenty "gut"sy—in fact, it has a gigantic stomach that can digest 500 pounds of vegetation in a single day. What is it?

Answers on page 330.

4-LETTER BIRDS

Don't get soar—just give us the bird!

1. What slow-flying, duck-like bird sounds like it might be some crotchety old guy?

2. Is it a chess piece? A card game? Nah, it's what member of the crow family?

3. What bird is the official state bird of Minnesota, and also depicted on the Canadian one-dollar coin?

4. Birds of this sort are believed to have vision as good as 20/2, about eight times more acute than humans with good eyesight. What's the bird?

5. Daisy, Daphne, Donald, or "Aflac!" Need we say more? What's the bird?

6. Her song "All I Wanna Do" was an unexpected smash hit in 1994. She has the same last name as what jackdaw relative?

7. Charles Darwin also called it a noddy, and said it was often so tame as to seem stupid. But this graceful seabird doesn't have to pay RENT—an anagram of its name.

8. It's a Studebaker compact model or a small terrestrial bird with an extravagant song and display flight. Shelley wrote a poem to a "blithe spirit" member of this species. What's the bird?

9. What perky bird shares its name with the architect of London's St. Paul's Cathedral?

10. What long-winged raptor's name is a word often associated with Benjamin Franklin?

11. This bird is an anagram of a 1980s American New Wave group. But enough about music. What's the bird, a pigeon relative?

Answers on page 330.

Animals

OUT OF AFRICA

*Go on a safari with us and identify these
beasts of the second-largest continent.*

1. This high-strung African beast can be crossbred with a donkey or a horse to create a domestic work animal. Can you name it?

2. Surprisingly related to deer and cattle, what spotted animal found throughout the African savannas dines on leaves atop acacia trees?

3. It can run at speeds of more than 65 mph for short bursts. What spotted African cat is it?

4. Which large African animal, with a horn long believed to possess aphrodisiacal properties, has been hunted to near extinction?

5. It inhabits Africa's grassy plains and is known as a gnu. What's another name for this beast?

6. One of Africa's four big cats is featured in *Bringing Up Baby*, starring Cary Grant and Katharine Hepburn. Which one?

7. Although no exact numbers have been established, what huge African animal, capable of galloping at 18 mph, has killed the most humans?

8. The most common large carnivore in Africa, what spotted animal with a "sense of humor" is both a skillful hunter and an opportunistic predator?

9. Which African predator, the second largest big cat on earth, was once found throughout Europe and Asia but today exists in the wild only in Africa and India?

10. The African version of this animal has large ears and a flat forehead, whereas the Asian version has smaller ears and a convex forehead. What is it?

Answers on page 330.

WOOF!

Get to know man's best friend.

1. What breed of dog continues to top the most-popular list in the United States, Canada, and the United Kingdom?

2. Every February, dogs and their owners take over New York's Madison Square Garden for this event.

3. This cowardly, drooling boarhound belongs to Hagrid in the *Harry Potter* series. What's the dog's name?

4. Name the Soviet space dog that died in flight during the 1957 orbit of *Sputnik 2*.

5. Greyfriars Bobby was a scrappy terrier who guarded his master's gravesite in what Scottish city?

6. What is the best-selling dog food in the United States?

7. What world-famous Great Dane made his television debut on CBS in 1969? In the more than 35 years since, his name has appeared on 10 different TV series.

8. This song was written in 1952 by composer Bob Merrill, but Patti Page's recording made it famous.

9. Who said, "Outside of a dog, man's best friend is a book. Inside of a dog, it is very dark"?

10. Although this famous collie character of the small and big screen was a female, she was always played by male dogs.

11. How much is the average American dog's annual vet bill: $100, $200, or $300?

12. What English bull terrier made her advertising debut in 1987 in a commercial for Anheuser-Busch?

Answers on page 330.

Animals

WHERE ARE HUE?

Identify these colorful names in geography.

1. The white cliffs of Dover refer to a geologic formation in what country?

2. The green of Ireland's countryside earned it what well-known nickname?

3. Yangtze or Huang He: What do the Chinese call the 3,395-mile-long Yellow River?

4. The "Orange Coast" stretches from Seal Beach to Dana Point in what state?

5. What wooded mountain range in the far southwest of Germany has a cake named after it?

6. Of Israel, Egypt, Lebanon, and Jordan, which country does not border the Red Sea?

7. What mountain range is mentioned in John Denver's hit "Take Me Home, Country Roads"?

8. What Norse explorer is commonly cited as the first European known to settle in Greenland? (He's named for his hair color.)

9. What's the official language of Africa's Ivory Coast?

10. What bridge in the United States has been painted orange vermilion (aka International Orange) since it opened in 1937?

11. It's been home to musicians Tom Waits, Beck, Jane's Addiction, and the Red Hot Chili Peppers, among many others. In what United States city is the district called Silver Lake?

Answers on page 331.

A CAPITAL IDEA

A world capital city is part of each answer.

1. He composed more than 3,000 songs in his lifetime, among them "White Christmas," "God Bless America," and "Alexander's Ragtime Band." Who was he?

2. One of the first Americans to make it big as an author, his book *The Sea-Wolf* sold out before publication. Name him.

3. What small green vegetable not only resembles a miniature cabbage but is also a close relative?

4. Name the behavior exhibited by a kidnapped victim who, over time, becomes sympathetic to his or her captors.

5. What generic name was given to the approximately 20 female broadcasters of Japanese propaganda during World War II?

6. Hormel, Armour, and Libby's all produce what hors d'oeuvre (and we use the term loosely) made of finely chopped meats, mustard, and spices formed into two-inch servings and packed tightly into cans?

7. Who made her film debut as a baby boy in *The Godfather* and grew up to win an Academy Award for writing *Lost in Translation*?

8. What knobby little tuber, resembling a ginger root, tastes like a cross between a radish and a potato?

9. What is the name of the "old man" in Ernest Hemingway's *The Old Man and the Sea*?

10. What is the name of the roasted beef tenderloin dish that's slathered with pâté and baked in puff pastry until it browns?

Geography

HIDDEN CITIES

Find the city "hiding" in the word or phrase.

1. What capital city can you find in "Czechoslovakia"?

2. What Peruvian city occurs in "Kilimanjaro"?

3. What's the Italian city hiding in "Andromeda"?

4. What's the city in "heathens"?

5. The city in "manufacturing" is . . . ?

6. What German city can be found in "timberline"?

7. What city might you locate in "Alyssa Milano"?

8. What city is located in "automobile"?

9. Can you find an Alaskan city in "astronomer"?

10. What's the southwestern United States city in "parmesan"?

11. What's the Nicaraguan city in "paleontologist"?

12. Can you see a French city in "Annette Funicello"?

13. What Taj Mahal city can you see in "anagram"?

14. Shouldn't take you long to find a lover's city in "comparison."

15. Visiting Einstein's birth city? It's right there in "culmination."

16. "Grenoble" is a French city with what American casino city inside?

17. Can you locate the capital of Latvia in "brigade"?

ISLAND HOPPING

Get to know the islands . . . fact and fiction.

Geography

1. Denpasar is the capital of what popular tourist island in the South Pacific?

2. What French painter is noted for having lived on Tahiti?

3. What island off the coast of Africa is the fourth-largest island in the world?

4. The 1988 film *Cinema Paradiso* is set on what large Mediterranean island?

5. What island was home to Mr. Roarke and Tattoo on a 1970s and '80s television show?

6. *Rapa nui* is the Tahitian name for a Pacific island better known by what "Christian" name?

7. Burt Lancaster, Bela Lugosi, and Marlon Brando all starred in versions of a film about this island based on an H. G. Wells novel?

8. In what sea is the island of Cyprus?

9. Alaska's Kodiak Island is sometimes wrongly cited as the largest U.S. island. What is actually the United States' largest island?

10. What is the only island shared by three countries?

11. The movie *Jaws* was filmed on Martha's Vineyard, which stood in for what fictional island in the book and movie?

12. Which island is the largest: Cuba, Haiti, or Jamaica?

13. Name one of the three largest islands in the Mediterranean.

Answers on page 331.

WELL STATED

Quiz yourself on the United States in song and story.

1. Reese Witherspoon starred in a movie with the same title as what Lynyrd Skynyrd song?

2. This patriotic march by John Philip Sousa was actually created for a newspaper of the same name.

3. The Osborne Brothers popularized what bluegrass song about one of three peaks of a mountain in a Smoky Mountains state?

4. This Rodgers and Hammerstein song is also the name of a state and a hit Broadway musical.

5. What Stephen Foster song is sung annually at the Kentucky Derby, which is sometimes also called "the most exciting two minutes in sports"?

6. The Mamas and the Papas and the Beach Boys are both known for what song of the Golden State?

7. "The stars at night/ are big and bright" . . . where?

8. The title of this film, one of Elvis Presley's most popular, includes the name of a tropical paradise.

9. What Bay State song did the Bee Gees record in response to the flower power movement?

10. What 1976 song did Billy Joel write about his beloved Empire State?

11. Al Jolson introduced what song about a state that's "round on the end and high in the middle"?

12. The Big Sky state appears in what 1909 song by Tin Pan Alley composer Luella Lockwood Moore?

Answers on page 332.

Geography

WHERE AM I?

Take a shot at geography.

1. What famous mausoleum is found in Agra, India?

2. You're looking up at "the world's tallest free-standing structure on land," though technically it's not considered a building. What's the structure, and what city and country is it in?

3. You're in Kenya, Africa, on a large savanna whose name means "Endless Plains" in the Masai language. What biannual event have you come to witness?

4. It stretches from Lop Nur to a place nicknamed "Old Dragon's Head." In Pinyin, it's called Chángchéng. What's the structure?

5. You're in an archipelago whose volcanic islands include Santiago, Santa Cruz, Fernandina, Isabela, and San Cristóbal. What's the name of the archipelago?

6. You're here to see the Roman Wall that once ran across the entire width of Great Britain. What's the correct name for this stone-and-turf fortification?

7. The Jefferson National Expansion Memorial, near the start of Lewis and Clark's landmark expedition, is maintained by the National Park Service. What's the memorial's popular name?

8. You've come to see Aberdeen Harbor, ride the Star Ferry, swim at Repulse Bay, and respectfully visit the Po Lin Monastery. Where are you?

9. You're in Suva, a capital city and the largest urban area in the South Pacific outside of Australia and New Zealand. You're visiting what island nation?

10. What European limestone promontory is sometimes called the Pillar of Hercules?

BABY, IT'S COLD OUTSIDE

Hot news about the world's coldest spots.

1. With a January temperature of –94°F (–70°C), a city in this barren region recorded the world's record low temperature outside of Antarctica. What's the name of this sparsely populated region?

2. Norwegian Roald Amundsen was the first explorer to reach what cold destination?

3. Arguably the coldest city in the contiguous United States, International Falls is located along the Canadian border of what state?

4. In which state was the infamous Donner party stranded by an October snowstorm in 1846?

5. Thule Air Base, the U.S. Armed Forces' most northerly installation in the world, is located on what Danish-owned island?

6. What geographic and cultural area extends across the northern regions of Norway, Sweden, and Finland?

7. The Klondike gold rush was centered in which northern region of Canada?

8. What is the name of America's northernmost point, with recorded temperatures as low as -50°F?

9. Punta Arenas, the city closest to Antarctica, is found in which country?

10. Which northernmost Canadian territory, established in 1999, is ranked first in area among the 13 provinces and territories, but is ranked last in population?

BAY WATCH

Time to test your estuarial knowledge.

1. Into which bay do the La Quebrada cliff divers plunge from heights exceeding 145 feet?

2. What is the smallest U.S. city (in population) to have its own NFL franchise?

3. A 1961 attempt to overthrow Fidel Castro bears the same name as what Cuban body of water?

4. Where is the Bay of Fundy, which boasts the highest tides in the world?

5. St. Petersburg and Clearwater are two of the three largest cities along which bay?

6. The U.S. Naval Academy lies along the western shore of which bay?

7. What Canadian trading company, established in 1670, is the oldest commercial corporation in North America?

8. Which large bay between western France and northern coastal Spain is notorious for its monster waves?

9. The iceberg-filled Baffin Bay separates northern Canada from what other country?

10. The waterfront street Cannery Row was made famous in a 1945 John Steinbeck novel. Can you name the California bay it's on?

11. What was the site of James Cook's landing in Australia and eventually became a penal colony?

12. The Massachusetts town of Plymouth is situated along the shore of which bay?

Answers on page 332.

Geography

HOT ROCKS

Get out your climbing boots.

1. What "pillar of Hercules" lies between Morocco and Spain and is home to 250 Barbary macaques?

2. The aboriginal people of Australia have always called this rock Uluru. What name did surveyor William Gosse give it in 1873?

3. When kings and queens of England are crowned at Westminster Abbey, they always sit on King Edward's coronation chair. What is the name of the stone that is set under the throne?

4. Called "the Rock" by lifers who spent their years staring across shark-infested waters at San Francisco, this prison's name is what?

5. What monolith rising 1,267 feet above Wyoming's Belle Fourche River played a key role in 1973's *Close Encounters of the Third Kind*?

6. According to legend, kissing this Irish stone endows a person with the gift of gab.

7. In 1620, William Bradford and the pilgrims supposedly stepped off the *Mayflower* onto what rock on Massachusetts Bay?

8. Often considered the greatest find in archaeological history, what is the name of this nearly four-foot-tall stone with the same text carved into it in three ancient languages?

9. Rising 3,000 feet off the floor of Yosemite Valley, what is the name of one of the world's favorite challenges for rock climbers?

10. Pioneers on the Oregon Trail would try to reach this sandstone rock in Wyoming by the Fourth of July. What did they call it?

11. The most sacred relic in Islam, the Rukn al-Aswad (Black Stone) rests in the Kaaba in Mecca. What do many Western theologians think it is?

"G"EOGRAPHY

All answers start with a G.

1. What British territory is known colloquially as "the Rock"?

2. This Colorado city was named after the editor who coined the phrase "Go West, young man."

3. The Quetzal is the currency of what country, the most populous nation in Central America?

4. According to the Gospels, what region of what is now Israel was the home of Jesus for at least 30 years of his life? It is also the place where he cured a blind man.

5. Christopher Columbus was a native of what northern Italian city and seaport?

6. What Netherlands city (not Edam) is famous for its cheese, which usually comes with a yellow or red wax coating?

7. Situated on the river Clyde, this is Scotland's largest city.

8. What Polish city is famous worldwide as the birthplace of the Solidarity movement under the leadership of Lech Walesa?

9. The largest number of casualties in the American Civil War occurred during what battle?

10. What capital of Jalisco and second largest city in Mexico is also famous for its mariachi festival?

11. What Swiss city is the seat of the European headquarters of the United Nations?

12. What capital of Guyana has the nickname "Garden City of the Caribbean"?

Answers on page 333.

BIG,
BIGGER,
BIGGEST

Which is the biggest, deepest, highest . . . you get the point.

1. What's the largest country, in square miles—China, Russia, or Canada?

2. What's the smallest country—Liechtenstein, Monaco, or Vatican City?

3. What continent has the highest mountain—Asia or Europe?

4. What country has the largest population—Africa, Europe, or Asia?

5. What country has the most billionaires—Japan, the United States, or Germany?

6. What's the largest continent, in square miles—North America, Asia, or Africa?

7. What's the largest ocean—Atlantic, Pacific, or Indian?

8. What's the biggest lake—Victoria, Superior, or the Caspian Sea?

9. What continent has the most countries—Europe, Asia, or Africa?

10. What has the largest desert—Africa or the Middle East?

11. Which ocean contains the deepest point: the Atlantic or the Pacific?

12. Where is the lowest point on land—in the Middle East, California, or Africa?

Answers on page 333.

Geography

NEW NAME, SAME PLACE

Geographic name changes.

Geography

1. Until 1972 it was Ceylon. What is it called now?

2. In 1930, Constantinople, once the capital of the Roman Empire, was officially renamed what?

3. This island nation in the Indian Ocean, once called the Malagasy Republic, is now known as what?

4. It was the French Sudan for a long time, but since 1960, it has been called what?

5. Until 1964, stamp collectors knew this African country as German East Africa. What do they know it as now?

6. It was Czechoslovakia until 1993. Now it's divided into what?

7. The region that is now Israel, the West Bank, Gaza, plus parts of Lebanon and Syria, was called what in ancient times?

8. After 1964, the country referred to as Rhodesia became what two African countries?

9. This African nation was Bechuanaland until 1966. What is it now?

10. It used to be called Upper Volta, but in 1984, its name was changed to what?

11. In 1980, New Hebrides became known by what name?

12. Known as Siam until 1949, what is this country called now?

13. Bangladesh was known by this name until 1971.

Answers on page 334.

TITLE TOWNS

United States cities that inspired hit songs.

1. This West Coast ditty quickly became Tony Bennett's signature song.

2. In 1964, Jan and Dean sang about this woman who lives in a community about 10 miles northeast of downtown L.A.

3. What city appears in the title of the Monkees' first release?

4. This home of baseball's spring training appears in the title of Glen Campbell's first release.

5. Graham Nash wrote this song in 1970 after the Democratic presidential convention that took place in this Midwestern city.

6. Liza Minelli originally sang this song from the film of the same name, but it took ol' blue eyes to popularize and forever link it with this Eastern seaboard city.

7. "Bright lights gonna set my soul on fire" is the opening lyric of which 1964 Elvis Presley release?

8. This Elton John song was named after and dedicated to the tennis team coached by Billie Jean King.

9. Johnny Horton's only number-one hit was what country ballad about the final battle of the War of 1812?

10. "Everything's up to date" in this city, according to a song in the musical *Oklahoma!*

11. Country singer Marty Robbins' biggest-selling hit was a 1959 ballad about which Texas border town?

12. What 1974 chart topper by Paper Lace is a fictional account of a gunfight between the Al Capone mob and the cops?

Answers on page 334.

WHERE IN THE WORLD?

In every answer, you'll find either a continent or country.

1. In what country is the only remaining wonder of the original Seven Wonders of the World?

2. When completed, it will be 72 times larger in volume than the world's second-largest dam. Where is the largest dam under construction?

3. On what continent is the highest non-Asian mountain?

4. Christopher Columbus first made landfall here during his initial voyage to the New World.

5. In what archipelago did the two deadliest volcanic eruptions in history take place?

6. The highest waterfall is in what country?

7. Where did the deadliest earthquake in history occur on May 22, 1960?

8. Outside of Africa, what continent is home to the largest sandy desert?

9. The temperature on this continent once soared to a steamy 136°F.

10. In what country will you find the deepest lake? (It's filled with one-fifth of the world's nonfrozen fresh water.)

11. You'll find the world's tallest building (as of July 2007) in this Middle Eastern country.

12. If you're looking for Bollywood, the world's most prolific movie-making area, you will have to visit what country?

LIFE'S A BEACH

America loves its beach towns. How many do you know?

Geography

1. What community in Miami, Florida, lends its name to a famous and trendy diet?

2. Located on South Carolina's coast, what city is best known as home to more than 100 golf courses? (Many of them are ranked among the best in the country.)

3. The first and most important NASCAR race each year is staged in what Florida city?

4. Name the town where the MTV reality show *The Real Orange County* takes place.

5. What East Coast city served as the setting for Brian De Palma's 1983 flick *Scarface* and boasts the largest collection of Art Deco architecture in the world?

6. What real city, 15 miles from NASA's Kennedy Space Center, served as the setting for the TV sitcom *I Dream of Jeannie*?

7. Speaking of TV sitcoms, what beach does Charlie Harper's back deck overlook on the CBS comedy *Two and a Half Men*?

8. What's the fitness-minded name given to an area of Venice, California?

9. Which Coney Island community is the subject of a 1983 Broadway play written by Neil Simon?

10. The AT&T National Pro-Am golf tournament is held each year in this small community in Monterey County, California.

11. The Chesapeake Bay and Atlantic Ocean converge along the coastline of what East Coast city known for its large naval base?

Answers on page 335.

BLESSED CITIES

*All of these American cities and towns
begin with "St.," "San," or "Santa."*

1. Every March 19, the swallows return to a Spanish mission in what California town?

2. Name the only Major League Baseball team whose name is composed solely of foreign words.

3. What California town has the same name as an 800-mile geographic fault that forms the boundary between the Pacific and North American plates?

4. Established by Europeans in 1565, what is America's oldest continually occupied town?

5. What tourist town on Florida's west coast is nicknamed "the Sunshine City" and shares its name with Russia's second-largest city?

6. What classic American music composition by W. C. Handy was adopted as the name of a National Hockey League team?

7. President Nixon's "Western White House" was located in what Orange County, California, city?

8. Newspaper magnate William Randolph Hearst's 56-bedroom mansion—Hearst Castle—is located in what California coast community?

9. Of all of America's "Blessed Cities," which one has the largest population?

10. This California metropolis served as the western terminus for the Pony Express.

11. And what Missouri town served as the *eastern* terminus for the Pony Express?

Answers on page 335.

VIVE LA FRANCE!

French contributions to world culture.

1. French fries are Belgian in origin, but that's not why they're called "French"—it refers to how the potatoes are cut. What's another name for "french-cut" food?

2. This style icon introduced the little black dress, the bikini, the shoulder bag, and a popular fragrance. What's her name?

3. A screenwriter, director, producer, and actor in more than 25 films, some of his gems include *Jules & Jim*, *Day for Night*, *The Wild Child*, and *The 400 Blows*. Who is this icon of the French cinema?

4. France wanted to give the United States a gift in 1876 to mark America's centennial of independence. Ten years late, the gift became a U.S. national treasure. What is it?

5. In 1963, the Singing Nun had the only song sung in French ever to go to #1 on the American pop chart. Name the song.

6. While obviously aliens, they told everybody they were from France. What was the collective name of these *Saturday Night Live* characters?

7. Of vermouth, cognac, and Grand Marnier, which spirit is not French in origin?

8. Along with Milwaukee, Detroit, and Des Moines, which Midwestern city is one of the "cardinal" cities settled and founded by French explorers?

9. This 2001 French film starring Audrey Tautou as a woman who performs good deeds for strangers became the third highest-grossing foreign film ever in the United States. What's its title?

10. As American as apple pie, it is also found at a lot of picnics. What condiment was invented by a French duke's chef in the 1700s?

Answers on page 335.

HIT THE ROAD

*Time for a trip down the world's most
famous roads and highways.*

1. Name the infamously fast German highway that is speed-limit-free for about half of its length, yet has an "advisory" maximum speed of 130 km/h (81 mph)?

2. On which three-block stretch of pavement between Los Angeles' Santa Monica and Wilshire boulevards is one of the most exclusive shopping areas in the world?

3. Which street serves as the address of the official residence of the British prime minister?

4. It's elementary. On which street did Arthur Conan Doyle's Sherlock Holmes and Dr. John H. Watson reside?

5. Blues clubs and restaurants line which famous street in downtown Memphis, Tennessee?

6. What famous route, renamed the "Will Rogers Highway" in 1952, ran from Chicago to Los Angeles for a total of 2,448 miles?

7. Screen and stage character Sweeney Todd was called the demon barber of what London area?

8. The longest thoroughfare in Washington, D.C., is also home to Embassy Row with its 45 foreign embassies. Can you name it?

9. Chuo-Dori and Harumi-Dori avenues are two of the main roads cutting through which major Asian shopping district?

10. What is the nickname of the Alaskan Highway, a 1,390-mile stretch of road that connects Dawson Creek, British Columbia, to Delta Junction, Alaska?

Answers on page 335.

Geography

PRESERVING PARKS

*Some of the world's most famous tourist attractions are
its parks and UNESCO World Heritage Sites.*

1. Half Dome, Sentinel Rock, and the giant sequoias are attractions
in this central California national park.

2. The Trans-Canada Highway connects all ten Canadian provinces.
In Alberta, it passes through what famous national park, well
known for its glaciers and ice fields?

3. A few miles north of Florida's Everglades National Park is what
highway, made famous by the amphibious creatures that lurk in the
water beside the road?

4. In 1975, Australia created a park to protect this attraction in
northern Queensland, one of the world's most diverse and delicate
offshore ecosystems.

5. Cheetahs, elephants, lions, buffalo—they're all protected at this
Tanzania national park.

6. Vanoise National Park was established in 1963 and was France's first
national park. In what famous mountain range is the park located?

7. A horseshoe-shaped glass skywalk, located 4,000 feet aboveground,
opened in 2007 to give visitors an incredible panoramic view at
what Arizona national park?

8. Royal National Park in New South Wales, Australia, was originally
called simply, the National Park. But after a visit by this queen in
1955, it was renamed.

9. This capital Scottish city's Old and New Town sections have both
been declared UNESCO World Heritage Sites.

10. Hawaii Volcanoes National Park includes these two active volcanoes, which helped form the islands of Hawaii hundreds of thousands of years ago.

Answers on page 336.

UNREAL ESTATE

You won't find these places anywhere outside your imagination.

1. When Fred Flintstone bellows, "Wilma! I'm home!" what town is he in?

2. What little village in Scotland appears only once every 100 years, and then only for one day? Hint: Lerner and Loewe wrote a musical about it.

3. Kyle, Kenny, Stan, Cartman, and Butters call what town home?

4. Before he was shipped off to Manhattan, what was the name of King Kong's Indian Ocean habitat?

5. First described by Plato, what legendary land completely disappeared in one day?

6. What fictional town, based on the real city of Rockford, Illinois, is home to TV's Dan and Roseanne Conner?

7. In *Gulliver's Travels*, our hero wakes up to find himself taken prisoner by miniature humans less than six inches tall. What's the name of their island nation?

8. What did Sir Thomas More call his fictional island that had perfect social and political systems?

9. When he's not holed up in his Fortress of Solitude, in what big city does Superman like to hang out?

10. Another "perfect" getaway is the focus of James Hilton's novel *Lost Horizon*. Can you name this hidden Tibetan village?

11. The four main characters in the 1986 film *Stand By Me* (based on the short story "The Body" by Stephen King) live in what fictional town in Maine?

Answers on page 336.

Geography

UNCLE JOHN

Each answer contains "Uncle" or "John."

1. Walt Disney's 1946 *Song of the South,* with tales of Brer Rabbit and Tar Baby, has never been released on home video because of fear of controversy. Who is the fictional narrator?

2. This blacksmith and steel plow manufacturer is known for green and yellow tractors.

3. A personification of the United States, he can be seen on World War I and II posters saying, "I want you."

4. Born in Illinois, this actor is famous for such films as *Sixteen Candles, The Sure Thing, Say Anything, Grosse Pointe Blank,* and *High Fidelity.*

5. If you want to give up, what do you say?

6. He's a hypothetical average man, or an unknown or fictitious man who is a party to legal proceedings. What's his name?

7. Napoleon Solo and Illya Kuryakin were the heroes of what 1960s spy show inspired by James Bond movies?

8. What West Indies folk song about an old sponger boat was recorded by the Weavers, the Beach Boys, and others? It contains the line, "I wanna go home."

9. This popular rice brand owned by Mars, Inc., has an image of an elderly African American man dressed in a bow tie.

10. He was Dan Conner on *Roseanne,* and since 2007, he's been the voice of Dunkin' Donuts. Who is the actor?

11. A 1994 movie version of this Chekhov play, starring Wallace Shawn and Julianne Moore, was called *Vanya on 42nd Street.* What's the name of the original Chekhov play?

Answers on page 336.

THE SCOOP ON POOP

You'd better sit down for this one.

1. Sir John Harington not only invented the flush toilet, he had the comfort station installed in the palace of which English royal?

2. What American president designed an indoor privy?

3. "Put a chicken in your tank" was the motto of Harold Bate, a British farmer who powered his vehicles with fuel made from what renewable resource?

4. The caterpillar of this butterfly fools hungry predators because it resembles unappetizing bird droppings.

5. Can you name the waste product that the Confederates mined during the Civil War and used to make gunpowder?

6. How many years would it take the average cow to fill a pasture with seven tons of "cow patties"—one, two, or three?

7. Even though it fed on feces, which species of dung beetle was considered sacred by the ancient Egyptians?

8. Maximus, a Sri Lankan company, produces beautiful, papyrus-like paper. What stinky substance do they use to make the paper?

9. The Bedouins taught the Nazi German soldiers serving in North Africa to cure dysentery by eating what substance?

10. What bodily substance colors human waste brown?

11. If your pooch suffers from *coprophagy*, what is he doing with poop?

12. The world's most expensive coffee is made with predigested beans collected from the droppings of the palm civet. Can you name this gourmet treat?

Answers on page 336.

The WC

GO WITH THE FLOW

*All answers contain the letters F-L-O-W, in that order—
but not necessarily one after another.*

1. This famous ship transported the Pilgrims from Plymouth, England, to Plymouth Colony, Massachusetts, in 1620.

2. A nine-letter word for the pleasant feeling that lingers after something is experienced or achieved.

3. What member of the cabbage family somewhat resembles broccoli?

4. It is filled with down and nice to rest your head on. What is it?

5. This widely recognized monument is also the tallest structure in Paris.

6. If you do this, it means you're drinking again. What's the four-word phrase?

7. An expression for someone or something that's suddenly but temporarily popular.

8. What 1969 movie starring Walter Matthau, Goldie Hawn, and Ingrid Bergman is named after a desert bloom?

9. Name the American poet who wrote *Paul Revere's Ride* and *The Song of Hiawatha*.

10. What hyphenated term means mature or completely developed?

11. "Politics makes strange" what?

12. The Goo Goo Dolls, pitcher Warren Spahn, singer Ani DiFranco, *Gunsmoke*'s Amanda Blake, and the host of *Howdy Doody* all hailed from what city?

Answers on page 337.

THE STRAIGHT POOP

In homage to Uncle John, all answers contain "poo."

1. She's been June Carter, Elle Woods, and Becky Sharp. Who is she?

2. What fictional character is sometimes known as "Bear of Very Little Brain"?

3. In *Moby Dick*, Ishmael agrees to share a bed with Queequeg. What is Queequeg's occupation?

4. What Valley-girl phrase means "You are so disgusting that you make me want to vomit"?

5. What's an eight-letter synonym that means sewage pit or covered cistern?

6. What breed of dog may come in toy, miniature, or standard size?

7. "It is kisstomary to cuss the bride" is an example of what kind of play on words?

8. A wet blanket, or someone who spoils the pleasure of others, might be called a what?

9. What college publication is the world's longest-running humor magazine?

10. "To the tables down at Mory's" is the first line of "The [what] Song"?

11. What's a two-word term for an informational document?

12. Inhabitants of what city are nicknamed "Scousers" in reference to the local meal known as scouse, a form of stew?

Answers on page 337.

THE THRONE ROOM

Let's see what happens when popular entertainment goes to the bathroom.

The WC

1. According to legend, *Leave It to Beaver* was the first network TV series to show a toilet. That's not quite true, but they did show the first toilet tank in which Wally and the Beav hid what?

2. The first toilet flush heard on television occurred on January 12, 1971, when Archie Bunker pushed the plunger on the debut of *All in the Family*. Who played Archie?

3. In 1997, a legal comedy-drama was the first TV series to feature a unisex bathroom, where all members of the law firm of Cage/Fish & Associates shared the same facilities. What series was it?

4. In a 1994 episode, Captain John Sheridan and his security chief talk strategy while taking a leak in the john. What syndicated sci-fi series may have been the first to feature a men's-room urinal scene?

5. The toilet is a plot device in this film, figuring in several scenes. And any time Vincent Vega uses a bathroom, things go wrong. What's the movie?

6. In the movie *Goodfellas*, how does Henry Hill's wife Karen dispose of his stash of cocaine?

7. In the 1962 film version of *Lolita*, Charlotte shows Humbert Humbert a room for rent, stops at the bathroom, and demonstrates what?

8. What 1994 film included the movies' first on-screen toilet flush, seen in close up?

9. The sound of a toilet flushing was commonplace on what series about the Bundy family that ran for ten years?

10. What character from what sci-fi sitcom said, "There are two kinds of toilet paper in this bathroom. I, and I alone, get the fluffy kind"?

CLOSE ENCOUNTERS OF THE "TURD" KIND

Birds do it, bees do it, let's do it, let's . . .

1. What manufacturer of widely selling Japanese toilets has the same moniker as Dorothy's dog?

2. On what day of the week can you always find a turd?

3. What company claims to be the world's largest manufacturer of bathroom and kitchen fixtures?

4. Can you translate the Spanish phrase "¿Donde ésta el baño"?

5. For what windy word are the following terms synonyms: Barking spider, Bucksnorter, Cushion Creeper, Poot, and Silent Horror?

6. How many rolls of toilet paper does the average American family go through each year—19, 119, 219, or 319?

7. In 1879 what U.S. company sold the first toilet paper on a roll, although the product was so "delicate" they didn't print the company name on the packaging?

8. In 1973 what talk-show host caused a three-week toilet-paper shortage after his joke scared consumers into hoarding supplies?

9. Loo roll, striking paper, bog roll, and bumfodder are synonyms in various countries for what?

10. In 1957 Procter & Gamble bought what toilet paper company in Madison, Wisconsin?

Answers on page 337.

PORCELAIN SWAN SONGS

They went "to the bathroom" and never came out.

1. The best-known celebrity bathroom death is probably Elvis Presley. In what year did he die?

2. What author of *Brideshead Revisted* died in the bathroom?

3. Comedian Lenny Bruce died in the bathroom, but not while answering the call of nature. He was discovered dead in his bathroom, having overdosed on what?

4. What Greek hero of the Trojan War, immortalized in a play by Aeschylus that bears his name, was killed by his wife Clytemnestra in the bathroom?

5. In the 1993 movie *Jurassic Park*, what fate awaits a lawyer using the facilities?

6. King of England from April to November 1016, Edmund II was stabbed in the bowels while using the toilet. What was Edmund's ironic nickname?

7. As an unknown, who beat out thousands of other actresses to play Scarlett in *Gone With the Wind*? She met her end ingloriously, dying of tuberculosis on the bathroom floor.

8. Jean-Paul Marat was stabbed to death while sitting in his bathtub. Marat was a revolutionary who played a major part in what conflict?

9. What famous Danish astronomer helped Newton develop his theory of gravity and supposedly died from a burst bladder because he thought it was rude to excuse himself from the banquet table?

Answers on page 338.

PATRIOT GAME

How well do you know America's founding fathers?

1. On June 12, 1776, Benjamin Franklin talked this reluctant lawyer into writing the first draft of the Declaration of Independence. Who was he?

2. What man is known more for his deadly duel with Aaron Burr than for his meritorious service as America's first Secretary of the Treasury?

3. Which president lent his name to a doctrine declaring that Europe would no longer be allowed to interfere with the affairs of the Americas?

4. Who was president of the Second Continental Congress and first to sign the Declaration of Independence?

5. Name the president who was the son of the second U.S. president.

6. Who was the oldest founding father to sign the Constitution and one of only six to sign both the Constitution and the Declaration of Independence?

7. The first Clinton in the White House was George Clinton, vice president under two presidents. Can you name one?

8. The Boston Tea Party was organized by which Boston brewer and political firebrand?

9. Which former president and vice president died less than four hours after Thomas Jefferson on July 4, 1826?

10. Known as the "Father of the Constitution," who was president when the British sacked and burned the White House in 1814?

11. *Common Sense*, which called for the independence of the colonies from Britain, was written by which patriot?

Answers on page 338.

THE WINDY CITY

Test your knowledge of this third-largest American city.

1. These two musical genres are often associated with Chicago.

2. In 1991, *Wall Street Journal* reporter Alex Kotlowitz published a nonfiction book called *There Are No Children Here*, the story of two young brothers growing up in what gang-infested Chicago neighborhood?

3. What "world's tallest building" dominates Chicago's skyline? (Bonus: In what year was its construction completed?)

4. Chicago is home to 17 professional sports teams, but five of these belong to major U.S. leagues. Can you name them?

5. Although he was from New York, this legendary gangster led the Prohibition-era crime syndicate, The Chicago Outfit?

6. What disaster killed 300 people, destroyed 18,000 buildings, and left 100,000 people homeless in 1871?

7. This improvisational comedy troupe, based in Chicago's Old Town neighborhood, has some well known alumni, including Dan Aykroyd, John Belushi, Joan Rivers, and Steve Carell. What's the group's name?

8. What long-running television show is set at the fictional County General Hospital in Chicago? (It's actually filmed in California.)

9. What children's writer and illustrator, best known for his books *Where the Sidewalk Ends* and *The Giving Tree*, was born and raised in the Windy City?

10. The year 1968 was a tumultuous one for the United States, and Chicago's mayor Richard Daley took a hard line against "agitators." At what historic summer event did Daley's police use "excessive force" to disperse protesters?

Americana

Answers on page 338.

AS AMERICAN AS . . .

*Like apple pie, all the items in this quiz have come
to symbolize the United States.*

1. Who was the heroic railroad engineer who always brought the
Cannonball in on time and is immortalized in a popular ballad?

2. What is the name of Grant Wood's iconic 1930 painting of a
sober-looking farm couple with the man holding a pitchfork?
Most people assume they are man and wife; they are in fact
siblings.

3. Farmers and free-range ranchers fought range wars over what kind
of fencing?

4. This classic American prefab eatery has been superseded by fast-
food joints? Hint: Same name as a movie with a Baltimore setting.

5. What is the "Green Monster" of Boston's Fenway Park made of?

6. On what famous road could you "get your kicks" from Chicago to
California? It was sometimes called "The Main Street of America"
and "The Mother Road."

7. Signs staggered along the side of the road with verses like "Within
this vale / of toil and sin / Your head grows bald / but not your
chin" were advertisements for what company?

8. What American artist is well known for his *Saturday Evening Post*
covers and such paintings as *Saying Grace, Rosie the Riveter,* and the
Four Freedoms series?

9. "The outlook wasn't brilliant for the Mudville nine that day" is the
opening line of what poem?

10. Bat Masterson visited Wyatt Earp in Tombstone, Arizona, and left
shortly before what famous event?

Answers on page 338.

CALIFORNIA DREAMIN'

*The reality is you don't have to visit the Golden State
to come up with the right answers.*

1. *Ursus arctus horribilis* can be found on the California state flag but it's no longer in the state itself (although plans are underway to reintroduce it). What is this animal found in only four states, with an estimated population of less than 150,000?

2. Identify the second largest city in California and the eighth largest city in the United States.

3. At 14,505 feet, what mountain has the highest point in the contiguous United States?

4. There are three national parks located in the Sierra Nevada region. Name two.

5. What does "Sierra Nevada" mean?

6. Nicknamed "Surf City, USA," what coastal city in Orange County is also the birthplace of moshing or slamdancing?

7. At 282 feet below sea level, the lowest point in the Western Hemisphere is found in what national park?

8. California is bordered by what three U.S. states?

9. What California county is more populous than 37 U.S. states?

10. What California city is roughly one-fifth Chinese, constituting one of the largest concentrations of Chinese outside of China?

11. More Nobel Prize laureates are employed at this university than any other institution in the world. What is the school?

12. The conspicuous hilltop mansion in San Simeon, California, named after its owner, a former newspaper tycoon, is known as what?

Answers on page 339.

THE STATE ON YOUR PLATE

We give you a present or former license-plate slogan, and you name the state.

1. What state has "Aloha State" on its license plates? (Duh!)

2. If you see "Unbridled Spirit" on a license plate, you may be heading to this state's famous horse race.

3. Nothing artificial here. This state's plates say it's "The Natural State." What is it?

4. What state's license plates have no slogan, just a silhouette of a cowboy on a bucking bronco?

5. You'll see "Vacationland" on what New England state's license plates?

6. Where in the South are you when the plate says "Stars Fell On" this state?

7. Y'all come back! What state liked to call itself "The Hospitality State"?

8. What skeptics like to proclaim they're the "Show-Me State"?

9. When you see "Land of Enchantment" on plates, look around. You might see a cactus. What state are you in?

10. Where are you when you see "Great Faces. Great Places" on the plates?

11. Not to be outdone, what Southern state's plates brag about its "Smiling Faces. Beautiful Places"?

12. If you are in "The Old Dominion," where are you?

Americana

ALL ABOUT ALASKA

This 49th state is the largest in the U.S. in terms
of area. How much do you know about it?

1. In what year did Alaska join the United States?

2. Alaska is a unique state because it doesn't border any other U.S. states. (Only the islands of Hawaii share this distinction.) What land areas does it border?

3. In 1989, an oil tanker hit a reef in Alaska's Prince William Sound, spilling more than 10 million gallons of oil and creating one of the worst manmade disasters in history. What was the name of the tanker?

4. What 58-mile-wide body of water is all that separates Alaska (and North America in general) from Russia?

5. This singer, songwriter, poet, and yodeler, who gained fame in the 1990s, lived most of her childhood in Homer, Alaska, in a house with no indoor plumbing. (This was all before she moved to San Diego, California, and lived in a van.)

6. The average high July temperature in this city (Alaska's largest) is just 65.3° F.

7. What's 800 miles long, connects Northern Alaska to Valdez in the South, and cost about $8 million to build? (Bonus: What does it transport?)

8. This tallest mountain in North America is located in Alaska's Denali National Park.

9. What animal, a Christmas-story favorite, roams free throughout Alaska's many parks and open spaces?

10. In 1925, a relay of sled dogs teams (about 150 dogs and 50 mushers in all) carried antitoxin serum and raced across the Alaska wilderness to save the town of Nome from what deadly disease?

Americana

Answers on page 339.

WE LOVE NEW YORK

Take a bite out of the Big Apple, and test your knowledge of America's most populous city.

1. Name New York City's five boroughs.

2. In 1609, Italian explorer Giovanni da Verrazzano was the first European to sail into New York Harbor. What explorer arrived 85 years later, named the settlement New Amsterdam, and claimed it for the Netherlands?

3. During the 1920s and 1930s, music and literature flourished in what New York City neighborhood? (Bonus: Name the artistic movement to which the neighborhood lent its name.)

4. In July 1863, a series of one of the worst riots in American history took place in New York City. What were the rioters protesting?

5. What "Yankee Clipper," who spent his entire career with the New York Yankees, has been called "Babe Ruth, Ty Cobb, and Shoeless Joe Jackson rolled into one"?

6. This New York cultural attraction opened in 1932 and has been home to the high-kicking Rockettes ever since.

7. Today, Wall Street is the center of the financial world. But how did the famous thoroughfare get its name?

8. What rock musical opened in 1996 and told the story of a group of young artist friends living, dying, and coping with AIDS and poverty in New York's East Village?

9. Held twice a year, this clothing showcase has been a New York City staple since 1943.

10. This three-term mayor (who served from 1978 to 1989) is often remembered for being tough on crime in New York and for pulling the city out of financial crisis.

Answers on page 340.

STATES OF THE UNION

How much do you know about the U S of A?

1. This mountainous state has the highest average elevation of any state east of the Mississippi River.

2. What state is home to the world's longest cave system and the oldest continuously held horse race in the country?

3. Which state produces more gold than any other and is second in production only to South Africa?

4. The country's first commercial radio station (KDKA), first oil well, first baseball stadium, and first daily newspaper are all accomplishments from this state.

5. Where is the world's largest volcano (by volume) located?

6. Where is the country's tallest freestanding manmade monument?

7. The geographic center of North America is located in the town of Rugby in which state?

8. This state is the birthplace of the most (eight) U.S. presidents.

9. What state hosts more than 500,000 motorcyclists each year at its annual "Bike Week" in the town of Sturgis?

10. This eastern state has the highest population density in America, with 1,134 persons per square miles—more than 14 times the national average.

11. Situated at 7,000 feet above sea level, which state's capital is the highest city in the United States?

12. Colorado has the highest mean elevation of the 50 states. What state is second in that category?

Answers on page 340.

Americana

WHAT'S IN A PRESIDENT'S NAME?

First, middle, last . . . how well do you know the U.S. presidents' names?

1. Which TV Texas Ranger's last name is the same as two presidential middle names?

2. President Gerald Ford's middle name is also the name of one of Santa's reindeer.

3. President John Kennedy's middle name is also the last name of what *The Great Gatsby* and *The Last Tycoon* author?

4. The first name of Bart Simpson's best friend is an alternate spelling of which former chief executive's middle name?

5. "Shock Jock" Stern's first name is the middle name of a president who became a Supreme Court chief justice?

6. The sixth president's middle name is the same as the name of which TV medical examiner?

7. President James Polk's middle name is the same as which Kentucky fort featured in the movie *Goldfinger*?

8. What 20th-century president and 20th-century assassin share the same first and middle name?

9. The author of *Walden* and a president who served in World War II share what middle name?

10. The last name of the third president is the same as the middle name of what 20th-century two-term president?

11. The last name of the man who said, "Give me liberty or give me death" is the middle name of this president, who lasted only 31 days in office.

Answers on page 340.

ALOHA!

Hawaii became the 50th U.S. state in 1959. See how much you know about its history and culture.

1. Who was the first known European to make contact with the Hawaiians in 1778?

2. What did he name the islands, and why did he call them that?

3. How many main islands make up the Hawaiian archipelago? (Bonus: What are their names?)

4. This Honolulu-born singer scored a hit in 1966 with the song "Tiny Bubbles." What was his name?

5. What last queen of Hawaii was deposed in 1893 by U.S. troops after she tried to dissolve the Bayonet Constitution, an 1887 law that stripped the royals of most of their power in favor of outsiders?

6. This "father of modern surfing" grew up in Waikiki. In his youth, his favorite surfboard was 16 feet long, weighed about 110 pounds, and was made from koa wood.

7. "Howzit," "da kine," and "broke da mouth" are expressions in what language that borrows words and phrases from Portuguese, Hawaiian, Chinese, and other languages?

8. The 1941 Japanese attack on what Hawaiian harbor was the catalyst for the United States' entering World War II?

9. One of the Hawaii's greatest monarchs, he united the islands under one government, ended the practice of human sacrifice, and instituted laws that protected civilians during wartime. The state of Hawaii celebrates a holiday in his honor every June 11.

10. Located on Oahu's North Shore, this might be Hawaii's best-known surf spot. In the winter, waves can rise as high as 30 feet.

Americana

PARTICULARLY PENNSYLVANIA

A keystone-state quiz.

1. Which Pennsylvania city, the fourth largest, is named for the body of water it borders?

2. "Chocolate Capital USA" is the nickname for what city?

3. What is the first name of Punxsutawney, Pennsylvania's, most famous resident?

4. Which Pennsylvania city once served as America's capital?

5. Over 2,200 people in which Pennsylvania city were killed in the Great Flood of 1889?

6. Pennsylvania is the only one of the 13 original colonies not to border what?

7. What famous fictional character is immortalized in a massive bronze statue at the bottom of the Philadelphia Art Museum steps?

8. With more than 2,000 spans, what city has more bridges than any other town in the world?

9. Which Pennsylvania city lends its name to the top-selling line of barbells and is home to the Weight Lifting Hall of Fame?

10. Which toy that "Walks downstairs, alone or in pairs" is made in Hollidaysburg?

11. This historic river forms the eastern border of Pennsylvania.

12. Of the six states that border Pennsylvania, which of the borders is the shortest?

Answers on page 341.

MADE IN AMERICA

The original American inventors.

1. The inventor of this classic weapon of the American West got his first big order from the U.S. War Department. What did he invent?

2. What founding father invented, among other things, bifocals, an iron furnace stove, and an odometer to measure the length of mail routes?

3. Philo T. Farnsworth and Vladimir Zworykin are the two men most often credited with inventing what "tube"ular device?

4. Before it became the generic term for women's stockings, nylon was first used commercially in toothbrush bristles. What company developed it in 1938?

5. In the 1950s, admiral and engineer Hyman G. Rickover was the first to use this vessel, which the United States now has many of.

6. Mary Anderson of Alabama wanted to improve drivers' vision during stormy weather, so she invented and patented what?

7. Willis Haviland Carrier invented this chilly "Apparatus for Treating Air" in 1902. What do we call it today?

8. Which came first—dry cleaning or blue jeans?

9. Walter Hunt perfected this handy item in 1849 and sold it for $400. People who plan for emergencies—like a broken shoulder strap at a prom—carry one. What is it?

10. The Home Insurance Building in Chicago, built in 1884–85 by Major William Le Baron Jenney, was the first modern what?

11. In 1960, using a manmade ruby, physicist Theodore H. Maiman created the first working one of these items. What did he invent?

Answers on page 341.

Americana

GEORGIA ON MY MIND

All things Georgia, and we're not just talking
Georgia, U.S.A. (but mostly).

1. Its Voronya Cave is the deepest known cave in the world. What country are we talking about?

2. What basketball team has "Sweet Georgia Brown" as its theme song?

3. Her first hit song was "If I Knew You Were Coming, I'd Have Baked a Cake," and in the 1940s, singer Garry Moore gave her a famous nickname. Who was she, and what was the nickname?

4. In 1945, she bought an abandoned hacienda in Abiquiu, New Mexico. It included the Ghost Ranch and became the setting for many of her paintings. Who is the artist?

5. The U.S. state of Georgia is bordered on the south by what state?

6. What is the body of water between Vancouver Island and the mainland Pacific Coast of British Columbia, Canada?

7. Written in 1930 by Hoagy Carmichael, what song was eventually adopted as the official song of the American state of Georgia?

8. What African-American author born in Eatonton, Georgia, won the 1983 Pulitzer Prize for *The Color Purple*?

9. What Georgia-born carpenter, former model, and furniture designer now hosts one of ABC's most popular reality shows? (Hint: Move that bus!)

10. What Georgia swamp was featured in the *Pogo* comic strip drawn by Walt Kelly?

11. Charlie Daniels will tell you that when the "devil went down to Georgia," he was looking to steal this.

Answers on page 342.

THE PRESIDENT'S INN

How much do you know about life in that big White House?

1. Which president kept fit by skinny dipping in the Potomac?

2. Who set fire to the White House in 1814?

3. What first lady coped with no running water and hung the laundry in the East room?

4. The White House has 132 rooms—and how many bathrooms?

5. What location in the White House became notorious as the place where President Warren G. Harding secretly met his mistress?

6. Whose ghost has been spotted by the current White House operations foreman?

7. Which president said, "The White House is the finest prison in the world?"

8. What president had electricity installed in the White House and then didn't touch the light switches for fear of electrocution?

9. When Archie's pony took a ride in the White House elevator, who was Archie's dad—and the president?

10. Kevin Kline plays the owner of a temporary employment agency who winds up impersonating the president in what White House comedy?

11. Which president never lived in the White House?

12. We all know that the West Wing is the president's domain, but the East Wing often houses the office of the first lady. What presidential wife was the first to set up shop there?

Answers on page 342.

Americana

DON'T MESS WITH TEXAS

*Test your knowledge of the notorious and noteworthy
people and events of the Lone Star State.*

1. Nine years before it became part of the United States, Texas declared its independence from what country?

2. This was first discovered below Spindletop, a salt dome near Beaumont, in 1901. What was the resource?

3. For what "father of Texas" is the state's capital city named?

4. What Gulf Coast city's theater district is ranked second in the world in terms of the number of theater seats (for movies and live performances) available in a downtown area? (The first is New York City.)

5. What folk song tells the story of Emily West Morgan, who seduced Mexican General Santa Anna and helped the Texans win the 1836 Battle of Jacinto?

6. Miss Ellie, J. R., Bobby, and Sue Ellen all lived on a ranch near this booming Texas city.

7. This towering icon of the Texas State Fair stands 52 feet tall, wears a size 70 boot, and sports a 75-gallon hat. He's represented the fair since 1952.

8. The defeat at this mission in San Antonio became a rallying cry for the soldiers fighting for Texan independence during the 1830s.

9. What first black Heavyweight Champion of the World was born in Galveston in 1878?

10. These notorious Depression-era bank robbers were Texas born (in Rowena and Ellis County) but died in Louisiana after they were ambushed by police.

STAR-SPANGLED PAST

Take a quiz through American history.

1. Name the world's largest museum complex comprising a zoo, eight research centers, and 18 museums.

2. A contemporary women's movement was ignited with the 1963 publication of what book by Betty Friedan?

3. It's sometimes known as branch water, rotgut, corn liquor, Portuguese grape juice, white lightning, or hooch. What is it?

4. In 1614, colonist John Rolfe married the daughter of Chief Powhatan. What was her name?

5. During the 1967 "Summer of Love," hippies, teenage runaways, and "flower children" from around the country flocked to what San Francisco neighborhood?

6. The Oregon Trail ended in Oregon. In what state did it start?

7. What photographer is best known for his Civil War photos?

8. Which state has "Home on the Range" as its state song?

9. During the Indian Wars, the last major armed conflict was between government troops and the Dakota Sioux. What is this event popularly known as?

10. In 1794, settlers in western Pennsylvania protested against a federal tax on liquor and distilled drinks. What's this uprising known as?

11. What was the first national park, established in 1872?

12. What two presidents received the Nobel Peace Prize in the 20th century?

Americana

Answers on page 342.

BORN IN THE USA

Test your knowledge of these great American achievements.

1. What singer has toured steadily since the 1980s on what has been dubbed the "Never Ending Tour"?

2. What folk artist took up painting at age 74 and became renowned for her scenes of American life in a style called "naïve art"?

3. On their way west, pioneer wagon trains usually included one wagon used for food, cooking equipment, and preparing meals. What was it called?

4. Name the poem by Edgar Allan Poe that begins "Once upon a midnight dreary" and includes the phrase "the lost Lenore."

5. Though it lasted only a year and a half, what mail service became part of the romance of the West?

6. Take a wild guess: What is the official state sport of Wyoming?

7. Another wild guess? What famous brand of cigarette lighter has shared the screen with Frank Sinatra, Lucille Ball, John Wayne, Bruce Willis, Sharon Stone, Nicole Kidman, and John Travolta?

8. In what classic American novel did the ravages of the 1930s Dust Bowl figure strongly? (The word "dust" was used 24 times in the first chapter alone.)

9. Roy Lichtenstein and Andy Warhol were prominent artists of what genre of painting?

10. William Faulkner called this man "the father of American literature." Who was he referring to?

11. What escaped slave helped more than 70 others escape slavery with the aid of the Underground Railroad?

Answers on page 343.

Americana

COWBOY STATE OF MIND

Americana, Wyoming style.

1. What first official national park is located in Wyoming?

2. The first designated national monument is also in Wyoming. What is it?

3. The author of *Brokeback Mountain* lives in this state. What is her name?

4. What large department-store chain started in Kemmerer, Wyoming?

5. What's so special about Wyoming's Black Thunder mine?

6. Wyoming's license plates feature a man on a what?

7. The federal building in Casper, Wyoming, is one of only two U.S. federal buildings named for a living person. Who is it named after?

8. The colorful Western figure "Buffalo Bill" Cody helped found what Wyoming city?

9. Besides "Cowboy State," why is Wyoming also called the "Equality State"?

10. Wyoming has an official "state mythical creature" that's a cross between a jackrabbit and an antelope. What is this creature called?

11. Residents of Wyoming are called . . . Wyomingians? Wyomingites? Wyomies?

12. What star of ABC's *Lost* grew up on a ranch in Crowheart, Wyoming?

13. Wyoming's state mammal is what Great Plains giant?

Americana

Answers on page 343.

THE SUNSHINE STATE

Grab your shades and test your knowledge of Florida's people and places.

1. What Spanish explorer first landed in Florida in April 1513? (His landing coincided with Easter, so he named his "discovery" *Pascua Florida*, which means "Flowery Easter" in Spanish.)

2. There are three national parks in Florida. Can you name one?

3. For what president is the South Florida U.S. space shuttle launch site named?

4. Ernest Hemingway spent many years on this southern-most Florida island. While there, he completed or worked on *A Farewell to Arms, For Whom the Bell Tolls,* and *The Snows of Kilimanjaro.* (He also liked to stop into Sloppy Joe's Bar for a drink.)

5. Go Gators! No . . . Go 'Noles! What two universities make up this age-old rivalry that defines college football in the state?

6. Florida was *the* swing state during the controversial 2000 presidential election. That year, George W. Bush defeated what political rival by only 537 votes, thus securing his place in the White House?

7. What "magical kingdom" opened in Orlando in 1971?

8. If you want to eat authentic fried plantains and hear traditional salsa music, you'll want to visit this Miami neighborhood. (The neighborhood's street fair made history in 1988, when it earned an entry in *Guinness World Records* for having the longest conga line: 119,986 people.)

9. The last measurable amount of this type of precipitation (.2 inches) in Tampa occurred in 1977. What kind of precipitation was it?

10. Don't forget where you are. In California, this town is best known for movie stars and glamour, but in Florida, it's a mid-sized city on the state's Atlantic coast.

Answers on page 343.

Americana

TEED OFF

Fore! Feel free to play through this quiz.

1. She may have been Queen of the Scots, but Mary brought golf to France where military cadets lugged her equipment around the course. Thanks to those guys, what do we call a golf assistant?

2. What's the name of the grassy fair play area between the tee and the green?

3. This golf course in Hawaii is regarded as the toughest in the world. It is named after a volcano on Oahu. Can you name it?

4. He's the sport's most famous player, but not too many people know Tiger Wood's first name. What is it?

5. Is the speed of the average male golfer's driving swing closer to 70, 80, or 90 miles per hour?

6. What Olympic medal-winning star of the high jump, javelin throw, and hurdles helped found the Ladies Professional Golf Association in 1949?

7. What do Shirley Temple and a modern golf ball have in common?

8. Who overcame a childhood case of polio to become widely regarded as the greatest golfer of all time?

9. Which pro golfer drew such big crowds that his mass of fans were called his "army"?

10. Of a golf shot, a golf club, or a golf course hazard, what's a "niblick"?

11. What's in the water that makes the 13th hole extremely hazardous at the Lost City Golf Course in South Africa?

Sports

FEELING PUCKISH?

How much do you know about the fastest game on Earth?

1. It was called the "miracle on ice" when an underdog hockey team upset the expected winners in the 1980 Olympics. What countries did the winners and losers represent?

2. What's a goalie doing when he "smothers" a puck?

3. What hockey player was a prodigy at six years old and grew up to become a superstar nicknamed "the Great One"?

4. When you see the Charleston Chiefs' flashiest player do a strip tease during the playoffs, you're watching what hockey movie?

5. The lyrics to Warren Zevon's comic hockey ballad, "Hit Somebody," were written by Mitch Albom, best-selling author of the inspirational *Tuesdays With* . . . who?

6. The Stanley Cup has been called the "holy grail" of hockey. Which hockey team has won the Stanley Cup more times than any other?

7. Which hockey team won the Stanley Cup three times by 1940 but had to wait 54 years before they won it a fourth time?

8. What was so special about Manon Rheaume's playing preseason games for the Tampa Bay Lightning in 1993?

9. How many goals does a hockey player have to score for it to be called a "hat trick"?

10. "Mr. Hockey," aka Gordie Howe, was famous for the "Gordie Howe hat trick," which consisted of a goal, an assist, and what else?

11. What is the term "sin bin" slang for?

12. In what Scandinavian country is hockey the most popular spectator sport?

Answers on page 344.

BASES LOADED

Do you know who's on first?

1. What United States city is known as the birthplace of baseball?

2. It's known "as the house that Ruth built" because, during the first game ever played at this ballpark, Babe Ruth hit a home run. What's the official name of this stadium?

3. What baseball great's records of the highest lifetime batting average (.367) and number of stolen home bases (54) still stand after more than 80 years?

4. Who said: "Baseball is 90% mental. The other half is physical"?

5. They call it *basebaru* but it's played the same. In what Asian nation is baseball the most popular team sport?

6. Who was the first player to have his number (4) retired in 1939?

7. In 1946, Jackie Robinson became the first African American to play for the minor leagues. For what team?

8. Of Felipe, Matty, Jesús, Moisés, and Mel, who is the eldest Alou in the family?

9. Hank Aaron and his brother played for the same team—the Milwaukee and Atlanta Braves—in the 1960s and early 1970s. Name the other Aaron.

10. Name that team: Eddie Stanky, Bobby Thomson, Wes Westrum, Whitey Lockman, and—Willie Mays.

11. President Bill Clinton said, "It's just a few hundred folks trying to figure out how to divide $2 billion." What was he talking about?

Sports

IT'S HALL IN THE GAME

All answers relate to sports Halls of Fame in North America.

Sports

1. What city is home to both the Pro Football Hall of Fame and the William McKinley Presidential Library & Museum?

2. Its address at 801 Hat Trick Avenue, Eveleth, Minnesota, provides a clue to the identity of what sport's United States Hall of Fame?

3. Canastota, New York, decided to honor two hometown world champions, Carmen Basilio (1950s) and Billy Backus (1970) and this knockout hall of fame was the result.

4. Only 14 miles apart, which two sports have halls of fame in Cooperstown and Oneonta, New York?

5. Olympic speed skaters Eric Heiden and Greg LeMond are two of the athletes enshrined in the hall of fame devoted to which sport?

6. Which association's hall of fame, due to open in Charlotte, North Carolina, in the spring of 2010, is the sanctioning body for the number one spectator sport in America?

7. Walter Hagan and Harry Vardon were among the first eleven inductees into which sport's hall of fame in St. Augustine, Florida?

8. Fort Lauderdale is home to what sport's international hall of fame with members such as Larry "Buster" Crabbe, Gertrude Ederle, and Johnny Weissmuller?

9. In which hall of fame do they honor the accomplishments of "The Destroyer," "Bruno Sammartino," and "The Fabulous Moolah"?

10. Which sport has a hall of fame in Holyoke, Massachusetts, where it was invented by William Morgan in 1895 at the YMCA?

Answers on page 344.

WOMEN ARE GOOD SPORTS

Test your knowledge of women in sports.

1. Who won two gold medals in track and field in the 1932 Olympics, had outstanding successes in golf and basketball, and has been called the greatest all-around female athlete?

2. What famous suffragette said, "Bicycling has done more to emancipate women than anything else in the world"?

3. Elizabeth Thible of Lyons, France, liked to soar above the ground and in the 18th century was the first woman to do what?

4. What sisters have both been ranked #1 in world tennis?

5. The most celebrated women's team in United States history won what 1999 international sporting event at the Pasadena Rose Bowl?

6. What Australian champion in women's swimming, arrested in 1909 for indecency in Boston for wearing a one-piece bathing suit, helped to liberate women from a bathing dress and pantaloons?

7. Known as the "Sparrow from Minsk," tiny Olga Korbut not only took home Olympic Gold with an amazing performance but also inspired young women to enter what sport?

8. What retired Olympic gold medalist is considered one of the all-time greatest heptathletes and was voted the number-one female athlete by *Sports Illustrated for Women*?

9. Sonja Henie holds the most gold medals in what Olympic sport?

10. Who has been described as the best woman hockey player on the planet and made history in 2003 as the first woman to register a point in a men's pro hockey game?

Answers on page 345.

ALL ABOARD!

Time for surfing, boogieboarding, and skateboarding, dude.

1. Hawaiian kings demonstrated their leadership by showing their skills on what type of board?

2. In Michigan, Sherm Poppen nailed two skis together so that his daughter could stand while she sledded down hills—creating what board sport?

3. Drummer Tom Morey fashioned the first modern bodyboard from scrap polyethylene foam. What did Morey name it?

4. Which sport combines sailing and surfing on a one-person board?

5. Which board sport was once banned in Norway?

6. Some people attend one of these when a loved one has died. Others ride them on a board named what?

7. The ollie takes a rider airborne with the board seemingly stuck to his feet. It was invented by Alan "Ollie" Gelfand and is used for the signature trick for what sport?

8. According to *Guinness World Records*, Flavio Jardim and Diogo Guerreiro made the longest journey (5,045 miles) ever traveled on what board?

9. In *Apocalypse Now*, Robert Duvall plays Lt. Col. William Kilgore who captures a Vietnamese village because it's a good place to enjoy what type of board sport?

10. What sport became part of the Olympics at the 1998 Nagano Games?

Answers on page 345.

Sports

HOOPLA

Can you make this basketball quiz a slam dunk?

1. Who led his team to six championships, holds the NBA record for highest career regular season scoring average, and was named ESPN's greatest North American athlete of the 20th century?

2. The fanatical following of the National Collegiate Athletic Association (NCAA) men's basketball championships is a "madness" that occurs in what month?

3. The madness began in 1957 when which player inspired a national following for the NCAA playoffs?

4. What Canadian-born professor invented basketball?

5. Which movie starring Gene Hackman is based on the true story of the Milan High School basketball team and their victory at the Indiana State Championships?

6. The most-watched televised college basketball was the 1979 victory of Michigan State over Indiana State. It launched a super-star rivalry between what two basketball greats?

7. What's the name of "the Wizard of Westwood" who coached the UCLA Bruins to an unmatched ten NCAA championships?

8. What NBA star is famous as a great rebounder, but notorious for dyed hair, tattoos, piercings, and cross-dressing?

9. What acclaimed documentary followed two gifted athletes from Chicago's inner city as they struggled to make it in the NCAA and NBA?

10. Which basketball franchise, with eight years of continuous NBA championships, holds the longest streak of consecutive championships in United States' pro sports history?

Sports

Answers on page 345.

SPORTIN' LIFE

For all you athletic supporters.

1. What baseball team holds the record for most World Series wins?

2. In what city—where they originated—were the 2004 Summer Olympics held?

3. In hockey, one player pushes another player into the wall, or boards, when the player being pushed is facing the boards. What's that called?

4. Football great Johnny Unitas is in the Pro Football Hall of Fame. What was his position?

5. In the United States, the term "Triple Crown" usually refers to thoroughbred horse racing, consisting of the Kentucky Derby, the Preakness Stakes, and what third race?

6. What retired baseball coach is famous for fracturing the language with comments like, "Nobody goes there anymore, it's too crowded"?

7. Barry Bonds broke whose long-standing career home-run record of 755?

8. President Gerald Ford was a star athlete in high school and college, despite his later image of being clumsy. What sport did he play?

9. What is it called when somebody walks with the ball in basketball?

10. What famous golfer's first name is Eldrick?

11. In 2007, what Swiss tennis player equaled Björn Borg's record of five consecutive wins at Wimbledon?

SPORTS TALK

Can you talk like the pros?

1. "Banana kick," "nutmeg," "hacking," and "overlap" are terms used in this sport that is one of the most popular around the world.

2. "Chief second," "neutral corner," "tomato can," and "hook" are a few of the terms used in this pugilistic art.

3. "Butt-ending," "head deke," "double minor," and "ragging" are terms in this cold weather sport that's popular in Canada.

4. "Eastern grip," "centerline," "mini-break," and "no man's land" are part of the terminology of what court sport that originated in 19th-century Europe?

5. "Albatross," "skull," "punch shot," and "chili dip" are terms belonging to what outdoor sport from Scotland?

6. "Chukker," "knock in," "pony goal," and "tail shot" are terms exclusive to this pastime of the upper classes.

7. "Forearm pass," "pancake," "dig," and "down ball" are terms used in which indoor or outdoor sport, six-players-to-a-team activity?

8. "Cylinder," "high post," "bang the boards," and "in the paint" all are terms relating to this sport invented by James Naismith in 1891.

9. "Scrum," "try," "maul," and "ruck" are part of this rough sport that the British say is a "gentleman's game played by hooligans."

10. We're taking bets that "bleeder," "break maiden," "juvenile," and "parked out" are part of the vocabulary of this activity.

11. "Cradling," "scooping," "wrap check," and "attack goal area" are all terms used in what college sport? (It's also Canada's national summer sport.)

Answers on page 346.

OFF TO THE RACES

Test your knowledge on the Sport of Kings.

1. What musical instrument plays the "call to the post" at the beginning of a thoroughbred race?

2. Who said, "Horse sense is the thing a horse has which keeps it from betting on people"?

3. Which breeder and jockey made horse racing "the sport of kings"?

4. What undefeated 18th-century stallion is in the pedigree of at least 80 percent of today's racing thoroughbreds?

5. What form of horse racing evolved in Ireland and England from the sport of fox hunting?

6. Who is the British jockey-turned-author that writes thrillers set against the background of horse racing?

7. At the Kentucky Derby and Belmont Stakes, what Triple Crown Winner set record times that remain unbroken?

8. Which early American president managed a race track and trained horses?

9. Who was the first female jockey to win a Triple Crown race and be inducted in thoroughbred racing's hall of fame?

10. What American horse is bred for sprinting short distances, typically a quarter mile or less?

11. What film tells the true story of an undersized thoroughbred whose unexpected victories made him a sensation during America's Great Depression?

12. What desert nation holds the world's richest horse race with a purse of $6 million?

Answers on page 346.

Sports

MORE SPORTIN' LIFE

When it comes to a quiz on sports, how do you score?

1. What is the most popular ball game in the world?

2. What cycling race has its finishing line on the Champs-Elysées in Paris?

3. What ancient philosopher said, "You can discover more about a person in an hour of play than in a year of conversation"?

4. Football is descended from what British game?

5. During the beheading of his second wife, Anne Boleyn, Henry VIII was playing what sport?

6. "Bending" a kick to make the ball swerve to the right or left is part of what game?

7. In what book does a queen play croquet with hedgehogs for balls and flamingos for mallets?

8. The foil, épée, and sabre are equipment for what sport?

9. The movie *Rudy* was inspired by Daniel Ruettiger's struggle to play for what college football team?

10. Though its name means "gentle way," what modern Japanese martial art has a goal of throwing one's opponent to the ground?

11. What song by Queen is a victory anthem at sporting events?

12. What U.S. team is the first professional franchise in any sport to reach 10,000 losses?

Sports

Answers on page 346.

VICTORY WITH DE FEET

Get a kick out of quizzes? Try this one on soccer.

1. The final match of what soccer tournament is the most widely viewed sports event in the world?

2. What Brazilian footballer said, "Every time I went away I was deceiving my mum. I'd tell her I was going to school but I'd be out on the street playing football. I always had a ball on my feet"?

3. In 1848, the first laws of soccer were drawn up at what university?

4. Soccer balls were made of inflated pigs' bladders—until who designed the first soccer ball made of vulcanized rubber?

5. After helping France win the World Cup, who had his image projected onto the Arc de Triomphe with the French public calling for him to be made president?

6. Which South American country has won the World Cup more times than any other?

7. Even the Pope rejoiced when the soccer team from which war-torn nation won the 2007 Asian Cup?

8. What English midfielder joined the Los Angeles Galaxy for the highest salary of any Major League Soccer player in history?

9. Which retired U.S. forward scored more international goals in her career than any other player, male or female?

10. What international soccer competition uses robots with the goal of developing an autonomous, humanoid robot team that can beat a human, championship soccer team?

Answers on page 346.

WHAT A RACKET!

Grand Slam your way through this quiz with your knowledge of tennis.

1. Tennis as we know it today was first played in France where players shouted *tenez*—which meant what?

2. What sporty king of England built a tennis court at Hampton Court Palace—where games are still held today?

3. Since 1877 The All England Lawn Tennis and Croquet Club has hosted what world-famous tennis event?

4. How many points have you scored in tennis if your score is love?

5. In tennis's 1975 "Battle of the Sexes" between self-proclaimed "male chauvinistic pig" Bobby Riggs and female athlete Billie Jean King, who won?

6. Which Italian Renaissance Baroque painter, considered "the greatest painter in Rome" in the early 1600s, killed a man over a quarrel about a tennis score?

7. Which tennis superstar said, "It's one-on-one out there, man. There ain't no hiding. I can't pass the ball"?

8. The U.S. Open is played at Flushing Meadows in a stadium named for what African American tennis great?

9. What's the top international team event in men's tennis and the largest annual, international team competition in sports?

10. *You Cannot Be Serious* is the title of his memoirs and the signature phrase of which tennis bad boy?

11. What athletic movie star donned her tennis whites and teamed up with Spencer Tracy in the comedy *Pat and Mike*?

12. What is the only Grand Slam tournament played on a clay court?

Answers on page 347.

TACKLE THIS

Are you on the ball when it comes to knowledge of the gridiron?

1. In the 1800s which Ivy League college played an early form of American football on "Bloody Mondays?"

2. When football became America's most popular spectator sport, it wrested the title from what other ball game?

3. What American president threatened to ban football unless the rules were modified to reduce the numbers of deaths during games?

4. What football-crazy town inspired the film and TV series *Friday Night Lights*?

5. Which football player has scored the most touchdowns (eight) during Super Bowl games?

6. What New York Jets quarterback was correct when he brashly predicted his team's victory in Super Bowl III?

7. Which coach led the 1953–57 Oklahoma Sooners through the longest winning streak (47 games) in college football history?

8. What running back Hall of Famer rapped: "They call me Sweetness and I like to dance. Running the ball is like makin' romance"?

9. What film was inspired by African American Herman Boone and his success as head coach of Alexandria, Virginia's, newly integrated high school football team?

10. In 1902 in Pasadena, spectators who watched the University of Michigan pummel Stanford 49-0 were watching the first of which college bowl game?

11. Which former Oakland Raiders coach became a color commentator and analyst for televised football games?

Answers on page 347.

EENY, MEENY, MINY, MOE!

Remember your childhood and name these outdoor games.

1. "Ghost in the Graveyard," "Sardines," and "Manhunt" are all variations of what popular game?

2. What colorful game requires two teams and has several lesser-known nicknames including "Forcing Open the City Gates" and "Bullrush."

3. Soldiers of the Roman Empire were the first to participate in this jumping activity (in full body armor to improve their stamina).

4. What water-based game shares its name with a 13th-century Italian explorer?

5. In Argentina, kids play "tiggy"; in France, it's "loup"; and in Bavaria, it's called "catch the man." What's its American name?

6. Although most often considered an activity for elementary school children, this baseball-like game was played by Allied soldiers during World War II.

7. Once a staple of P.E. class, what game has disappeared from many U.S. curriculums because school officials deem it too dangerous?

8. Armed with just $10 for the registration fee, anyone can head to Maine in February for the annual national championship of this game, whose only needed piece of equipment is a ball.

9. In some countries this game is called "sneaking up on granny," but in the United States, it's more like directing traffic.

10. This game was played as long ago as ancient Rome, and over the centuries, its playing pieces have been made of stone, metal, ceramics, and glass.

Answers on page 347.

IT'S BOXING DAY

Score a K.O. in this boxing quiz.

1. In what ancient culture did criminals and slaves use boxing to win their freedom?

2. Who was England's first bare-knuckle champ and the father of modern boxing?

3. The match that made Gentleman Jim Corbett world heavyweight champion in 1892 was fought according to what rules?

4. When boxing in the Olympics, how many rounds do competitors go?

5. Who fought only 138 minutes as world champion, but during that time made $15,000 a minute?

6. What German pugilist (a symbol of the Nazis), who had a famous bout with Joe Lewis, actually risked his life to save Jewish children from that regime?

7. The 1974 "Rumble in the Jungle" between Muhammad Ali and George Foreman took place in what nation?

8. What heavyweight champion said: "Everyone wants to go to heaven but nobody wants to die"?

9. Though Muhammad Ali called himself "the greatest," whom did he rate as the best pound-for-pound boxer of all time?

10. Who won a Best Actor Oscar for his portrayal of Middleweight Champion Jake La Motta in *Raging Bull*?

11. The 1893 match between Andy Bowen and Jack Burke established a record when it went how many rounds?

12. What female world welterweight champ—described as one of the most feared and avoided champions in boxing—goes by the nickname Island Girl?

Answers on page 347.

GOLD FEVER

Go for the gold in this quiz on the Olympic Games.

1. The Ancient Olympics took place in the sacred stadium of what country?

2. The main fashion difference between the modern Olympic athlete and the Ancient Olympic athlete is that the latter didn't wear what?

3. What Frenchman founded the modern Olympics so that young people could compete in sports rather than in war?

4. What group of athletes were allowed to compete in the Olympics for the first time at the 1900 Paris Games?

5. Hitler promoted the idea of African inferiority, so in 1936 the Fuhrer was humiliated when what African American athlete took four gold medals at Berlin?

6. At the Sydney Games, marathon champ Naoko Takahashi gave credit to what highly unusual substance, for helping her win?

7. What winner of seven gold medals in the 1972 Summer Olympics said, "I swam my brains out"?

8. Who won the light-heavyweight gold medal at the Rome Olympics before he went on to become "the greatest" world heavyweight champion?

9. Soviet gymnast Larissa Latynina holds an Olympic record with how many medals?

10. Runner Paavo Nurmi won a record 12 Olympic medals representing what country?

11. What Academy Award winner for Best Picture is based on the story of Olympic athletes Harold Abrahams and Eric Liddell?

Sports

Answers on page 348.

AAARGH!

Avast me hearties, it be time to take this pirate quiz . . . or walk the plank!

1. What color pirate flag signaled an attack where no one's life would be spared?

2. Treasure from Black Sam Bellamy's sunken pirate ship Whydah, was discovered off what Massachusetts island?

3. What theme parks contain the ride that inspired the film, *Pirates of the Caribbean*?

4. Who said, "Now and then we had a hope that if we lived and were good, God would permit us to be pirates"?

5. While running a criminal fleet of 800 junks in the China Sea, what made powerful Ching Shih different from most other pirates?

6. Frederick is apprenticed to failed pirates in what Gilbert and Sullivan musical?

7. To terrify his enemies, what pirate not only brandished swords and pistols but had flaming hemp woven into his hair?

8. Which pirate's corpse was placed in an iron cage hanging over the Thames River as a warning to would-be buccaneers?

9. The fast-food chain Long John Silver is named after the pirate in what adventure story?

10. Which swashbuckler got himself a knighthood and a post as Lieutenant Governor?

11. Every March brings a re-enactment of Robert Searles's raid and ransacking of what Florida harbor?

12. What cruise liner was attacked in 2005 by modern Somali pirates with rocket-propelled grenades and automatic weapons?

IT HAPPENED IN 1800

We weren't there at the time, but it was a very busy year.

1. In 1800, the American capital moved to Washington, D.C., from what city?

2. This man, born in 1800, is credited with being the first American to vulcanize rubber.

3. What unit of electricity was named for Alessandro Volta, who in 1800 demonstrated what is considered to be the first electric battery?

4. On January 8, 1800, the Wild Boy of Aveyron—thought to be about 12 years old—emerged from the woods where he had presumably spent most or all of his life. In what country is Aveyron?

5. In 1800, Congress earmarked $5,000 to buy books for research and a place to store them, thereby creating what?

6. As a result of the work of England's Edward Jenner, what vaccine was first administered in North America in 1800?

7. A little tomato sauce, eggs, and cognac and—and voilà!—chicken Marengo was born. What French general ordered his chef to rustle up this quick meal with whatever was on hand before the Battle of Marengo in 1800?

8. The first president to live in what is now called the White House took up residence there in 1800. Who was he?

9. Nat Turner and John Brown both were born in 1800, both led unsuccessful slave uprisings in Virginia, and both died in the same way, Turner in 1831; Brown in 1859. How did they meet their deaths?

10. The area around it was first settled by American Royalists in 1800, and in 1857 England's Queen Victoria chose it to be Canada's capital city. Name it.

History

Answers on page 348.

WAR! WHAT IS IT GOOD FOR?

Well, maybe it's good for quizzes—you'll find a "WAR" in each answer.

1. What horse's 27-year career as a stud produced a grandson named Seabiscuit?

2. What was Civil War Union General William Tecumseh Sherman's three-word opinion of war?

3. Castor oil, vitamin C, and duct tape are just three of the suggested ways of getting rid of what contagious skin lesion?

4. "Werewolves of London" was a 1978 hit single for what artist?

5. What's the most commonly used word for a male witch?

6. What *Time* magazine 1977 Man of the Year was assassinated in Cairo in 1981?

7. Bill Clinton's presidential campaign served as the basis for what 1993 documentary?

8. Who announced in 2006 that he would donate more than $1 billion a year to the Bill and Melinda Gates Foundation, the largest charitable donation in history to date?

9. What Virginia senator was Elizabeth Taylor's next-to-last husband—so far?

10. Though actually a colony of organisms called a *siphonophore*, this creature is often mistaken for a jellyfish. What is it?

11. Who was Little Orphan Annie's benefactor?

Answers on page 348.

History

1900s: **BY THE DECADE**

How well do you know the people and events of the 20th century?

1. What archipelago became a United States' territory on February 22, 1900, but waited another 59 years to become the 50th state?

2. Often called the "greatest American athlete," this Native American won two Olympic gold medals in 1912 before going on to play professional football, baseball, and basketball. Name this man who was also the first president of what became the National Football League.

3. After this founding member of the renowned Algonquin Round Table was fired from *Vanity Fair* in 1920 (because her criticism was too critical), colleagues Robert Benchley and Robert Sherwood quit in protest. Who was this lady known for her sharp tongue?

4. Classics including *Gone with the Wind*, *Stagecoach*, *Mr. Smith Goes to Washington*, and *The Wizard of Oz* were all released during this "most spectacular year in film."

5. What Allied general and future U.S. president commanded the D-Day invasion of France on June 6, 1944?

6. The Soviets' answer to NATO, this organization held its first meeting in 1955. What is this organization's name?

7. *To Kill a Mockingbird*, Harper Lee's 1960 Southern coming-of-age novel, featured this young girl as its heroine.

8. Born in England in 1978, Louise Brown is best known for being what kind of medical miracle?

9. The first months of 1986 were dramatic for the superpowers' space programs. What were two events of this sad and exciting year?

10. Who became the first female United States Secretary of State on January 23, 1997?

THE WORLD'S WORST

. . . disasters on the roads, rails, and in the air.

1. How many voyages had the *Titanic*, the world's largest and supposedly safest passenger liner, taken before it collided with an iceberg and sank in 1912?

2. Margaret Brown survived and rescued others to become a heroine of the *Titanic*. Name the Broadway musical based on her story.

3. In 1937, after a trans-Atlantic flight from Frankfurt, the *Hindenburg* was destroyed by fire while landing in New Jersey. What type of aircraft was the *Hindenburg*?

4. During World War II, which attack sank more United States ships and caused the most damage to the war effort: the Japanese attack on Pearl Harbor or Nazi U-boat attacks near the coast of New Jersey?

5. What sunken Great Lake freighter, nicknamed "The Fitz," was memorialized in a hit song by Gordon Lightfoot?

6. Ontario's Highway 401 is the site of Canada's deadliest automobile pile-up. Within 10, how many vehicles were involved?

7. Only four people of 524 passengers and crew survived the deadliest single-aircraft crash in history when Flight 123 crashed into a mountain in 1985. Name the airline.

8. In Sri Lanka about 17,000 people died in the world's worst known railway disaster. What natural phenomenon was to blame?

9. When another train collided with the *Cannonball Express*, its engineer died trying to save the lives of others. A ballad sung in vaudeville theaters made his name a legend—who was he?

10. What's the title of the airline disaster spoof, with Kareem Abdul-Jabbar in one of his few movie roles, that became a cinema comedy classic in 1980?

Answers on page 349.

CURSES!

Try not to get hexed by these questions.

1. What fairy-tale princess was doomed by a curse to prick her finger on a spinning wheel and die (though the curse was later modified by a good fairy)?

2. According to Confucius: "It is better to light one small candle than to curse . . ." Can you finish the quote?

3. This team sold Babe Ruth to the Yankees, triggering the Curse of the Bambino, which kept them from winning the World Series for 86 years. Can you name the team?

4. Which Pharaoh's tomb is said to have brought untimely death to the British explorers who discovered it?

5. What play, featuring three witches, has been so plagued with disaster that actors are afraid to ever name it aloud in the theater?

6. The Hope Diamond is said to bring bad luck to its owners—including the beheading of which beautiful French queen?

7. Citizens of which nation curse an enemy by secretly placing an offering on their back steps—thus inviting in supernatural demons?

8. A certain Porsche Spyder broke the legs of two mechanics, killed one driver who raced it, and badly injured another. But this "death car" is most famous for speeding which Hollywood star to his demise?

9. More than 1,700 ships and planes allegedly have disappeared or lost their crews in what "hexed" area of the Atlantic Ocean?

10. Many cultures believe that an envious stare can curse your health, your children, and your possessions. What is this curse called?

History

Answers on page 349.

HEADACHES

Don't lose your head over this quiz!
(Though these folks did.)

1. This biblical future king defeated the behemoth Goliath with nothing more than a slingshot and five smooth stones . . . then cut off the giant's head with his own sword.

2. "Off with her head!" screams this foul-tempered monarch. Who is she and to whom is she referring?

3. What hunchbacked Shakespearean king shouts, "Off with his head," when he accuses his former friend, Lord Hastings, of treason?

4. Who is the Old Testament female who seduces Holofernes and then chops off his head while he sleeps in a drunken stupor?

5. This New Testament beauty whose dance for her stepfather, King Herod Antipas, so pleased him that he offered to grant her anything she desired. (Her request: John the Baptist's head.)

6. What French doctor, credited with inventing a beheading machine, actually only promoted its use as a more humane means of execution?

7. This 20th-century bad guy ordered more people decapitated than were killed during the entire French Revolution.

8. Name Washington Irving's famous short story in which Ichabod Crane is pursued by a ghostly headless horseman.

9. English history is filled with beheadings. Name the English king who had two of his six wives "lose their heads" over him.

10. The tradition of offering prisoners one last cigarette before execution originated with what New World explorer who requested one last smoke before his beheading?

Answers on page 349.

History

DOING BATTLE

These decisive battles made their way into history.

1. Fought over three sweltering summer days, this bloody battle marked the turning point of the Civil War.

2. What was the name of Napoleon's last battle? (Hint: It's become synonymous with "defeat.")

3. Before William the Conqueror earned his fierce-sounding moniker at the 1066 Battle of Hastings, he was known by what less noble-sounding name?

4. The disastrous Crimean War Battle of Balaclava—where English forces were led by the Earl of Cardigan and Lord Raglan—was immortalized in what famous poem by Alfred Lord Tennyson?

5. Although there's a debate about who said it, "Don't shoot until you see the whites of their eyes," was first uttered during what Revolutionary War battle?

6. What long foot race was named for a 480 B.C. battle after which a Greek messenger ran about 25 miles to Athens to announce victory over the invading Persian army?

7. The most reproduced war photograph of all time is of Marines raising the U.S. flag during what World War II battle?

8. To this day, the first day of what World War I battle holds the record for the most casualties?

9. Shakespeare's Henry V rallied his troops before the 1415 Battle of Agincourt with the stirring cry, "We few, we happy few, we band of brothers," because the British were vastly outnumbered by what powerful army?

10. A series of battles during the Vietnam War was named the Tet Offensive because it began during what annual celebration?

History

A ROYAL MESS

Can you flush out the royals in these historic scandals?

1. Which grandmother to Queen Elizabeth II was too miserly to buy her own nice things, so she'd pinch them from friends and hapless subjects?

2. What Prince of Monaco disapproved of his daughter's liaisons with gardeners, bodyguards, and married elephant trainers—before she finally settled down with a circus acrobat?

3. What new invention was installed in the palace of King Louis XIV so he could get to his mistresses faster?

4. Hilary Swank starred in what film about "an affair" that could have cost France's Louis XVI and Marie Antoinette their heads?

5. What fertile English monarch had enough illegitimate children to make him the butt of this joke: "A king is supposed to be the father of his people, and our king is father to a good many of them"?

6. During World War II, the Duke and the Duchess of Windsor were so chummy with the Nazis that Winston Churchill sent them where?

7. What Empress of Ancient Rome murdered her husband to put her son Nero on the throne—only to have the boy assassinate her?

8. What queen scandalized 16th-century Europe when she married Baron Bothwell, the chief suspect in her husband's murder?

9. What not-so-beloved British prince was fingered as Jack the Ripper by conspiracy theorists?

10. Now admired for her devotion to a healthy lifestyle, what Duchess was once best known for photos with a beau who paid too much attention to her toes?

Answers on page 350.

BANKS AND ROBBERS

True accounts of some serious criminals.

1. In 1831, in America's first recorded bank robbery, Edward Smith stole $245,000 from City Bank on what New York City street?

2. Frank and Jesse James led a band of Civil War veterans through a stunningly successful series of bank robberies. Which side had the gang members fought for during the war?

3. Woody Guthrie wrote an ode for this depression-era bank robber who gave his ill-gotten gains to the poor.

4. Which other depression-era bandit took his girlfriend on crime sprees, making them the Romeo and Juliet of bank robbers?

5. What doting mom covered for her sons and went to the movies while they robbed banks?

6. What gang pulled off the world's biggest bank heist—filling three tractor trailers with about $1 billion from what bank?

7. Name the legendary bank robber who admitted, "I have been hunted for 21 years, have literally lived in the saddle, have never known a day of perfect peace. It was one long, anxious, inexorable, eternal vigil."

8. In what classic comedy does Alec Guinness portray a timid bank employee who pulls off the (almost) perfect bank heist?

9. Israeli folk hero Ronnie Leibowitz robbed more than 20 banks, but his sentence was shortened because the judge was impressed by Roni's unusual action. What did repentant Roni do?

10. Albert Spaggiari tunneled into a supposedly impregnable bank in Nice, France, and made off with 60 million francs. From where did the bandit tunnel into the vault?

Answers on page 350.

History

LET'S PLAY FAMILY FEUD!

*Do you know the players
in these familial battles?*

1. A squabble over a pig started a feud between what two Appalachian families?

2. According to the Bible, his jealous brothers sold him to a spice caravan.

3. Which two sisters, both nominated for the Best Actress Oscar in 1941, were permanently estranged after the eldest sister won?

4. Half-brothers Julian and Sean gave peace a chance when they ended their eight-year feud. What is their last name?

5. Some MacDonalds still resent what other clan for murdering their ancestors centuries ago?

6. He killed family members for the throne, and his son tossed him in prison. But feuding Shah Jahan is best remembered as a lover because he built what monument to his wife?

7. DNA results showing he could have fathered children by his black slave sparked a feud between the white and black descendants of what U.S. president?

8. A feud between brothers Peter and Robert Mondavi impacted what California product?

9. During the 15th century's War of the Roses, the House of Lancaster took on the House of York for what prize?

10. What European mythology pits the Children of Llyr, the powers of darkness, against the Children of Dôn, the powers of light?

Answers on page 350.

HISTORY'S MYSTERIES

*Can you solve this quiz
about unsolved mysteries?*

1. What legendary island civilization (first mentioned by Plato) supposedly sank into the ocean and has never been found again?

2. In 1888, his murders of women terrorized the East End of London. What's the alias of this still-unidentified serial killer?

3. Ingrid Bergman won an Oscar in the film about which daughter of Tsar Nicolas II—the lost Grand Duchess of Russia?

4. Who was the first explorer to notice that there was something really spooky about the Bermuda Triangle?

5. Inspired by the mystery of a Bastille prisoner whose identity was kept secret by King Louis XIV, Alexandre Dumas wrote a novel entitled what?

6. What Canadian brigantine became the "ghost ship" after it was found in Spanish waters in pristine shape—but whose captain and crew had vanished?

7. In 2007, Gordon Holmes took videos of what unknown creature that's said to swim beneath the waters of Scotland's largest lake?

8. There's no written record of the once-thriving town of Gede, and no one knows why this sophisticated Swahili enclave (it even had flush toilets!) was abandoned in the 1600s. Where is it?

9. What former convict and leader of the Teamsters Union disappeared in 1975 from a Detroit parking lot and hasn't been seen since?

10. Although they agree it is somewhere along North America's Pacific Coast, historians still squabble about the exact location of New Albion. Who claimed it for England in 1579?

Answers on page 351.

LOST!

*Can you find your way through this
maze of wayward travelers?*

1. Though he wound up in America, Columbus was actually heading for what country?

2. The first woman to fly solo across the Atlantic vanished over the Pacific. Who was she?

3. Douglas "Wrong Way" Corrigan claimed navigational mistakes when he flew from New York to Ireland. Where was his plane supposed to be heading?

4. According to the Brothers Grimm, what kids were lost in the woods when they found a cottage made of bread, cakes, and sugar?

5. Dr. Livingstone (of "Dr. Livingstone, I presume" fame) found the source of the Congo River. Too bad—he thought he'd found the source of what?

6. The popular TV drama *Lost* tells the story of castaways who survived the crash of what flight from Sydney to Los Angeles?

7. When his expedition was lost in the Arctic, John Franklin was searching for what route between the Atlantic and Pacific?

8. On the African island of Pate, folks claim to be descendants of shipwrecked sailors who couldn't get home to where?

9. Hitler's lost U-boat 869 was presumed to have sunk off the coast of Morocco, but it was actually found off the shore of what U.S. state?

10. What explorer, who disappeared while climbing Mt. Everest, said he wanted to reach the summit "Because it is there"?

11. What author of *The Little Prince* disappeared while on a World War II Allied mission?

Answers on page 351.

HOW DARE THEY?

Those dastardly politicians! Do you know what they've done?

1. What scandal is named for the hotel where a 1972 break-in at the Democratic National Committee headquarters led to the resignation of President Nixon?

2. And which two *Washington Post* reporters were instrumental in exposing the Nixon Administration's cover-up of the break-in?

3. Which powerful politician hushed up his affair (with a woman whose first name began with "M") until the media exposed the scandal . . . in 1797?

4. Which trigger-happy U.S. Vice President shot a man in 1804?

5. Who wrote, "It could probably be shown by facts and figures that there is no distinctly native American criminal class except Congress"?

6. When Glaucia needed re-election to the Senate, he and colleague Saturninus instigated the murder of an opposing candidate, infuriating the citizens of which Republic?

7. What first lady of the Philippines became a worldwide symbol of greed when she announced that she owned 2,700 pairs of shoes?

8. Which American first lady drew fire for using her astrologer to dictate the president's appearances?

9. Posthumous scandal tainted Canadian Prime Minister Mackenzie King, who governed with advice from what beloved—and dead—relative?

10. The Cold War turned hot in the early 1960s after John Profumo dallied with a call girl who two-timed him with a Soviet Embassy official. Profumo's passions brought down the Conservative Government in what nation?

History

Answers on page 351.

THAT'S NO LADY

These fatal femmes have caused a lot of trouble throughout history.

1. According to medieval rumor, lovely Lucrezia had a hollow ring for poisoning the drinks of her family's enemies. What powerful Papal family did Lucrezia belong to?

2. Anne Bonny wore breeches and outfought the men while she plied what trade on the Caribbean Sea?

3. In the 17th century, Ann Putnam's testimony instigated the executions of 20 people. Later she apologized for falsely accusing them of what?

4. Which New England Sunday school teacher inspired the schoolyard rhyme "she took an axe and gave her mother forty whacks. And when she saw what she had done; she gave her father forty-one?"

5. Which devout North Carolina granny was surrounded by deaths from "gastroenteritis"—until she got caught with the arsenic?

6. Cowgirl Pearl Hart became the only female bandit to commit what crime and live to tell the tale?

7. Sharon Stone portrayed a brilliant and seductive serial murderess in what steamy film about the ultimate femme fatale?

8. Iva Toguri D'Aquino did time for allegedly broadcasting Japanese propaganda to Allied soldiers during World War II. What was the nickname connected with Iva and those broadcasts?

9. Slovakia's Countess Elizabeth Báthory was often portrayed as bathing in the blood of her murdered victims. What was her legendary motive for replacing bubble bath with gore?

10. Who was just a convicted horse thief in Texas—until legends and Hollywood made her into the West's "Bandit Queen"?

WHERE IS IT?

Can you dig up the answers to these hidden treasures?

1. Treasure hunters still hunt for millions in gold and diamonds hidden by what retreating commander of the Nazi's Afrika Korps?

2. In *Roughing It,* what famous American author hunted for California's lost Cement Mine because it held gold nuggets "as thick in it as raisins in a slice of fruit cake"?

3. When people think of buried treasure they think of pirates. But who was the only pirate actually known to bury his loot?

4. On Nova Scotia's Oak Island, treasure hunters have dug for buried treasure since 1795, making a 200-foot-deep hole nicknamed what?

5. What 1715 disaster was great for treasure hunters and lousy for King Philip V because it sank his Spanish treasure fleet off Florida's coast?

6. Treasure hunters still search the area of Washington, Georgia, for hastily hidden gold—stolen in 1865 from what government?

7. Indiana Jones hunts for biblical treasure in what films?

8. No one's busted the code of an 1885 cipher-text mapping the secret location of Thomas Beale's buried millions. But a cipher-text describing the treasure can be decoded with what historic United States document?

9. An estimated 750 tons of gold are reputed to lie buried in Ecuador— a treasure that once belonged to the ruler of what empire?

10. During French Colonial Rule, Malians hid treasures to prevent looting. In 2006, what priceless, unearthed Timbuktu treasure was brought to the U.S. Library of Congress?

History

Answers on page 352.

ON TRIAL

When it comes to courtroom drama, how will you be judged?

1. In what series of trials did the Allies charge the Nazis with crimes against humanity?

2. What TV defense attorney played by Raymond Burr often proved his client's innocence by exposing the real murderer on the witness stand?

3. What was the nickname for the trial of the Chicago baseball players who confessed to throwing the World Series?

4. In the Scopes "monkey" trial, Clarence Darrow defended a teacher who was prosecuted for teaching what theory?

5. What South African defendant said at his trial, "I have cherished the ideal of a democratic and free society…it is an ideal for which I am prepared to die"?

6. In what courtroom drama does an alcoholic lawyer (Paul Newman) find his moral center during a malpractice trial?

7. Oliver L. Brown sued the school district of Topeka, Kansas, and the resulting Supreme Court decision paved the way for what social change in American schools?

8. What philosopher and "gadfly of Athens" was tried, convicted, and executed on charges of corrupting the youth and not believing in the ancestral gods?

9. The Supreme Court case of *Marshall vs. Marshall* (involving jurisdiction of tort claims) was no yawner because the petitioner was what former Playboy Playmate?

10. What railroad heiress—now famous for designing jeans—was once the object of a bitter custody battle with rumored weeping and wailing coming from the courtroom?

Answers on page 352.

REMEMBRANCE OF THINGS PAST

Here's one for the history books.

1. The Sons of Liberty protested the tax on tea with an action that later became known as the what?

2. Who was president of the United States during the Great Depression and most of World War II?

3. What civil-rights figure refused to give up her seat on a bus to a white man?

4. The Treaty of Panmunjon ended what conflict?

5. Columbus knew the Earth was round, and thought he could sail in what direction from Europe to reach Asia?

6. Ancient Greece, Rome, and Egypt traded across what sea?

7. What explorer, trying to find the Fountain of Youth, ended up giving Spain claim to Florida by exploring St. Augustine?

8. What international organization was the first to win the Nobel Peace Prize twice?

9. Greece was known as the birthplace of what form of government?

10. A runaway slave was killed by British soldiers in the Boston Massacre. Was it Crispus Attucks, John Henry, or Nat Turner?

11. He was born in Greece, and was founder as well as the first president of Republic of Turkey. Who was he?

12. Where did General Robert E. Lee surrender to General Grant to effectively end the Civil War?

Answers on page 352.

PETER, PAUL, AND MERRY

*Each answer contains one of the title words.
Some may even have two!*

1. His real name was Simon, but he was nicknamed "the rock." His emblem is two keys. Who is he?

2. What's another name for a carousel?

3. *The Cardplayers* is an iconic work by what post-impressionist painter?

4. Who was the Russian czar from 1672 to 1725?

5. Robin Hood's outlaw followers were known as what?

6. The most popular version of "Vaya con Dios" was recorded by who and Mary Ford?

7. What fictional detective was created by Dorothy L. Sayers?

8. Charles II of England was popularly known as what?

9. This 15th-century Flemish painter of religious and allegorical scenes is perhaps best known for his voluptuous and fleshy women. Who is he?

10. Established by Peter the Great, this fortress is the final resting place of all of the Russian tsars. What is the building called?

11. What was the epithet of Ken Kesey's group, chronicled in *The Electric Kool-Aid Acid Test*?

12. What French existentialist philosopher and author wrote *Being and Nothingness*?

Answers on page 352.

RANDOM ACTS OF HISTORY

A potpourri of world history.

1. Caesar was assassinated on the "Ides of March." What date of the month was that?

2. The world's first civilization developed in Mesopotamia, which is now mostly what country?

3. During the Cold War years, what was the most visible symbol of the "Iron Curtain"?

4. Who was the queen consort of France, as the wife of Louis XVI?

5. A conflagration that started in a bakery in 1666 and destroyed more than 13,000 houses is now known as what event?

6. What German-born Swiss painter produced nearly 9,000 works of art, including *The Embrace* and *Twittering Machine*?

7. On August 27, 1926, a ticker-tape parade was held in New York for Gertrude Ederle. What was her accomplishment?

8. Modern human beings—*homo sapiens*—originated around 200,000 years ago, on what continent?

9. *The Vitruvian Man* is a famous drawing of a nude male figure in two superimposed positions with arms and legs apart and inscribed within a circle and square. Who made the drawing?

10. The Singing Revolution was the bloodless overthrow of communist states in what three Baltic countries?

11. The Third Reich was Nazi Germany. What did Germans consider the First Reich?

History

Answers on page 353.

FIRST LADIES

Test your knowledge of women (real and mythological) of the ancient world.

1. When she was unearthed in Ethiopia in 1974, it was discovered that this petite woman lived between 3 and 4 million years ago. What is her name?

2. Because she could not restrain her curiosity, this woman was blamed for releasing all the evils upon the world. What is her name?

3. What group of women warriors terrorized North Africa, Asia Minor, and the lands around the Black Sea?

4. The statue of this Egyptian was so widely photographed in the early 1900s that it influenced the standard of Western beauty for the rest of the century. Can you name her?

5. What wife of the lost Greek adventurer Odysseus said she would re-marry as soon as she finished her weaving—and then unraveled the weaving every night?

6. Himiko, the Queen of Wa, is credited with uniting dozens of warring clans to become the first person to rule this island nation. What country did she unite?

7. What Greek poet, some of whose work was discovered in ancient trash heaps, is often called "The Tenth Muse"?

8. Whose loyalty to the pagan gods earned her such a bad reputation that her name became a synonym for all disobedient and immoral women?

9. The Trung Sisters repelled invasions from neighboring China in A.D. 39–41, making them the national heroes of what country?

10. To end the bloody Peloponnesian War, what character in a play by Aristophanes persuaded women to withhold sex from their husbands until peace was secured?

Answers on page 353.

History

THE USUAL SUSPECTS

A rogues' gallery of fictional evildoers.

1. Angela Lansbury played Laurence Harvey's politically ambitious—and murderous—mother in what 1962 thriller?

2. What wisecracking criminal, nicknamed Gotham City's "clown prince," taunted the authorities by leaving playing cards at the scene of his crimes?

3. What black-clad woman sought revenge on her sister's accidental death by threatening that she "could cause accidents too"?

4. What criminal mastermind enjoyed having old friends for dinner—especially "with fava beans and a nice Chianti"?

5. What rogue scientist and self-described Prometheus is obsessed with annihilating his high-flying nemesis, obliterating Metropolis, and ruling the planet?

6. Who's the two-toned, fur-loving, evil diva who is so cruel that her country home is nicknamed "Hell Hall"?

7. What brilliant professor and mathematician, known as the Napoleon of Crime, hides an air rifle in his cane?

8. What Asian villain with "a face like Satan," created by British author Sax Rohmer, was the inspiration for James Bond's nemesis, Dr. No?

9. What is the name of the squat, toadlike woman whose interests in the dark arts include taking sadistic pleasure in terrorizing her students?

10. What 1988 action film features Alan Rickman as Hans Gruber, a techno-terrorist who plots to steal bank bonds from the vault of a skyscraper?

History

Answers on page 353.

WHAT'S HER NAME?

Famous floating transports.

1. Name the ship that spilled 11 million gallons of oil in Alaska's Prince William Sound on March 24, 1989.

2. Which of Christopher Columbus's three ships never made it back to Spain after his first voyage to the New World?

3. The SS *Stockholm* struck and sank what Italian ocean liner off the coast of Nantucket in 1956, resulting in the death of 46 passengers and crew?

4. What is the name of the raft used by Thor Heyerdahl in 1947 to travel 4,300 miles from Peru to Polynesia?

5. More than 1,170 lives were lost when what U.S. battleship sank during the Japanese attack at Pearl Harbor on December 7, 1941?

6. Fletcher Christian led a 1789 mutiny, casting adrift the captain and 18 crewmen of which British Royal Navy ship?

7. The sinking of which ship in 1898 precipitated the Spanish–American War and also instituted a famous rallying cry?

8. Which luxury ocean liner that sailed the North Atlantic from 1936 to 1967 is today a 365-room, three-star Art Deco hotel in Long Beach, California?

9. Which sister ship of the RMS *Olympic* and RMS *Titanic* sank in 1916 after hitting a mine with the loss of 30 lives?

10. What was the name of Robert Fulton's ship that was the first steamship built in the Unites States and the first commercially successful steamship in the world?

Answers on page 353.

QUARTER BACKS

Rifle through your pockets and you might find some answers.

1. What does the three-word caption on the back of the Delaware state quarter say?

2. What animal is found on Kentucky's state quarter?

3. Washington crosses the Delaware on which state's quarter?

4. A keystone is one of several designs on this state's quarter. What's the state?

5. What state's quarter shows a trumpet, fiddle, and guitar?

6. Keep the trumpet, replace the fiddle and guitar with a pelican, and you'll be looking at the back of which state's quarter?

7. An American bison and sunflowers grace the back of which quarter?

8. Which state's quarter has a lighthouse and schooner?

9. Who are the two flyboys pictured on North Carolina's quarter?

10. The completion of the Transcontinental Railroad, along with the "Golden Spike," adorn which state's quarter?

11. Name the 1607 event's quadricentennial celebrated on Virginia's quarter.

12. A portrait of Helen Keller along with her name written in Braille can be found on which state's quarter?

13. What state has the incongruous combination of a diamond, rice stalks, and a mallard duck flying over a lake?

History

Answers on page 354.

TO ERR IS DIVINE

Some of the world's best inventions and discoveries were found by mistake.

1. What office supply was created in 1968 as a result of a 3M scientist accidentally creating a semi-sticky adhesive?

2. Which popular metal toy—fun for a girl or a boy—accidentally sprang into department stores in 1945?

3. Pharmacist John Pemberton found the real thing by accident when looking for a medicinal cure-all. Instead, which popular carbonated beverage did he invent?

4. What tasty snack was discovered in the 1600s when a baker fell asleep and let these "little rewards" bake too long?

5. What accident cleanly floated its way to the top of Proctor and Gamble's products, all 99 $^{44}/_{100}$% of it?

6. In 1943, a test tube full of boric acid and silicone oil was thrown onto the floor by an excited scientist, only to bounce back up and become what National Toy Hall of Fame plaything?

7. In the early 1940s, inventor George de Mestral took his dog for a walk in a field full of cockleburs, which ended up in his dog's coat and his own pants. Upon closer inspection, he noticed their hook-like shape and invented which modern fastener?

8. What popular plastic toy was inspired by a metal pie tin?

9. In 1901, Wilhelm Conrad Röntgen received the first Nobel Prize in Physics for which accidental discovery?

10. In 1853, a dinner guest in Saratoga Springs, New York, complained about his food, and chef George Crum decided to "fix" the dinner. The guest loved it. What popular snack food did Crum accidentally invent out of spite?

NATIVE SONS

Famous Native American men and women throughout history.

1. Credited for successfully laying siege to Fort Detroit in 1763, which Ottawa chief's name lives on as a General Motors brand?

2. On June 25, 1876, General George Custer and the 7th Cavalry were pitted against which great Lakota chief and over 2,000 braves at Little Big Horn?

3. Which Patuxet tribe member, along with Native American Samoset, is best known for teaching the Pilgrims survival skills during their first difficult winter in the New World?

4. Which trees are named after the Native American silversmith who was the first to create a written list of symbols for the Cherokee language?

5. Three American towns are named after which Apache war chief, whose name continues to this day to be a fierce battle cry?

6. "From where the sun now stands, I will fight no more forever" is the last line of a famous surrender statement by which Nez Perce chief, known for his pacifism?

7. Which well-known Apache chief successfully prevented both the Mexican and American governments from taking control of Arizona between 1856 and 1872?

8. Which Native American athlete is the only person to win both the Olympic pentathlon and decathlon in the same year?

9. Which full-blooded Mohawk played the part of Tonto, the Lone Ranger's faithful companion, on TV from 1949 to 1957?

10. Which leader of the Mohawk nation around 1410 was made famous 450 years later in an epic poem written by Henry Wadsworth Longfellow?

History

Answers on page 354.

KEEP THE FAITH!

We've got questions about religions.

1. The word "Thursday" comes from the name of what Norse deity?

2. The story of Zao Jun, a domestic deity, gets a feminist spin in what Amy Tan novel?

3. A cross is the symbol of Christianity and a six-pointed star is the symbol of Judaism. A crescent and smaller star is the symbol of what religion?

4. Of all religions, which one claims the largest number of adherents worldwide, with more than 33 percent of the human population?

5. In this evangelistic Hindu sect, male believers wear white or saffron robes, shave their heads except for a topknot, and chant, dance, and sing in public. What's the religion?

6. Native American tribes such as the Anasazi, Hopi, and Zuni venerate a humpbacked, flute-playing trickster god who represents fertility and music. What's his name?

7. A small case containing a parchment inscribed with Hebrew verses is affixed to the doorposts of many Jewish homes. What is this religious article called?

8. What German monk and reformer is considered to be the founder of Protestantism?

9. What religion accepts Haile Selassie I, the former Emperor of Ethiopia, as God incarnate?

10. In the New Testament, these godly messengers are agents of revelation and are most prominent at the birth of Jesus, the resurrection, and in the Apocalypse. What are these heavenly ministers called?

11. *The Watchtower* and *Awake* magazines are distributed by what religious group?

Answers on page 354.

THAT'S SO FIVE CENTURIES AGO!

Test your knowledge of fashion history in everything from hair to underwear.

1. Until the 1830s what did fashionable women wear under petticoats?

2. In the 17th century what makeup was used to give complexions a fashionable pallor, even though it caused digestive and neurological troubles?

3. The Oppian Law limited the extravagance of upper-class female fashions. Where was the first recorded demonstration by women hoping to repeal it?

4. In 1776, with homespun farmer's clothing and his long, unpowdered hair, what American diplomat became France's fashion icon?

5. What would a Civil War belle like Scarlett O'Hara wear under her hoop skirt just in case those skirts flew up in a high wind?

6. What medieval eye drops were used to make a lady's eyes brighter, though they had the unfortunate side effect of possible blindness?

7. When King George II imposed the 1746 "Dress Act," he outlawed what Highland article of clothing worn by English royalty to this day?

8. What Victorian fashion gave ladies loads of derriere?

9. Why did Alexandra, Princess of Wales, introduce choker necklaces and jeweled collars into Victorian fashion?

10. Who said, "Beauty of style and harmony and grace and good rhythm depend on simplicity"?

11. In the 1700s, why were British soldiers routinely given a pound of flour?

History

CURSED KING HENRY

According to Mel Brooks, "It's good to be the king!" But it wasn't good to be anywhere near King Henry VIII of England.

1. What Spanish royal couple and Columbus backers were the parents of Henry VIII's first wife, Catherine of Aragon?

2. Which of Henry's wives, the one rumored to have six fingers on one hand, was widely thought to be a witch?

3. Henry agreed to marry his fourth wife based on an "embellished" portrait of her. When he finally saw her, he described his bride-to-be as a "Flanders mare."

4. Catherine Howard, Henry's fifth wife and 30 years his junior, lost her head as a result of doing what?

5. Henry's last wife, Katherine Parr, was shrewder than the rest—she kept her head and survived her royal husband. She also served as his nurse because he suffered from what medical condition?

6. Jane Seymour (wife #3) didn't last long as queen, but unlike most of the others, she died of natural causes. What killed her?

7. Which wife got him to marry her by insisting they "wed before bed"? (She'd learned her lesson by watching Henry dump his many mistresses, including her own sister.)

8. What was the nickname of Henry's elder daughter who tried to restore Catholicism in England?

9. Known as the Virgin Queen, Henry's younger daughter ruled England for 45 years and is widely considered to have been one of the country's best monarchs. Who was she?

10. Beheadings were a popular form of entertainment in Tudor England. What was the name of Henry's powerful minister whose severed head was mounted on a spike and displayed on London Bridge after he recommended Henry's disastrous fourth marriage?

Answers on page 355.

THEY RULED!

These 20th-century leaders left their marks on the world.

1. In the 1980s, he introduced the ideas of *glasnost* and *perestroika* to the former Soviet Union and was implored by United States president Ronald Reagan to "tear down this wall!"

2. These two world leaders made history in September 1978 when they signed the Camp David Accords, pledging peace between long-time enemies Egypt and Israel.

3. What general led a military coup during the late 1930s, took control of Spain, and installed himself as dictator and head of state? His regime lasted until his death in 1975.

4. During the 1960s, '70s, and '80s, she served four terms as India's prime minister and remains the first and only woman to hold that office.

5. He won the Nobel Prize in Literature in 1953, but is best remembered as the prime minister who led Great Britain to victory in World War II.

6. This emperor authorized the daring attack at Pearl Harbor but ultimately saw his country surrender unconditionally to the United States. (He was the only Axis leader to survive World War II.)

7. What prime minister of Great Britain from 1979 to 1990 is credited with revitalizing the country's economy during her time in office?

8. This "iron lady" was one of the founders of Israel. (She also served as the country's fourth prime minister.)

9. What dictator's antagonistic relationship with the United States has lasted more than 45 years, since he overthrew General Fulgencio Batista in 1959 and established communism in his nation?

10. When the Nazis invaded France in 1940, this military leader fled to London, where he directed the French resistance.

History

BATTLE CRY

Here's another opportunity to test your battle savvy.

1. Churchill called what battle his country's "finest hour?" When it was over, he said, "Never in the field of human conflict was so much owed by so many to so few."

2. In what Civil War battle, named after a nearby creek, was the retreat of the Union forces called "The Great Skedaddle?"

3. What novel by a German World War I veteran recounts the horrors of war and its after-effects as experienced by the individual soldier?

4. With what famous expletive did General McAuliffe respond to a German surrender ultimatum during the Battle of the Bulge?

5. What novelist drew on his experience as a POW captured during the Battle of the Bulge for his novel *Slaughterhouse Five*?

6. What London landmark commemorates the battle where a British fleet defeated the French and Spanish navies?

7. What fierce barbarian king was defeated by the Romans in the Battle of Chalons, leading one historian to write, "It should never be forgotten that in the summer of 451 and again in 452, the whole fate of Western civilization hung in the balance"?

8. The 1840 presidential campaign slogan "Tippecanoe and Tyler too" reminded voters of what candidate's heroism during his victory over Chief Tecumseh's Native American alliance?

9. During the Second Punic War, what Carthaginian and one of history's greatest military strategists defeated superior Roman forces by marching an army—including war elephants—over the Alps?

Answers on page 355.

History

OH, MUMMY

*Don't be in de Nile when it comes to
knowledge of ancient Egypt.*

1. When seducing Julius Caesar or Marc Antony, Cleopatra dissolved what jewels in vinegar as an aphrodisiac?

2. Believing it to be the center of a person's being and intelligence, Egyptians left which organ inside an embalmed body?

3. As far as those seven wonders of the ancient world go, what's so unique about the Great Pyramid of Giza?

4. The Great Sphinx of Giza is the largest single stone statue on Earth—with the face of a man and the body of what animal?

5. Rising about 390 feet above the Egyptian island of Pharos, what was the only wonder of the ancient world with a practical use?

6. Who fueled rumors of a mummy's curse when he died only seven weeks after he'd entered the sealed tomb of King Tutankhamen?

7. Theories that Tutankhamen was murdered by a blow to the head were quashed when a CAT scan of his mummy indicated the teen king died from complications of what?

8. Her sculptured likeness has made what ancient Egyptian queen renowned for her beauty?

9. When Egyptian women urinated on grains to see if they sprouted, they were performing the first-known (and surprisingly accurate) version of what medical test?

10. The ancient cities Menouthis and Herakleion disappeared over 1,500 years ago but have finally been located—at the bottom of what sea?

History

Answers on page 356.

THE CRUSADES

*What do you know about all those busy knights . . .
and bloody days of crusading?*

1. Byzantine Emperor Alexius I Comnenus was nearly overwhelmed by fervent crusaders after he asked for Western mercenaries to help vanquish what foe?

2. Which pope launched the crusades with a fiery speech demanding that Christians take the Holy Land out of the hands of the Turks?

3. After the pope's speech, many men, not to mention women and children, left home to fight. What priest is famous for leading this People's Crusade?

4. After the crusaders marched off, their first actual battle (which started over the cost of supplies) took place with fellow Christians in what country?

5. Most crusaders believed that by retaking Jerusalem they were guaranteed access to what reward?

6. When the first crusaders finally did take Jerusalem, they massacred what two religious groups already living there?

7. According to legend, what French queen on the Second Crusade dressed like an Amazon warrior and urged people to fight?

8. St. Marks in Venice is still graced today by the rich booty stolen from what Christian city by participants in the Fourth Crusade?

9. Crusaders may have disdained the enemy, but they loved the enemy's horses—and bred Arabian stallions to English mares to create what breed of horse?

10. What celebrated king of England spent most of his time either fighting in the Holy Land or living in France and used the country's fortunes to finance his crusades?

Answers on page 356.

History

FOUND!

Historical finds.

1. A popular Beatles song inspired the name of one of the greatest anthropological finds. What's the name of the "missing link" discovered by Dr. Donald Johanson and a team of paleontologists in 1974?

2. A piece of fabric was first historically recorded in 1357 in Lirey, France, and has become history's single most-studied artifact. "Sindonology" describes the in-depth analysis of what relic?

3. Abducted from her Salt Lake City home and missing for more than seven months in 2002, what 14-year-old girl was found alive?

4. What famous Da Vinci painting was stolen from the Louvre in 1911 and found in 1913?

5. What was the most unusual thing about Egypt's King Hatshepsut, who was found in 1881 amid a royal cache of mummies in the Valley of the Kings?

6. Comprised of roughly 900 documents, what was found in 11 caves near a settlement in Qumran by a Bedouin sheepherder?

7. What hieroglyphic relic was found in 1799 by the French in a small village near Alexandria, Egypt?

8. The Mildenhall Treasure is hoard of 4th-century silver Roman pieces found by a ploughman in 1943 in the English county of Suffolk. What famed Welsh author wrote a story called "The Mildenhall Treasure," first published in *Ladies' Home Journal* in 1946?

9. In 1952, physician and researcher Jonas Salk found the cure for which disabling disease?

10. This Civil War Confederate ironclad warship fought the Union's ironclad *Monitor* in an 1862 battle that redefined naval warfare.

History

WHAT'S THIS QUIZ ABOUT, EH?

Good-natured wordplay for Canadians only: all answers contain "eh."

1. The 1994 Olympics in this town are considered one of the greatest Winter Games ever. What's the town?

2. It's the birthplace of David, the birthplace of Jesus of Nazareth according to the gospels, and the traditional site of Rachel's tomb. What West Bank city is it?

3. It's a hairdo, a word in the Utah state nickname, or something found in an apiary. What is it?

4. He rebuilt the walls of Jerusalem, and his Old Testament book precedes Esther's. Who is he?

5. It's a really big but unspecified amphibious animal, and one word for it can be found in Job 40:15–24. Hippopotamus? Water buffalo? Crocodile? Dinosaur? We don't know. What's the word?

6. A fictional cockroach named Archie had an alley-cat pal named what? You have to love her indomitable spirit; she would always say, "There's a dance in the old dame yet."

7. Let's get serious now. What is Canada's oldest independent brewery, whose labels include Clancy's Amber Ale and Ten-Penny Old Stock Ale?

8. The mascot of the Japanese video game company Sega is Sonic the . . . what spiny mammal?

9. Two of the three creators of this long-running rural comedy, taped at Opryland USA, were Canadian. What was the series?

10. It's time to say goodbye, just as they'd say it in Göttingen. What would they say?

Answers on page 357.

UP NORTH

Canadiana revisited.

1. Canada has its own version of the Loch Ness monster. What's it called, and where is it supposedly found?

2. What British Columbian town sounds like a TV teen drama that starred James Van Der Beek and Katie Holmes?

3. Where in Canada would you find the Big Nickel, listed in *Guinness World Records* as the world's largest coin?

4. What small Prince Edward Island town is famous for its *Anne of Green Gables* house?

5. Shania Twain is the most famous native of this city, which until 2001 was Canada's largest municipality in land area. What's the city?

6. Two places in Canada lay claim to having the highest tides in the world. Can you name one?

7. The Montreal Expos relocated from Canada to Washington, D.C., after the 2004 season. What are they called now?

8. This Canadian city is nicknamed the City of Gardens. What is it?

9. The residents of Moose Jaw, Saskatchewan, are called what?

10. What Canadian city is famous—or infamous—for having a notoriously windy intersection?

11. What city is home to the annual Canadian Tulip Festival every May?

12. What national animal is depicted on the Canadian five-cent piece?

Answers on page 357.

Canada

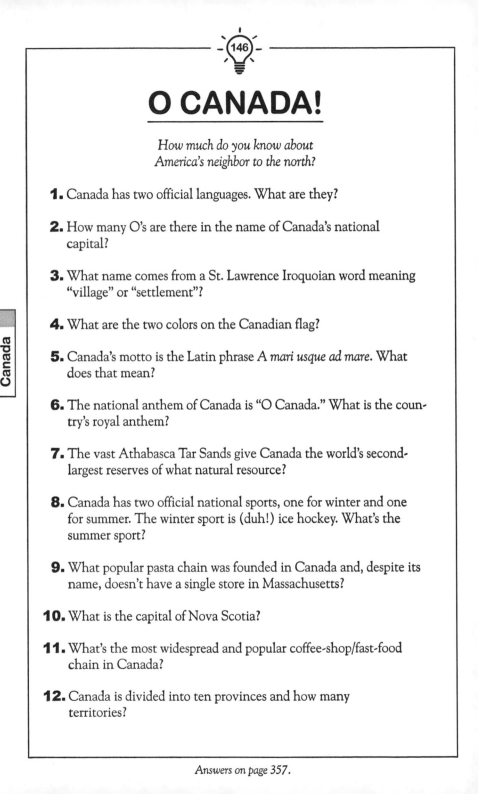

O CANADA!

*How much do you know about
America's neighbor to the north?*

1. Canada has two official languages. What are they?

2. How many O's are there in the name of Canada's national capital?

3. What name comes from a St. Lawrence Iroquoian word meaning "village" or "settlement"?

4. What are the two colors on the Canadian flag?

5. Canada's motto is the Latin phrase *A mari usque ad mare*. What does that mean?

6. The national anthem of Canada is "O Canada." What is the country's royal anthem?

7. The vast Athabasca Tar Sands give Canada the world's second-largest reserves of what natural resource?

8. Canada has two official national sports, one for winter and one for summer. The winter sport is (duh!) ice hockey. What's the summer sport?

9. What popular pasta chain was founded in Canada and, despite its name, doesn't have a single store in Massachusetts?

10. What is the capital of Nova Scotia?

11. What's the most widespread and popular coffee-shop/fast-food chain in Canada?

12. Canada is divided into ten provinces and how many territories?

Canada

Answers on page 357.

IN THE PROVINCES AND THE TERRITORIES

Provincial Canada.

1. Banff National Park is Canada's oldest national park. In what province is it located?

2. What are Canada's three "prairie provinces"?

3. Which is the largest of Canada's provinces in area?

4. What are the four original Canadian provinces, federated in 1867?

5. Which province is largest in population?

6. Mount Logan is Canada's highest mountain. In what province or territory is it located?

7. What's the longest river in Canada, and what province or territory is it in?

8. At Magnetic Hill, Canada's third most visited natural attraction, cars appear to "mysteriously" roll uphill. In what province is it located?

9. When the *Titanic* was struck by an iceberg and sank in 1912, it was southeast of which Canadian province?

10. What is Canada's smallest province?

11. What's the capital of Nunavut?

12. Which province is known as Canada's "energy province"?

Canada

Answers on page 358.

NORTH STARS

Canadian celebrities.

1. He's been called "the most recognized face in Canada" and "the biggest mouth in sports." Who can that be?

2. What Russian-born Canadian entrepreneur founded the distillery empire that later took the name of Seagram?

3. What world-famous entertainment empire was founded by Canadian entrepreneur and former street performer Guy Laliberté?

4. What Ontario-born director-producer-screenwriter directed the top-grossing film of all time—and what's the film?

5. What ice-hockey star is the founder and namesake of Canada's largest fast-food chain?

6. What Canadian pop/rock singer had big hits with "Sundown," "Carefree Highway," and "If You Could Read My Mind"?

7. What Fort Saskatchewan–born actress lived in a grass hut in the Philippines at age 18 and then became a star on ABC's *Lost,* although she says she doesn't watch television or own a TV set?

8. What NFL placekicker set and still holds the record for kicking the longest field goal ever made in Super Bowl history—54 yards in Super Bowl XXVIII?

9. Which head of a major Hollywood studio was born in Canada?

10. In the latter part of the 18th century, Simon McTavish was perhaps Canada's most influential businessman in what industry?

11. What Canadian-American sports entrepreneur built the oval-shaped arena the Forum in the Los Angeles suburb of Inglewood?

Answers on page 358.

O CANADIANS!

More famous folk from Maple Leaf country.

1. What Ontario-born hockey player is nicknamed "the Great One"?

2. What media baron and art collector was Canada's richest person at the time of his death in 2006?

3. This Toronto-born architect's works include the Experience Music Project in Seattle, the Walt Disney Concert Hall in Los Angeles, and the Fish Dance in Kobe, Japan. Who is he?

4. Yousuf Karsh was a famous Canadian (though born in Armenia). What was he famous for?

5. Born in Quebec, Marc Gagnon has won three Olympic gold medals—in what sport?

6. Most Canadians probably know the name of Roberta Bondar. What is she famous for?

7. What do the performers Mary Pickford, Howie Mandel, Guy Lombardo, Jim Carrey, and Alex Trebek all have in common— besides being Canadian?

8. What longtime *60 Minutes* correspondent was born in Canada?

9. *The Handmaid's Tale* and *The Blind Assassin* are novels by what Canadian author?

10. What adventure-loving Canadian became a buffalo hunter, frontier marshal, gunfighter, fight promoter, and sports columnist?

11. Former Canadian prime minister Lester B. Pearson was awarded a 1957 Nobel Prize in what category?

12. What was the nickname of the publishing tycoon and entrepreneur Max Aitken?

Canada

Answers on page 358.

NORTHERN HIGHLIGHTS

Test your smarts about all things Canadian.

1. How many oceans does Canada border?

2. Two of the three capitals of Canadian territories have colors in their names. Can you name them?

3. What is the standard abbreviation for Manitoba?

4. Who is Canada's head of state?

5. How many main parties are there in the Canadian parliament?

6. What are the two largest cities in Canada, by population?

7. What are "beaver tails"?

8. In what Canadian territory is the magnetic North Pole found?

9. Where is the world's largest skating rink?

10. The world's longest city street begins in Toronto. What is its name?

11. What Canadian territory has almost no trees?

12. Who represents the queen when she is not present in Canada?

13. What is the tallest mountain in the Canadian Rockies?

14. The biggest waterfall in Canada is located in Ontario. Can you name it?

15. Canada is the second-largest country in the world in terms of what?

Answers on page 359.

Canada

CHOCOLATE-COVERED QUIZ

Tasty but not very fattening.

1. The scientific name for the cacao (cocoa) tree is *Theobroma cacao.* That's fitting because *Theobroma* is Latin for what?

2. About 1500 BC, in the rain forests of Central America, which clever folks started making drinks from cacao beans?

3. What conquistador loaded up his ships with New World cacao beans and sailed home to turn the Spanish into chocaholics?

4. Chocolate syrup is the fake blood flowing through the famous shower scene in what Hitchcock film?

5. Whose mother taught him that "life is like a box of chocolates, you never know what you're going to get"?

6. Dark chocolate contains flavonoids that are known to protect the health of what bodily organ?

7. Chocolate also contains the alkaloid theobromine, which makes the treat poisonous for what important family member?

8. Wanting to whip up something special for patrons of her Massachusetts restaurant, Ruth Wakefield cut a semisweet chocolate bar into her cookie dough and invented what in the 1930s? (Bonus: Name the restaurant.)

9. What is the only U.S. state that grows cacao trees to make chocolate?

10. At 24 pounds per person annually, which country's citizens chow down the most chocolate?

Food and Drink

Answers on page 359.

THEM'S DRINKIN' WORDS

A spirited quiz for the over-21 crowd.

1. The name of what liquor is the Russian word for water?

2. It sells for around $1,500 a bottle. What kind of alcoholic beverage is Louis XIII de Remy Martin?

3. What is the American name for the classic Latin cocktail, the Cuba Libre—served with or without lime juice?

4. What liquor, the main ingredient in the original martini, gets its distinctive flavor from juniper berries?

5. If you're drinking mezcal con gusano, a close relative of tequila, what's that thing lying there at the bottom of the bottle?

6. What is the Greek national drink, an 80-proof anise-flavored beverage that is manufactured nowhere else but its home country?

7. Barley dried by peat-fueled fires gives what liquor its distinctive smoky flavor?

8. What gives a Cosmopolitan its pretty pink color?

9. The popular beverages Seagram's VO and Crown Royal are two of the best sellers in which liquor category?

10. In what state is Lynchburg (population 361), home of the Jack Daniel's distillery?

11. Sure, there's a Manhattan, but what is a Bronx cocktail?

12. If you add a miniature onion to a martini, what is the drink called?

Answers on page 359.

SWEET TALK

The yummiest quiz in the book.

1. Choo Choo Charlie used to fuel his train with what coated licorice candy that happens to be the oldest branded candy in the United States?

2. Launched in 1941, what colorful candy originally appeared in brown, yellow, orange, red, and (believe it or not) violet?

3. What candy bar is named after a street in the town of Reading, Pennsylvania, not the fancy Manhattan street you probably thought it referred to?

4. What candy brand's 50 official jelly bean flavors include Toasted Marshmallow, Jalapeno, and Buttered Popcorn?

5. Those chewy jellied Chuckles come in five flavors. Can you name four of the five?

6. Introduced in 1938 by a dramatic skywriting campaign, what candy bar offers four distinct sections (fudge, caramel, peanut, and vanilla), each covered in chocolate?

7. What candy bar originally came in three pieces so that you could share it with friends—like the trio it was named for?

8. It's the best-selling candy bar of all time—what is it?

9. Do you know what makes Red Hots so darn hot?

10. What bar made by Nestlé, if its name were taken literally, would constitute enough money to buy a Mercedes-Benz CL?

11. On an episode of *Seinfeld*, what small, chocolate-covered candy did Kramer accidentally drop into a patient during an operation?

Food and Drink

Answers on page 360.

TV DINNERS

Famous food on the boob tube.

1. What TV family's daily diet might include such appetizing entrées as marinated gizzard of lizard and tongue of yak?

2. Buzz Beer was brewed in a microbrewery located in a Cleveland garage on what show?

3. A character on *Happy Days* enjoyed a garnish of parsley with his sandwich, but he hated liver. Who was he?

4. What rumpled 1970s TV detective liked chili with ketchup and crackers and sparkling cream soda?

5. One of the two female leads on this show (the ditzy one) liked to eat peanut butter and sauerkraut on raisin bread. Name her.

6. On an episode of this 1960s series, kitchen-challenged Elly May makes a sponge cake—using real sponges. What was the series?

7. Two of Lisa Douglas's gourmet specialties were "eggs fried in the shell" and "upside downside up cake." Name her series.

8. What TV character has eaten a tiny bicycle, a huge log of gummy worms, a rotten hoagie he found in the trash, a bar made of five pounds of concentrated spaghetti, Vaseline, and his own soul disguised as a donut?

9. On what sci-fi series do the alien races partake of such delicacies as *breen*, a meat dish akin to the Swedish meatballs made on Earth, and *hot jala*, a thick, milky-green beverage made from the sap of the jalwah tree?

10. "Who wants to try my garlic tuna with bananas?" asks Dad. "I'd rather eat mulch," says Randy. "Then you'll love my lemongrass chili pudding," Dad answers. What was the series?

Food and Drink

SAY CHEESE

Break out the crackers and wine, because after
you read about all these different kinds of
cheese, your mouth will be watering.

1. What American cheese product, introduced in 1928, is named for its extremely smooth consistency when melted?

2. *Everybody Loves Raymond* is based on the real-life experiences of what comedian whose last name is a popular Italian cheese?

3. This cheese is made exclusively in three counties in England: Derbyshire, Leicestershire, and Nottinghamshire. What is it?

4. According to the kid's riddle, which cheese is always made backward?

5. In America, roped or braided mozzarella formed in half-inch cylinders about six inches long is called what?

6. What generic name is often given to Emmentaler and Gruyère cheese?

7. The milk of what animal is used to make Roquefort cheese?

8. What state is second after Wisconsin in U.S. cheese production?

9. What Mediterranean cheese is salted and cured in a brine solution for weeks before serving?

10. Geitost, Graddost, and Jarlsberg all come from which country?

11. Its protected designation of origins include Parma and Reggio Emilia, and the true version is made from cow's milk produced only from May to November. Name this cheese.

12. What cheese takes its name from Britain's biggest gorge (and is the United States' favorite cheese)?

Food and Drink

Answers on page 360.

OUR DAILY BREAD

No matter how you slice it, it's the staff of life.

1. With its origins in Mexico and Central America, what unleavened flatbread is made with either cornmeal or wheat flour?

2. Johnnycake is another name for this Southern side dish traditionally baked in a cast-iron skillet.

3. What is the name of the braided or round, very sweet, golden yellow bread served on Jewish holidays?

4. Which bread became a northern California staple during the Gold Rush era and has remained a San Francisco specialty?

5. What rounded specialty yeast breads get their unique taste from the practice of boiling the dough before baking?

6. Made with flour, baking soda, buttermilk, salt, and no yeast, what European bread is traditionally baked with a cross imprinted on the top crust?

7. A Southern staple, what crunchy, dark breads are the result of deep-frying buttermilk batter that may include beer, onions, and chopped peppers?

8. What American steamed bread, made with a blend of wheat, rye, and corn flours, is named for a state capital on the East Coast?

9. First created in Germany more than 500 years ago, what cakelike bread served during Christmas is filled with fruits, nuts, and spices and sprinkled with sugar?

10. The name of what popular German sourdough sandwich bread translates into "the devil's fart"?

11. Used as a scoop for dip or the base for a gyro, this Mediterranean bread's name is Greek for "pie."

Answers on page 360.

TIME TO SPICE THINGS UP

Test your knowledge of herbs and spices.

1. What culinary flavoring is called "the stinking rose"?

2. Credited with "discovering" America, Columbus also "discovered" what popular bean that flavors ice cream?

3. What Ivy League college was founded with profits from the East Indian spice trade?

4. Indonesia's Moluccas—home of nutmeg, mace, and cloves—were once known to Westerners by what name?

5. Soldiers in ancient Rome were paid part of their salary with what seasoning?

6. This spice that tastes like licorice is used to flavor everything from liqueur to mousetrap bait?

7. What spice (popular for Thanksgiving turkey dressing) was once used to cure snakebites in ancient Greece and Rome?

8. Put it in apple pies if you must, but Antony and Cleopatra used this spice to liven up their love life. What is it?

9. What is the world's most expensive spice (by weight)?

10. What country suffered a culinary crisis when paprika (its national spice) was banned for safety reasons?

11. Black pepper is what Asian country's gift to the world?

12. What spice in curry powder has been shown to slow the progress of leukemia?

Food and Drink

Answers on page 361.

HAIL TO THE CHEF

If this quiz doesn't make you hungry,
then you may not have a stomach. Bon apétit!

1. Thanks to Paul Hogan commercials, if you're barbecuing for an Aussie, you might want to throw another ____ on the ____, even if they almost never say that Down Under!

2. Shish kebab is a popular BBQ entrée. What does "shish kebab" mean, literally?

3. Who created the long-popular cooking show *The French Chef*, even though she was neither French nor, at the time, a trained chef?

4. What term is used for the person who is second in command to the head chef?

5. Although he was rumored to have trained under Escoffier, this famous revolutionary worked as a baker in Boston before going on to become prime minister and then president of Vietnam. Who is he?

6. In what 1978 comedy that stars George Segal, Jacqueline Bisset, and Robert Morley is someone killing the chefs in the manner of his or her most famous dish?

7. In a large hotel or professional kitchen, what is the *pâtissier*?

8. In Australia it's called "reef and beef." What is this entrée called in the United States?

9. If a waiter brings your minestrone and apologizes that they were out of cannellini, what's missing from your soup?

10. It's called "mahi-mahi" in Hawaii, but what is another name for this fish?

11. If you order chicken cordon bleu, how will it be served?

Answers on page 361.

COUNTER INTELLIGENCE

*Know what a cup of joe is? Then this quiz on
diner lingo ought to be a piece of cake.*

1. Rather than leaving them swirling in hot water, it takes the cook just three minutes to put "Adam and Eve on a raft." What is it?

2. It's hot outside, and your throat's parched—so parched that it's time to get an "M.D. with hail." What did you order?

3. What dish was known briefly as "foreign entanglements"?

4. "Mike and Ike" are usually found sitting on every table in a diner.

5. "Wax on"—what's this addition to a burger?

6. When the waitress says "draw one with life preservers," what's she getting for you?

7. "Bossy in a bowl" is a hearty meal for a winter day. What is it?

8. On a hot afternoon, kids love "houseboats," especially if you "throw in the mud." What's this special treat?

9. If the kitchen is "in the weeds," what's the cook's problem?

10. Name this all-American meal: "one cow on the hoof, make it cry, with a side of frog sticks."

11. What's this meal, straight off the children's menu: "hounds on an island"? (The "island" alone is sometimes called "whistleberries")

12. What dinner includes a "first lady with a Murphy, a side of cow feed, and lots of napkins"?

Food and Drink

Answers on page 361.

BOOZE CLUES

Can you name the liquor?

1. Which liqueur—a mix of Mexican coffee, vanilla, sugar, corn syrup, vodka, and cane spirits—is the second best-selling cordial in the world?

2. Toasted hazelnuts, toasted cocoa, toasted coffee, vanilla berries, and orange flowers are all combined to create what northern Italian liqueur?

3. What beverage is a slightly thick and rich combination of malt whiskey, honey, herbs, and spices created at a boutique distillery on the Isle of Skye.

4. This green European spirit, whose sale is illegal in the United States, contains 15 different herbs, including wormwood, which shares a toxic element also found in marijuana.

5. A popular dark and bitter German 70-proof "J" liqueur, this drink's name translates to "Master Hunter." (It's usually served straight and chilled.)

6. What cordial, made with fine French cognac infused with tropical oranges, sells for between $40 and $225?

7. Sold under a number of brands in both white and black varieties, what anise-flavored liqueur is traditionally served straight with three roasted espresso beans?

8. A ruby red, intensely sweet French cordial, this liqueur is made with raspberries, honey, blackberries, vanilla, cognac, and herbs.

9. According to its makers, only two monks know how to blend the 130 plants that go into which classic French 100-proof liqueur?

10. What clear Italian cinnamon-flavored schnapps has about $2 worth of 24-carat gold leaf flakes is each 750 ml bottle?

Answers on page 361.

JUNK FOOD FOR THOUGHT

Would you like some fries with this quiz? Please drive through.

1. Jared Fogle, who once weighed over 400 pounds, was used in their ads after he claimed to have lost 245 pounds eating only this chain's food.

2. What American chain is named after a Rolling Stones song?

3. This coffee chain is named after a character in Herman Melville's *Moby Dick*.

4. The first modern drive-through window was introduced in 1971 by what fast-food franchise?

5. What burger chain was founded first: Burger King, McDonald's, or In-N-Out Burger?

6. Square, five-hole burgers known as "Slyders" are the product of what fast-food chain visited by Harold and Kumar in 2004?

7. This fast-food chain perpetrated an April Fool's hoax in 1996 by claiming in a *New York Times* ad that it had purchased the Liberty Bell and renamed it after itself.

8. How many herbs and spices are in Colonel Sanders' secret blend for his original fried chicken recipe?

9. *Fast Food Nation: The Dark Side of the American Food Industry* by Eric Schlosser has been compared to what famous work by Upton Sinclair about the meat-packing industry?

10. Which chain prints book, chapter, and verse numbers (but not the text) from the Bible on its paper products as a reflection of its owners' Christian beliefs?

Food and Drink

Answers on page 362.

WHAT'S FOR DINNER?

Snack time for your brain.

1. In Canada, what product is commonly called "Kraft dinner" regardless of whether or not Kraft is the manufacturer?

2. You dry what fruit to get a prune?

3. What man invented flash-freezing, which made modern frozen food possible? (There's still a line of frozen foods bearing his name.)

4. On average, each citizen of Guam consumes 16 cans of this spiced ham product annually. Hawaii, another place where it is popular, has the only McDonald's that serves it. What is it?

5. Celery, chocolate, apple, and coffee are discontinued flavors of what popular dessert?

6. Haddock and cod are the typical types of fish used in what product?

7. Although his company manufactures many more products than its slogan implies, Henry John Heinz liked the way two specific numbers looked together, so he used them instead. What's the company's well-known slogan?

8. Milano, Bordeaux, Geneva, and Lido are all what?

9. Male model Fabio was a spokesman for what margarine product?

10. According to his lawyers, Dan White's consumption of this creme-filled spongecake and other "junk" foods diminished his mental capacity and were a contributing factor in his murders of San Francisco Mayor George Moscone and City Supervisor Harvey Milk. What has this defense become known as?

Answers on page 362.

Food and Drink

BEER BLAST

Have some frothy fun with this quiz on domestic and imported brews.

1. In 1997, this Mexican beer, which was already the top-selling beer in its country, became the top-selling import brand in the United States.

2. Can you name the best-selling imported beer in the United States between the repeal of Prohibition and 1997?

3. What brewery produces the Sam Adams ales?

4. "The beer that made Milwaukee famous" is the catchphrase used for years by which popular brand?

5. What foreign beer is synonymous with its unique container, popularly referred to as an "oil can"?

6. Its label displays a buxom serving girl holding two beer steins. What is this second best-selling German beer in the United States?

7. Which American beer brand, when spelled backward, is a popular article of summer clothing?

8. What thick and hearty Irish brew is used to mix such drinks as a Black Velvet, Irish Car Bomb, and Miner's Lung?

9. Established in Pennsylvania in 1829, what is the oldest continuously operating brewery in the United States? (It made nonalcoholic beer during Prohibition.)

10. What was Pennsylvania's Latrobe Brewing Company's best-selling beer between 1939 and 2006 (when Anheuser-Busch purchased the brewery)?

11. A brewer is a male beer maker. What do you call a female beer maker?

Food and Drink

Answers on page 362.

EATING ABROAD

Signature and national dishes of other countries.

1. Which country lays claim to haggis: a sheep's lung, heart, and liver cooked in its stomach with oatmeal, spices, and kidney fat?

2. Although it is popular throughout Eastern Europe, borscht—the blood-red soup of beetroots, meat, and cabbage—is typically associated with what country?

3. Found in most Mexican kitchens, this sauce is made from dry chili, nuts, spices, vegetables, and chocolate.

4. Kimchi, which is made of cabbage and other vegetables that have been buried underground until they ferment, is a staple dish in which country?

5. Which main course, associated with Greece and Turkey, is a baked dish of eggplant, ground lamb, onions, tomatoes, and spices covered in a white sauce?

6. Meanwhile in Poland, the locals are enjoying what signature bite consisting of small dumplings with potato, cheese, sauerkraut, mushroom, or spinach fillings?

7. Sauerbraten and kartoffelklosse are the "meat and potatoes" of which European country?

8. Apple pie is to America as Sacher torte is to what country?

9. Colcannon, a dish of mashed potatoes and cabbage seasoned with butter, is likely to be served up where?

10. What delicacy, whose name translates to "fat liver," was officially declared a part of France's cultural heritage by legislators in 2005?

11. This vitamin-rich sandwich spread made of yeast extract and vegetables has become an Australian icon.

Food and Drink

POP QUIZ

Famous soda brand names.

1. Which soft drink, an anagram of "Episcopal," was invented in New Bern, North Carolina, and trademarked in 1903?

2. Initially introduced in 1958 as a "dietetic product," what is the brand name of the first diet cola produced in the United States?

3. What caffeine-intensive, fruity soft drink did Coca-Cola invent in 1979 to go up against Pepsi's Mountain Dew?

4. Which root beer brand was responsible for the first franchised restaurant chain in 1919, but wasn't available in stores until 1971?

5. This latecomer cola brand, introduced in 1934, was the first to be distributed nationally in cans in 1954 and the first to hit the shelves in 16-ounce bottles in 1959.

6. Which major soft drink brand, a combination of 23 soda fountain fruit flavors, was developed at Morrison's Corner Drug Store in Waco, Texas, in 1885?

7. Wet Planet Beverages introduced this novelty cola in 1985. It has more than twice the caffeine of Coca-Cola and over 50 percent more than Mountain Dew. Yikes! What is it?

8. In contrast to a hard drink, what does a soft drink imply a lack of?

9. Which soda manufactured by Pepsi features a root beer-drinking bulldog on the label?

10. What brand, developed in 1876 in Union, Maine, was the first mass-produced soft drink and one of the few products advertised in *Mad* magazine?

11. The first soda pop was created in the in Detroit, Michigan, in 1866, and is still sold today. What is it?

Food and Drink

Answers on page 363.

MANGEZ-VOUS FRANÇAIS?

How much do you know about French food?

1. Americans call it French dressing. What do the French call it?

2. The French call it *pain perdu*. What do Americans call it?

3. When you ask someone to pass the *sel et poivre*, what are you asking for?

4. If a French dish is called *à la Florentine*, which of these does it include: basil, spinach, mushrooms, tomatoes, or none of these?

5. A *fromagerie* is a cheese shop. A *patisserie* is a pastry shop. What is a *boucherie*?

6. Which of the following is *not* originally a French wine: Chablis, Vouvray, Graves, Zinfandel, or Sauternes.

7. Foie gras is a delicacy, and it's made from what organ of the goose?

8. What's the name of the long, skinny, crusty French bread you often see standing upright at the bakery?

9. And speaking of bread, what does the French word *croissant* mean?

10. If you started your meal with *escargots*, moved on to a main course of *filet mignon* with *pommes frites*, and finished up with a dish of *glace*, what would you be eating?

11. Boursin, Boursault, Camembert, and Reblochon are the names of what kind of food?

Answers on page 363.

Food and Drink

THE COOKIE JAR

All your favorite cookies, homemade and store-bought.

1. Take a pair of toasted marshmallows, four squares of chocolate, and squish them between two graham crackers. What is the result?

2. A box of Nabisco Animal Crackers has 18 different kinds of animals, but only four have been there since the cookies first appeared in 1902. Which animals are they?

3. Can you supply the missing name from this advertising slogan used for the third most popular cookie in America? A cookie is just a cookie, but a _____ is fruit and cake.

4. Most people think *biscotti* is Italian for "biscuits." It isn't. What does it mean?

5. What classic chocolate cookies, virtually unchanged by Nabisco since 1924, can be stacked and frosted with sweetened whipped cream to make a popular no-bake refrigerator cake?

6. In England, cookies are called what?

7. Not every cookie gets its sweetening from sugar. Besides sugar, what ingredient gives gingersnaps their old-fashioned sweetness?

8. Which of the following is the top-selling Girl Scout cookie in America: Caramel deLites, Thin Mints, Lemonades, Peanut Butter Sandwiches, or Shortbread?

9. True or false: Fortune cookies originated in China.

10. What cookie was invented as a health food and is often crushed to make a pie crust?

11. What sandwich cookie was originally sold in Britain in 1912 in two flavors: lemon meringue and cream?

Food and Drink

Answers on page 363.

EAT YOUR VEGGIES

Test your vegetable I.Q.

1. What green vegetable was banned from the White House and *Air Force One*'s menus by order of President George H. W. Bush during his term in office?

2. True root vegetables are plant roots that we use as vegetables. Carrots are root veggies; potatoes are not. Name two more true root vegetables.

3. Sauerkraut is made from what vegetable?

4. Which salad green is also called rocket, rucola, and roquette?

5. It's sometimes called an alligator pear. California grows 95 percent of the American crop. What is it?

6. Can you name two of the vegetables included in the group called "nightshades"?

7. The annual U.S. production of this field crop is more than twice that of any other American crop. We eat it soon after picking, but it's also a component in peanut butter, potato chips, ketchup, and soft drinks. What is it?

8. What homegrown squash grows so well that gardeners try to get rid of it by giving it to their neighbors or baking it into loafs of bread?

9. Eating what vegetable will give your urine a distinctive and rather strange odor?

10. Dr. Brown's Sodas is famous for making a soft drink flavored with what vegetable?

11. The "roots" of this vegetable can be found in Afghanistan, and it was originally grown for its fragrant leaves.

LADIES IN THE KITCHEN

Real and not-so-real girls and women in the food business.

1. She was eight years old when her daddy named his new line of cheesecakes after her. Nobody doesn't like her! What's her name?

2. Even her 1-800-266-5437 number spells her story. What's the name of this married lady who opened her first bakery in 1977 and now has a nationwide chain?

3. If that famous grandma-shaped plastic bottle of syrup came to life and reminded you that she's "so thick, so buttery, and still just as sweet," who would be talking to you?

4. What chewy little chocolate roll was named for the five-year-old daughter of Austrian immigrant Leo Hirshfield?

5. True or false: Betty Crocker was a real person.

6. In 1889, this African American aunt wore a head scarf and was a spokesperson for a pancake mix. Today, with a modern look, she sells frozen breakfast foods. Who is she?

7. Ann Page and Jane Parker, fictional homemakers, became the brand names on dozens of in-house products stocking the shelves of what gigantic supermarket chain?

8. Another fictional Ann became the symbol of a huge flour company. What was the company's (and Ann's) name?

9. Pies, pie shops, a chain of West Coast restaurants (including East Side Mario's), and a line of frozen foods and salad dressings all come from a company named after what talented lady?

10. What woman baked the first Pepperidge Farm breads, founded the company, and was its first public face in TV ads of the 1950s?

Food and Drink

Answers on page 364.

SUSHI, ANYONE?

How much do you know about Japanese food?

1. Miso, tofu, and shoyu are products of what legume?

2. Made from fermented rice, this "wine" is served hot in tiny ceramic cups or cold in little wooden boxes. What is this alcoholic drink?

3. Protein-rich, paper-thin sheets of shiny dark green *nori* are used to form rolls containing sushi or other tasty tidbits. What is *nori*?

4. Soba, udon, and ramen are varieties of what kind of food?

5. Dried bonito tuna flakes are an important ingredient in Japanese cooking. When they're cooked with water, the resulting soup stock is called what?

6. What's the difference between sushi and sashimi, both of which are made with raw fish or other seafood and garnished with pickled ginger?

7. Small pieces of seafood and vegetables coated in special light batter and deep-fried very quickly are called what?

8. What popular sauce (a sweet-salty mixture of soy sauce, sake, and mirin) is brushed onto chicken, meat, or fish before grilling or pan-frying?

9. To pack on the pounds, certain Japanese sportsmen load up on gigantic quantities of a one-pot dish called *chanko-nabe*, a rich broth full of meat, seafood, veggies, tofu, and other delicious items. What is the profession of these big guys?

10. If you're eating enokis, namekos, and shiitakes, what vegetable are you enjoying?

Answers on page 364.

BEYOND APPLES AND ORANGES

The world of uncommon fruits

1. Name the fruit native to the Pacific islands that was featured in the book *Mutiny on the Bounty*?

2. Though it sounds lustful, the name of this fruit (also called *granadilla*) actually refers to the crucifixion of Christ.

3. What fuzzy little fruit shares its name with New Zealand's national bird?

4. It looks like a tiny orange, but the rind tastes sweet and the juicy interior is tart. It's often used as a Christmas wreath decoration.

5. Slice it crosswise and it's got the shape of a five- or six-pointed star, which is why it's popularly called a star fruit. What is its real name?

6. True or false: papaya and pawpaw are two names for the same fruit.

7. In its native Southeast Asia, it's called the "King of Fruits." In other parts of the world, it's reviled for its repulsive smell. What is it?

8. What Chinese fruit has a bright red bumpy shell surrounding soft sweet pulp, and—when it's dried—a tough, brown, bumpy shell surrounding a raisinlike "nut"?

9. Moses assured the Hebrews that when they reached the Promised Land, they'd find plenty of these hard-shelled red fruits that are eaten seed by seed. What fruit is he talking about?

10. You can eat its seeds and rind, but most people areas grow this tropical fruit for its sweet-tasting flesh.

Food and Drink

Answers on page 365.

OH, NUTS!

We're nuts about nuts. Had enough? Nuts!

1. What nuts are traditionally used in the Louisiana and Texas style of pralines?

2. This nut is used to produce Barr's Red Kola and Cricket Cola, but are not used to create Coke, Pepsi, or Royal Crown Cola.

3. Originally dyed by producers to hide stains on its shell, what beige nuts are still artificially colored for tradition's sake?

4. What nuts are mentioned in the holiday classic "The Christmas Song," first recorded by Nat King Cole in 1946?

5. Often added to white-chocolate-chip cookies, this exotic nut has a shell so hard that a vice is usually needed to crack it.

6. Also called a *pignoli*, what nut is combined with basil, garlic, olive oil, and grated cheese to create a traditional pesto?

7. India and Vietnam are the largest exporters of this kidney-shaped nut with a sweet, buttery flavor and a 48 percent fat content.

8. The liqueur Frangelico and the spread Nutella get their distinctive flavor from which nut?

9. In the United States, only California commercially produces this nut, the major ingredient in the sweet confection marzipan.

10. The ice cream topping commonly called "wet nuts" is made from which nuts mixed with a thick sugar syrup?

11. What South American nut's saturated fat content is among the highest of all nuts? (Despite its name, it's actually from Bolivia.)

12. This nut is also called a groundnut, manila nut, jack nut, and goober pea.

Answers on page 365.

NO MUGGLES HERE

How well do you know J. K. Rowling's wizarding world?

1. What's the name for someone who has magical parents but no powers of his own?

2. Muggle-born Hermione Granger is considered by some to be the "greatest witch of her age." What do her parents do for a living?

3. What's the given name of Harry Potter's archenemy?

4. There are eight other Weasleys in Ron's immediate family. What are their names?

5. In the first book, Hagrid acquired a dragon egg and reared the baby dragon. What was the animal's name?

6. Bully Draco Malfoy has two sidekicks—name them.

7. In *The Prisoner of Azkaban*, the Hogwarts students learn to defeat boggarts (shape-shifting creatures that take on the appearance of a person's greatest fear). What did the boggart reveal that Harry Potter was most afraid of?

8. What Death Eater so tortured the parents of Neville Longbottom that they were forever confined to a mental institution? (Bonus: What was the hospital?)

9. Name the four houses of Hogwarts and their heads of house.

10. In *The Goblet of Fire*, Hermione Granger started a social welfare organization called S.P.E.W. What does the acronym stand for?

11. In *The Half-Blood Prince*, Harry and Professor Dumbledore ventured into a haunted cave where Harry was attacked by the Inferi (enchanted corpses). How did Dumbledore save him?

Answers on page 365.

The Arts

STORYBOOK ROMANCE

Ain't love grand? Especially the fictional kind.
Identify the character or the novel.

1. The Butler did it—Rhett Butler that is. He really does it for Scarlett in what Civil War saga?

2. In Bram Stoker's famous tale, Jonathan Harker nearly loses his devoted wife to a count with a deadly, oral fixation. Who is this demonic aristocrat?

3. In a lonely manor on the moors, passion and misery engulf Catherine after she falls for the quintessential bad boy—who just happens to be her foster brother. What's his name?

4. *Pride and Prejudice*—these faults nearly deep-six the love between Fitzwilliam Darcy and Elizabeth Bennet. Which half of the couple suffers from pride and which from prejudice?

5. She inspired love at first sight in 12-year-old Tom Sawyer and made him forget that he already had another sweetheart. What was the name of this strawberry blonde?

6. Who is the "lady" in D. H. Lawrence's racy saga of a woman and her lover?

7. What literary sleuth is often found on the couch, getting love—not therapy—from psychologist Dr. Susan Silverman?

8. Jane Eyre is just about to marry when she discovers that the groom already has a mad wife locked up in his mansion. Who is this secretive fellow?

9. Despite their spotty looks and the problems of their 15 offspring, Pongo and Missis have a loving relationship. What makes this couple different from the other loving couples in this quiz?

10. In *The Accidental Tourist*, Macon Leary gets another chance at love with offbeat Muriel Pritchett. What kind of animal brings them together?

The Arts

FRAMED

Picture this: art and the people who make it.

1. Leonardo Da Vinci called her *La Gioconda* (Italian for Mrs. Giocondo), but by what simple name is this most famous of all paintings known?

2. What artist's mother is depicted as a somber old woman in a painting whose formal name is *Arrangement in Grey and Black Number 1*?

3. Andy Warhol, one of the leaders of the 1960s Pop Art movement, found fame using images of what grocery item?

4. In Thomas Gainsborough's most famous painting, *The Blue Boy*, why does the subject hide one of his hands in the folds of his clothes?

5. What abstract expressionist has been called "Jack the Dripper" by critics?

6. What Dutch painter and etcher's most famous painting, *Night Watch*, portrayed neither a watch nor a night scene?

7. A German guide to the 1937 World's Fair in Paris described this Pablo Picasso mural as, "a hodgepodge of body parts that any four-year-old could have painted."

8. What Impressionist so hated using the color black that on his death, his friend refused to allow the coffin to be draped in a black sheet? (A flowered cloth was used instead.)

9. Norwegian Expressionist Edvard Munch's iconic painting *The Scream* inspired an ad campaign for what 1990 movie?

10. Henri de Toulouse-Lautrec was as famous for his decadent personal life as for his art, and he hung out at what Paris nightclub that gave its name to two Oscar-winning films?

The Arts

DANCING MACHINES

See if you can identify these lords and ladies of the dance.

1. What Russian, who defected to Canada in the 1970s, has been called "the greatest living male ballet dancer"?

2. Although he'd been dancing since childhood and had appeared in movies and on TV, this tap dancer found fame when he performed in the 1996 Broadway production, *Bring in 'Da Noise, Bring in 'Da Funk*.

3. She's the best-known pioneer of modern dance and a founding member of Juilliard's dance division.

4. What dancer and instructor taught such famous clients as Eleanor Roosevelt and Jack Dempsey? Today, the nearly 200 dance studios that bear his name teach a variety of ballroom styles.

5. What dancer and choreographer found *Fame* in the early 1980s playing the role of Lydia Grant in the movies and on TV?

6. Formerly with the New York City Ballet, she joined the American Ballet Theater in 1974, becoming the long-time dance partner of #1.

7. What Dutch dancer and courtesan was executed by the Allies during World War I because they believed she'd been spying for Germany?

8. This world-famous tap dancer and movie star won the 1992 Tony award for Best Actor for his role in the musical *Jelly's Last Jam* about the life of jazz musician Jelly Roll Morton.

9. She's been called the greatest ballerina of all time, and he was a renowned Russian ballet dancer who defected to the West in 1961. They became close friends and dance partners, pairing most famously in *Giselle*, *Swan Lake*, and *Romeo and Juliet*. Who are they?

10. This dancer created more than 75 ballets during his lifetime, but his most lasting legacy is the African American modern dance company that bears his name.

BANNED BOOKS

Be careful what you read.

1. China banned what Lewis Carroll classic because it portrayed animals and humans as equals?

2. What classic resource has been banned in Eldon, Missouri, and by the Anchorage (Alaska) Board of Schools for including slang definitions for words like "bed," "knocker," and "balls"?

3. West Marion High School in Mississippi removed what "hot" Ray Bradbury classic? (Go figure, the book is about censorship.)

4. Shel Silverstein detractors accused this poetry collection of promoting drug use, the occult, and suicide, among other things. What is the work called?

5. Thomas Paine was indicted for treason for *The Rights of Man*, but what "logical" work was banned because it preached Deism.

6. World War II dictators burned many books. Curiously, Jack London's novel about a sled dog was one of the most-often burned. Name it.

7. The term "bowdlerize" (meaning "to expurgate prudishly") is an named after Thomas Bowdler, a 19th-century author who wrote a family-friendly version of which playwright's work?

8. What children's book was banned because it contained a tiny picture of a topless woman on a beach? (The offended must have spent an extra long time searching for the sunbather.)

9. This 1930 William Faulkner novel was banned in Kentucky for obscenity, passages about abortion, and other affronts despite the fact that no one on the school board had read the book. Name it.

10. This pro-environment Dr. Seuss story is his most controversial, having been banned in various schools for supposedly being a story that made the logging industry look bad.

The Arts

Answers on page 366.

DANCING WITH THE STARS

When celebs get down—and sometimes dirty.

1. What cartoon character does Gene Kelly dance with in the 1945 film *Anchors Aweigh*?

2. What future star of the sitcom *Friends* shared a stage with Bruce Springsteen in his "Dancing in the Dark" video?

3. What kind of household machine did Fred Astaire dance with in a TV commercial that first aired during the 1997 Super Bowl?

4. Paula Abdul dances with an animated cat in the video for what song?

5. For what TV series finale in 1992 did Cliff and Clair Huxtable break the fourth wall by dancing off the set and out the studio doors?

6. After receiving an honorary Academy Award in 1998, director and choreographer Stanley Donen danced with his statuette while singing what song performed by Fred Astaire in *Top Hat*?

7. What actor and movie "disco king" was photographed dancing with Princess Diana at a White House dinner in 1985?

8. In the film *Ferris Bueller's Day Off*, star Matthew Broderick gets a parade crowd grooving by singing what Beatles hit, first recorded by the Isley Brothers?

9. What song does the cast sing and dance to at the close of the film *The 40-Year-Old Virgin*?

10. In an embarrassing 1995 *Late Show with David Letterman* appearance, who climbed onto the host's desk, did a brief dance, and flashed him with her back to the camera?

Answers on page 367.

The Arts

BUILDING BLOCKS

All about architecture.

1. The house built over a waterfall in rural Pennsylvania by Frank Lloyd Wright is named what?

2. Louis Sullivan, the 19th-century architect of skyscrapers, promoted the precept that "Form follows . . . " what?

3. Doric, Ionic, and Corinthian are three types of what?

4. The Rotunda is the focal point of whose design for the University of Virginia?

5. Denver's Mile High Center, the JFK Library, and the Pyramids of the Louvre were all designed by what master architect?

6. Germany's most influential school of art, architecture, and design is called what?

7. "Less is more" and "God is in the details" are aphorisms of what famous German architect?

8. What English architect designed 53 London churches, including, notably, St. Paul's Cathedral?

9. At 21, this undergraduate artist—still not a legally registered architect—won a public design competition for the Vietnam Veterans Memorial in Washington, D.C. Who is she?

10. Among this architect's best-known works are Spain's Guggenheim Museum; his Santa Monica, California, residence; and the Prague's Dancing House, originally named "Fred and Ginger." Who is he?

11. This Mesopotamian structure at Ur is a terraced pyramid of successively receding stories supporting a shrine. What is the structure called?

Answers on page 367.

CULTURE VULTURES

Art, ballet, classical music—
This one's for the cultured among us.

1. Where would you go to see Michelangelo's the *Pietá*?

2. The works of Bach, Beethoven, and Brahms belong to what musical genre?

3. What Dadaist artist submitted an actual urinal, titled *Fountain*, to an art exhibit in 1917?

4. In what city is the Museo del Prado located?

5. What author of *Dover Beach* wrote that having culture means to "know the best that has been said and thought in the world"?

6. *The Thinker* is one of the most recognized sculptures in the world. Who was the sculptor?

7. What French artist is well known for his paintings of ballet dancers?

8. "Jaunty John joked about the jolly jack-o'-lantern." Is that an example of assonance, alliteration, or onomatopoeia?

9. Who wrote *The Rape of Lucrece*?

10. Jacques Derrida founded (and coined the term for) what process in literary criticism and philosophy?

11. The Temple of Athena on the Acropolis of Athens is better known by what name?

12. *Grand jeté* and *petits sauté* are part of what art form?

JUST ONE BOOK

These authors composed one classic or best-seller . . . and no more.

1. What Southern author wrote a novel about racial tolerance, won the Pulitzer Prize, and then never published another book. Boo who?

2. John Kennedy Toole couldn't get his novel published and committed suicide in 1969. His mother persisted and published it in 1980. What's the name of the book about kooky characters in New Orleans?

3. Who wrote *Gone With the Wind*?

4. Oscar Wilde is famous for his comic plays, but he also wrote a Victorian novel about an aging portrait. What's its title?

5. Carl Sagan published several works on space and science but only one novel. His 1985 tale about space travel became a popular sci-fi movie in 1997. What is the name of the book and movie?

6. *Save Me the Last Waltz*, published in 1932, is the sole literary effort of what wife of the much-published author of *Tender Is the Night*?

7. This early 20th century French author wrote one book, but it's a big one. *Remembrance of Things Past* is 3,000 pages across seven volumes.

8. Anna Sewell was a one-hit-wonder, but it could be due to the fact that she was gravely ill for most of her life and died at age 59. Name her classic children's novel about a horse.

9. Charlotte Bronte wrote *Jane Eyre* and Anne Bronte wrote *Agnes Grey*. The third Bronte sister wrote the classic novel *Wuthering Heights*. What's her name?

10. *Das Kapital* isn't a novel, but the outline of the political philosophy of Communism. What politically influential 20th-century figure wrote it?

Answers on page 367.

The Arts

PICTURE THIS

Famous photographs and the people who take them.

1. A teenage Afghani girl with piercing blue eyes famously appeared on the cover of what magazine in 1985?

2. What actress appeared fully nude and pregnant on the cover of *Vanity Fair* in 1991?

3. What photographer is best known for sweeping black-and-white images of mountains and forests?

4. On VE Day, a sailor grabs a random woman in New York City's Times Square and kisses her in this famous photograph by whom?

5. *Time* and *Newsweek* used the same photo of a murder suspect in June 1994. *Time* was lambasted for darkening the subject's skin tone, making him appear more "menacing." Who was it?

6. In this famous picture from the 1968 Olympics, two American track and field athletes perform what controversial gesture during their medal awards ceremony?

7. What World War II monument is a re-creation of a Pulitzer Prize-winning photograph?

8. Who was the young man photographed standing firm against military tanks in the 1989 pro-democracy Beijing protests?

9. Whose famous photographs feature babies inside flowers or dressed up like fruit and vegetables?

10. Taken the day John Lennon died, her photo of him naked and hugging a clothed Yoko Ono appeared on *Rolling Stone's* cover.

11. What French photographer stuck his lens through a gap in a fence to obtain his most famous image—a man leaping over a puddle?

The Arts

FAMOUS FIRST LINES

*Can you name the books that open
with these famous first lines?*

1. "Call me Ishmael."

2. "It was the best of times, it was the worst of times . . . "

3. "All happy families are alike; each unhappy family is unhappy in its own way."

4. "It was a pleasure to burn."

5. "They're out there."

6. "All children, except one, grow up."

7. "As Gregor Samsa awoke one morning from uneasy dreams he found himself transformed in his bed into a giant insect."

8. "The primroses were over."

9. "Mother died today."

10. "Midway, in our life's journey, I went astray from the straight road and woke to find myself alone in a dark wood."

11. "All this happened, more or less."

12. "Nothing to be done."

13. "I am a sick man . . . I am a spiteful man . . . "

14. "It is a truth universally acknowledged, that a single man in posses-sion of a good fortune must be in want of a wife."

15. "Call me Jonah."

The Arts

FIRST REJECTED— NOW COLLECTED

These authors were all turned down before they became world famous.

1. Eight publishers said no to J. K. Rowling's first book. What was its British title?

2. *The Mysterious Affair at Styles*, this author's first book, was rejected by six publishers, but she went on to write 70-plus novels.

3. What Frederick Forsyth novel was passed up by nearly 50 publishers before it became a bestseller?

4. This Ayn Rand novel was turned down by 12 publishers before it was accepted by Bobbs-Merrill over the objections of the company's president. What was it?

5. *And to Think That I Saw It on Mulberry Street* was passed up by 28 publishers before it went on to become a children's classic. Who is the author?

6. A book by Robert W. Pirsig was rejected 121 times (!) before it became a big best seller in 1974. What was the book?

7. This book, Tom Clancy's first, was turned down by more than two dozen publishers before it became a huge best seller.

8. The author of *The Thomas Berryman Number*, which was rejected by 26 publishers, has since become one of the world's best-selling authors. Who is the writer?

9. This Southerner's first novel, turned down by 28 publishers, was called *A Time to Kill*. His next book was a bestseller. Who is the author?

10. Irving Stone's biographical novel of Vincent Van Gogh was rejected by 17 publishers over three years. What was the title?

WRIGHT STUFF

A quiz on America's most influential and controversial architect—Frank Lloyd Wright.

1. Wright coined what word to describe the overhang for a car to park under?

2. What well-known toy still being manufactured did Wright's son, John Lloyd Wright, invent in 1918?

3. Wright revealed his ability to think outside the box when he designed a radical, innovative floor plan for residential homes with his Prairie Houses. What was it called?

4. Although Ayn Rand denied it, many people believe that she based this architect, the main character in her novel *The Fountainhead*, on Wright.

5. Wright's personal homes shared the same name as an early Welsh poet. What is that name?

6. Unlike most architects of the time, Wright designed homes for average income families. What original name did he give these designs?

7. Wright asserted that form and function are the same and that a building should grow naturally from its environment. What did he call this concept?

8. Name Wright's most famous private residence built over a stream and waterfall in Bear Run, Pennsylvania?

9. With what office building did Wright have to prove to officials that his "flower columns"—the reversed tapered columns look like giant lily pads—would withstand the weight of the roof?

10. When an official complained that the walls of this curved museum were not high enough to display some of the art, Wright suggested they cut the pieces in half. Name this building.

The Arts

Answers on page 369.

DOUBLE TROUBLE

O.K. Sherlock—how well do you know your fictional detective teams?

1. Control called on these intelligence officers when K.A.O.S. reigned. What are the code names of their two star agents?

2. Created in 1927 by the Stratemeyer Syndicate, who are the two teen Bayport sleuths who managed to solve 58 crimes in 52 years without aging a day?

3. In Tony Hillerman's novels, these members of the Navajo Tribal Police patrol the Southwest's Four Corners area. The methodical lieutenant is assisted by an impetuous medicine man in training. Name the duo.

4. This former Navy Seal turned P. I. and his British sidekick live at a posh estate, "Robin's Nest," in Hawaii. Who are they?

5. What husband-and-wife team have fun teasing the prime suspects, even if they're thin on clues or suffering from a hangover?

6. Englishman Captain Hastings likes to follow the rules to solve a crime, but assists what French-speaking egghead (known to lie, cheat, and steal to get his "little grey cells working")?

7. Elizabeth George paired D. S. Havers, a working class detective with what suave aristocrat who was the Eight Earl of Asherton?

8. No criminal can out-fox this eccentric, homebound orchid grower (who weighs a "seventh of a ton") and his milk-drinking legman.

9. In books by Janet Evanovich, what New Jersey bounty hunter is assisted by Lula, a sassy filing clerk and ex-hooker? This heroine's adventures are all numbered.

10. When this humble, aphorism-spouting detective teams up with eldest son, the two chase down cases in one exotic locale after another, but rarely in Honolulu, their home town. Who are they?

Answers on page 369.

THE PLAY'S THE THING

Some of the most popular musicals and plays
to make it on the Great White Way.

1. In what show do the songs "Springtime for Hitler" and "Prisoners of Love" appear?

2. This musical, originally titled *Welcome to Berlin*, has the Kit Kat Klub as its major setting.

3. What musical was created especially for ABBA fans?

4. George Bernard Shaw's *Pygmalion* serves as the basis for what 1956 Broadway play?

5. "Oh, What a Beautiful Mornin'" and "The Surrey with the Fringe on Top" are two numbers in this Rodgers and Hammerstein musical.

6. What "singular sensation" premiered on Broadway in 1975, won nine Tony awards, and had more than 6,000 performances during its original run? (It held the record for the longest-running musical until 1997, when it was surpassed by *Cats*.)

7. A young theatrical agent desperately tries to reunite his elderly uncle (a former vaudeville star) with his long-time stage partner in this Neil Simon play.

8. What Broadway retelling of the King Arthur legend features killer rabbits, dancing girls, and knights who say "Ni"?

9. Actress Idina Menzel won a 2004 Tony award for her lead role in what bewitching musical?

10. This play's subtitle is *The American Tribal Love-Rock Musical.*

11. What musical, set in 19th-century Germany, premiered on Broadway in December 2006? (It's based on a play of the same name.)

The Arts

Answers on page 369.

LITERARY BRAIN TEASERS

Some of these answers will surprise you.

1. What famous person did Helen Keller dedicate her biography to?

2. What are the names of Don Quixote's horse? Sancho Panza's donkey?

3. Ezra Pound was charged with treason for what activity during World War II?

4. The *Eloise* books about a young girl who lives at New York City's Plaza Hotel were based on author Kay Thompson's god-daughter who grew up to me a famous singer. Who was the inspiration for Eloise?

5. Ernest Hemingway said a man should do four things: "plant a tree, fight a bull, write a book, and" what?

6. One of the most reclusive American authors ever, this man hasn't published a book since 1965. He's best known for a 1951 novel that's one of the most often banned books in the United States. What's his name and what's the book?

7. In 1880, he began writing a weekly newspaper story about a marionette that became Pinocchio. Who is the author?

8. Dick and Jane had two pets in the classic children's reading primers. What kind of pets were they, and what were the animals' names?

9. In Frank L. Baum's *The Wonderful Wizard of Oz*, what color were Dorothy's slippers? (Hint: They were not ruby red.)

10. What was the first American novel to sell more than one million copies?

Answers on page 370.

BOOK LEARNIN'

Literary trivia.

1. What pachyderm-like creature is imagined in *Winnie the Pooh* books but is never actually seen, though Pooh and Piglet bravely try to capture one in a trap?

2. The author of what epic poem says that his purpose is to "justify the ways of God to men"?

3. In *Ali Baba and the Forty Thieves*, what was Ali Baba's occupation— stone-cutter, woodcutter, or hair-cutter?

4. The fictional utopian valley of Shangri-La was created by James Hilton in what novel?

5. Who was Dante's guide through Paradise in the *Divine Comedy*, and his lifelong love and inspiration?

6. Dr. Faust sells his soul to the devil in a classic work by what great German author?

7. "Carolyn Keene" was the author pseudonym used on stories about what teen-age detective?

8. "She walks in beauty, like the night" is a line from . . . Shakespeare, Lord Byron, or Keats?

9. Natty Bumppo is the hero of what series of novels by James Fenimore Cooper?

10. Rip Van Winkle sleeps for 20 years in the story by what American author?

11. Sancho Panza was the devoted companion of what literary character?

12. "Water, water, everywhere / Nor any drop to drink" is a line by what English poet?

Answers on page 370.

The Arts

PLAY RIGHTS

Are you a drama queen (or king)? Check it out with this quiz about famous plays.

1. Psychoanalyst Sigmund Freud believed that all little boys secretly want to get rid of their dads and marry their moms. He named this famous "complex" after what tragic Greek title character?

2. In what Arthur Miller play did peddler Willie Loman sell out his principles in a bid for success and riches?

3. What Pulitzer Prize–winning play by Thornton Wilder chronicled the lives of everyday people and is the most-performed American drama of the 20th century?

4. The 1956 Broadway musical about a cockney flower girl taught to pass for a member of the British upper crust was based on what George Bernard Shaw play?

5. Speaking of Shaw's plays, what was Mrs. Warren's profession?

6. In Reginald Rose's play about jury deliberations (later turned into a Sidney Lumet film), how many "angry men" were there?

7. What German scholar was willing to do anything for knowledge and power, so he traded his soul in a pact with the devil?

8. *Kiss Me, Kate*, the 1949 Tony Award–winning musical about the tempestuous relationship between a pair of actors, was based on what Shakespeare play?

9. In a short one-act play entitled *For Whom the Southern Belle Tolls*, Christopher Durang parodied what Tennessee Williams play about the relationship between a fading flower of Southern womanhood and her painfully shy daughter?

10. What classic French character could be said to have won his fair maiden Roxanne by a nose?

Answers on page 370.

The Arts

WRITE ON

All answers deal with the art of writing.

1. This 1876 system of book classification used by libraries attempts to divide knowledge into ten major categories, which are then further subdivided. What is it called?

2. After he invented movable type in 1445, what was the first book that German goldsmith and printer Johannes Gutenberg published?

3. This epic poem from Babylon written in cuneiform in about 2500 BC is considered one of the earliest books written. What is the title?

4. Japanese noblewoman Murasaki Shikibu wrote the first novel in 1007. Can you name the title?

5. What is the best-selling book in the world?

6. Ian Fleming's dashing James Bond character made his debut in what 1952 novel?

7. Located in Mesopotamia (modern-day Iraq), what ancient civilization is credited with the invention of writing in the 4th century BC?

8. In 1755, Samuel Johnson (a poet, essayist, literary critic, and lexicographer) accomplished what unique literary feat?

9. This largest library in the world contains more than 30 million books, 1 million newspapers, and the largest rare book collection in North America. What's it called?

10. Blank pages at the beginning and end of a book that can be plain or decorated are known as what?

Answers on page 371.

TEST YOUR METAL

A mine of information for trivia fans.

1. The Statue of Liberty owes her fashionably greenish tinge (and girlish figure) to 179,220 pounds of what metal?

2. The oxide of what metal protects a baby's bottom from rashes?

3. What contemporary term for the movies came from the precious metal that reflected the images transmitted by movie projectors?

4. What is encased in a copper or steel alloy shell when it's called a full metal jacket?

5. Who didn't write "All that glitters is not gold," because he actually wrote "All that glisters is not gold"?

6. Thanks to high thermal conductivity, your wet tongue will do what when it touches a metal pole in subfreezing temperatures?

7. What poisonous metal used by hat manufacturers in the 19th century brought on hallucinations and other psychotic symptoms, giving rise to the term "mad as a hatter"?

8. What fancy-schmancy metal is almost twice as valuable as gold, and needs ten tons of mined ore to produce a single ounce?

9. Sterling silver is an alloy of 92.5% silver and 7.5% of what other metal?

10. Because deadly cyanide is used to leach it out of ore, environmentalists are on the march against the "dirty" mining of what precious metal?

11. What common metal used to be so valuable that Emperor Napoleon III made forks out of it for his honored guests—while lesser folk used golden forks?

Answers on page 371.

WHAT'S UP, DOC?

Stick out your tongue and say "ah."

1. Before the advent of modern pharmaceuticals, willow tree bark was routinely used for fever, muscle aches, or headaches. Its active ingredient is found in what medicine cabinet staple?

2. Rhinoplasty (nose jobs) is a popular plastic surgery procedure. Surprisingly, it was invented over 2,000 years ago by Sushruta, who was already performing the surgery in what country?

3. Though it's commonly prescribed for impotence, Viagra was actually developed to cure what much different condition?

4. Queen Victoria popularized anesthesia when she used what substance to knock her out during childbirth?

5. F. G. Banting, a Canadian doctor, saved millions of lives when his diabetes research led to what discovery?

6. Today he's a Nobel Prize winner, but Dr. Barry Marshall was called crazy when he drank *H pylori* to prove that it caused what kind of stomach trouble?

7. Untidy Alexander Fleming found one of his petri dishes filled with mold. What wonder drug was the result of that dirty-dish discovery?

8. Dr. Ignaz Semmelweis saved the lives of thousands of mothers when he instituted what practice for delivery-room doctors and nurses?

9. Dismissed as deluded females, Katherine McCormick and Margaret Sanger affected millions when they launched the development of what little pill?

10. Why was Christiaan Barnard's 1977 operation on 53-year-old Lewis Washkansky such a big deal?

Science

SUBSTANCE ABUSE

How much do you know about the elements?

1. What Greek philosopher first used the word "elements," and maintained that there were only four of them: fire, earth, air, and water?

2. Because so much of the earth is made up of water, what gas is the most common element in the earth's crust?

3. An element's rate of decay is known by what term?

4. What gas is so light that it constantly escapes the earth's atmosphere and is replenished by the decay of radioactive elements?

5. Diamond, the hardest known substance, and pencil "lead" (or graphite, one of the softest) are pure forms of what element found in all living things?

6. Two of King Tut's three coffins were made of what gleaming and precious malleable metal?

7. The best known conductor of heat and electricity, this metal has been used to make jewelry since antiquity.

8. What is the name of the painful condition that occurs when a sudden drop in pressure causes the nitrogen dissolved in the bloodstream to bubble out of solution?

9. This precious metal, worth twice as much as gold and used to make jewelry, is also found in automobile exhaust systems and catalytic converters.

10. The fall of the Roman Empire has been blamed in part on what poisonous metal used in their water pipes, which leached into their drinking supply?

Answers on page 371.

BODY LANGUAGE

*While not exactly CSI, each answer
does include a body part.*

1. The narrow part of a guitar along which the strings of an instrument extend to the pegs is also known as what?

2. Which "pointed" word also means to accuse an individual of guilt?

3. Throw one of these in a basketball game and you'll get called for a foul. What is it?

4. A person who's up on all the latest trends is said to be this.

5. Because of the weight placed on it, this has the thickest skin of any body part. It also is one of only two areas of the body that does not grow any vellus hair or "peach fuzz." What is it?

6. What kind of morally reprehensible cad is so low you could step on him?

7. Venture capitalists always seek new projects to do what to?

8. When pirates bury their loot, what do they put it in first?

9. Another name for a toilet, especially on a boat, is what?

10. Name the part of a golf club head farthest from the shaft.

11. To give someone the brush-off, give them a cold one of these.

12. What unit of poetic meter consists of stressed and unstressed syllables in any of various set combinations?

13. Cypress and other swamp-growing trees have this rounded protrusion growing from their roots.

Science

Answers on page 372.

GETTING BETTER ALL THE TIME

It's the survival of the fittest in this quiz on evolution.

1. What key player in Darwin's theory of evolution died in 2006 at the age of 170?

2. This Beatles tune inspired the name of the 3-million-year-old fossil of a female who resembled a chimpanzee but walked upright.

3. What contemporary of Darwin's, who studied fossils and even coined the word *dinosaurus* (dinosaur), was a major critic of the theory of evolution?

4. Where did scientists discover Tiktaalik, the "missing link" in the evolution of fish that went from swimming in water to crawling on land?

5. In 2005, courts barred a Pennsylvania public school district from teaching this alternative to the theory of evolution in biology.

6. Name the son of Christian missionaries who had a major role in demonstrating the human evolution that took place in Africa.

7. Neanderthals have been extinct for 30,000 years, but on TV they're making a comeback in ads for what company?

8. Charles Darwin published his ideas of the theory of evolution at age 51 in what famous book?

9. Who said, "All the ills from which America suffers can be traced to the teaching of evolution"?

10. The fossil *Archaeopteryx* is thought to help demonstrate how reptiles evolved into what?

11. Who is known as "the father of modern genetics" for his study of the inheritance of traits in pea plants?

Answers on page 372.

KEYS TO THE GEEKDOM

Test your nerd knowledge on this computer quiz.

1. What's another name for the information superhighway? (Yeah, it's a gimme.)

2. In what film does the computer HAL 9000 say, "I know you and Frank were planning to disconnect me, and I'm afraid that's something I cannot allow to happen"?

3. In 1997, the IBM computer Deep Blue beat world champion Garry Kasparov at what game?

4. When Berkeley Systems released these airborne appliances, they were an instant hit. What were they?

5. This science-fiction author said, "I do not fear computers. I fear the lack of them."

6. What furry, computer-driven toy was banned from intelligence agencies because officials feared it could repeat state secrets?

7. What company created "Lisa," the first commercial personal computer to use a mouse?

8. Advanced computer-generated imagery created hordes of supernatural creatures and an army of the dead in what *Lord of the Rings* film?

9. This Japanese company started off making handmade cards and went on to become a powerful video game producer.

10. What film portrays a future where people live in a computer-simulated reality created by machines?

11. *Tennis for Two*, created by William Higinbotham, is believed to be the world's first what?

Science

Answers on page 372.

MOTHER NATURE GETS TOUGH

Oh, the disasters she has wrought.

1. In 2004, what event in the Indian Ocean triggered the world's deadliest tsunami with hundred-foot killer waves?

2. The eruption of what volcano in 1980 was the deadliest and most destructive volcanic event in United States history?

3. Some scientists believe that the dinosaurs disappeared 65 million years ago, when the Yucatán peninsula got slammed with what?

4. In 1923 Tokyo suffered shock waves equivalent to 300 times the power of the 1945 Hiroshima bomb. What caused that catastrophic event?

5. What makes a waterspout destructive when it reaches land?

6. Surviving the bitter winter of 1783, Benjamin Franklin was the first to note that dust from what natural event could cause deadly climate change?

7. What disease took 20 to 50 million lives in 1918 and caused the worst recorded natural disaster?

8. When you see a smooth, rounded slope of snow that might signal a wind slab, you should head elsewhere to avoid what disaster?

9. What film starring George Clooney is based on the true story of a fishing captain and his crew fighting the combination of three weather events in a mean nor'easter?

10. The worst known flood in recorded history happened in China when this river overflowed its banks, leading to approximately four million deaths.

Answers on page 372.

STARRY, STARRY QUIZ

Test your astronomical skills in this quiz about the night sky.

1. What constellation of stars is named for a winged horse?

2. What's the brightest star in the night sky?

3. Who painted *The Starry Night*?

4. What planet is the Evening Star when it's in the west and the Morning Star when it's in the east?

5. What candy bar is named after the galaxy that holds our solar system?

6. Within the constellation Orion, you can see a red giant that's one of the largest stars known. What is its name?

7. In what science-fiction film saga is the Death Star capable of destroying a planet with a single shot?

8. Who said, "We are all in the gutter, but some of us are looking at the stars"?

9. Falling stars or shooting stars are actually meteoroids burning up where?

10. The Earth's sun is a middle-aged star and has about how many years left until it reaches old age and dies?

11. What color are the most frequent and inconspicuous stars in the universe?

12. In the animated Disney movie *Pinocchio*, what character sings "When You Wish Upon a Star"?

13. The first moon landing occurred in what year: 1959, 1969, or 1979?

Science

Answers on page 373.

MEDICAL EXAM

From chompers to stompers,
do you know your body parts?

1. Here's a shocker—you're a creature with two brains! Okay, one's inside the skull but the second—called the enteric nervous system—is where?

2. What nerve connects your "two brains" and allows them to communicate?

3. Dem bones, dem bones—how many are in the normal human skeleton?

4. What type of cell is a source of political and religious controversy as well as the building block and repair kit for the body?

5. Three bones (the humerus, the paired radius, and the ulna) form what hinge joint?

6. Ouch! Where will you find painful swellings called bunions?

7. What gland organ manufactures enzymes so you can digest your food and insulin to control your blood sugar levels?

8. We all have what daily rhythm to our sleep and wake cycles?

9. That noise you hear when people crack their knuckles is from the bursting bubbles in what thick, clear lubricant around the bones?

10. Where is your largest organ located?

11. No matter how strong you get, you'll still have only three types of these—striated, smooth, and cardiac. What are they?

12. Talk about tough—what are the hardest substances in the body?

Answers on page 373.

TIN MEN
AND WOMEN

Test your artificial intelligence quotient in this quiz on robots.

1. In the animated TV series *The Jetsons*, what was robot Rosie's job?

2. You can buy an iRobot Roomba to perform what household chore?

3. Who invented Clocky, a robot alarm clock that shrieks to wake you up and skedaddles when you try to shut it down?

4. The robot rovers Spirit and Opportunity study the barren terrain of what planet?

5. In what 1984 film does a cyber-assassin from the future try to murder a woman who stands between machines and their goal of exterminating mankind?

6. In 1495, what famous painter and sculptor designed an armor-clad robot-knight?

7. Sony's AIBO is what type of robot pet?

8. Unimate, the world's first industrial robot, worked on an assembly line to create what product?

9. Who said, "The robot is going to lose. Not by much. But when the final score is tallied, flesh and blood is going to beat the damn monster"?

10. What do you call a robot designed to resemble a human?

11. Robot comes from *robota*, which means drudgery in what language?

12. Robots invaded the music world when Sony QRIO did what with a Beethoven symphony?

Science

Answers on page 373.

ELEMENTARY, MY DEAR WATSON

Can you detect the answers to this forensic science quiz?

1. Even after a crime scene is cleaned by a tidy crook, investigators can use Luminol to find traces of what?

2. When the only witness to murder is the fly on the wall, what type of scientist can use flies or other insects to establish time, location, and sometimes the manner of death?

3. What mystery writer noted, "Whereas a gentleman was expected to put on gloves to dance with a lady, he may now be expected to put on gloves in order to strangle her"?

4. The largest forensics laboratory in the world is run by what United States federal agency?

5. In ancient Greece, at the first known demonstration of forensics, who measured the density and buoyancy of a king's (allegedly golden) crown to prove the goldsmith was a swindler?

6. The Innocence Project has sprung more than 200 folks from prison. What evidence does it use to prove innocence?

7. Jurors who are fans of *Crime Scene Investigation* or *Law and Order* sometimes expect forensics to work in court like it does on TV. What's this mistaken expectation called?

8. Whorl, arch, and loop are the three basic patterns for what?

9. The world's most famous shoe print evidence was found at the Nicole Simpson and Ron Goldman murder scene in Los Angeles. Experts found prints from what brand of size-12 shoes?

10. What was the only physical evidence that linked serial killer Ted Bundy to his crimes?

Answers on page 373.

Science

ALL ABOUT ANATOMY

See if you can complete this quiz without using your head.

1. Of the more than 200 bones in the human body, which is the largest?

2. The word *patella* comes from the Latin, meaning "shallow dish." What is a more common term for this bone?

3. Blood vessels that transport blood to the heart are commonly referred to as what?

4. What's the major artery that is located on either side of the neck?

5. Stroking what part of the body will produce the Babinski reflex?

6. A feature of the human neck clinically known as the laryngeal prominence is more commonly called what?

7. Histology is the study of what?

8. Hormones and glands are part of what bodily system?

9. When you swallow food, this special flap closes the opening of your windpipe to make sure the food enters the esophagus and not the windpipe.

10. This scientist studied the gall wasp before he began to study human sexual behavior.

11. What are the names of the two bones that are found in the forearm?

12. The malleus, incus, and stapes are three small bones located where?

Science

AT THE SCIENCE FAIR

Just think: a lot of third-graders can answer most of these.

1. As opposed to invertebrates, vertebrates are animals that have what?

2. When the moon is in its new moon phase, what do we see?

3. Insects go through a series of changes as they mature, from egg to larva to chrysalis (cocoon) to adult. What is this called?

4. The three main types of teeth in humans are incisors, canines, and what?

5. Which are smaller, bacteria or viruses?

6. Would you feel heavier on the earth or the moon, or equally heavy on both?

7. Is the claw of a claw hammer a lever, a wedge, or an inclined plane?

8. Coal, oil, and natural gas are examples of what types of fuels?

9. An animal that eats both plants and animals is called a what?

10. Weight is a force—is it measured in newtons, kilograms, or meters?

11. In medieval times, alchemy was a pseudoscientific forerunner of what modern science?

12. Decayed leaves, twigs, or animals make up what component of soil?

13. Adults have 32 permanent teeth. How many are molars?

Science

Answers on page 374.

THAT'S MY INVENTION

These inventors were so proud of their achievements,
they named their creations after themselves.

1. This German count invented an airship in 1901 that was used to bomb England in World War I and then later for luxury passenger transport until it was abandoned after several famous disasters.

2. In 1862, he invented a hand crank–powered machine gun with 10 barrels that could shoot up to 320 rounds per minute. Name the man and the machine.

3. A disposable razor blade (instead of the existing straight razor) was whose brainchild in 1895? He began its production in 1903.

4. Who invented an internal combustion engine in 1892 that created fuel combustion via high pressure, thereby making spark plugs unnecessary?

5. This Belgian invented the single-reed woodwind instrument made famous by such artists as John Coltrane and Stan Getz. Who was he?

6. He invented a unique electronic musical instrument in 1964—an organ-style keyboard connected to a generator, a sequencer, and an oscillator. Who was this innovator?

7. Who created a whole line of containers in 1945 after he was introduced to a substance called polyethylene?

8. To better maintain his 20,000-square-foot ice-skating rink, who invented a large mechanical device in 1949?

9. This German physicist who studied under Ernest Rutherford invented what device that detects and measures nuclear radiation?

10. Who improved (but didn't invent) a common piece of science lab equipment in 1855 that mixes air and gas to provide a very hot flame for heating and sterilization?

Science

Answers on page 374.

IT'S ELEMENTARY

Remember studying the periodic table back in school? Hope so . . .

1. Which extremely flammable element (atomic #1) was used to fill the *Hindenburg* instead of the element it was designed to use—helium?

2. The famed Anaconda mine in Butte, Montana, produced 94,900 tons of which element (#29) between 1881 and 1947?

3. First uncovered in 1798 from inside a mineral called pitchblende, which element (#92) is named after the planet discovered eight years earlier?

4. This metallic element (#22), strong as steel but 45 percent lighter, is primarily used in aircrafts and missiles, yet also finds its way into golf clubs and tennis rackets—what is it?

5. Which element's (#36) name is more widely known as the birthplace of Superman than as the rare gas used in specialized high-speed photographic flashlamps?

6. Can you name this common element (#6) that has an isotope that has been used for years to date archaeological finds?

7. What is the rare and short-lived element (#102) that is named after the inventor of dynamite?

8. Which element (#27) has been used for centuries to impart a permanent rich blue color into glass, porcelain, pottery, and enamels?

9. What is the second most abundant element (#14) on earth (exceeded only by oxygen) and is the principal ingredient of glass?

10. Which element (#13), the most abundant metal in the earth's crust, is extensively used in compact discs, kitchen utensils, and house exteriors?

Answers on page 374.

IT'S REIGNING DINOSAURS

Test your knowledge of these prehistoric creatures.

1. Some 2,000 years ago, dinosaur fossils were discovered in Wucheng, Sichuan, China. What did folks think they'd found?

2. Most scientists believe Dr. Gauthier's theory that these modern-day animals ae the descendents of dinosaurs.

3. Paleontologist Jack Horner discovered the first evidence that some dinosaurs do what?

4. "Warm" or "cold" are the sides scientists take in what hotly debated question about some dinosaurs?

5. Who wrote the dinosaur techno-thriller that was adapted into the film *Jurassic Park*?

6. Able to look into a six-story window, what dinosaur was likely the tallest creature to walk the earth?

7. "Sue," sold for more than $8 million to the Field Museum of National History in Chicago, is famous because she is the most complete skeleton found of what dinosaur?

8. Who wrote, "If we measured success by longevity, then dinosaurs must rank as the number one success story in the history of land life"?

9. What dinosaur, related to Tyrannosaurus rex, was found in and named for a Canadian province?

10. Megalosaurus, the first dinosaur fossil to get a scientific identification, was discovered in 1824 in what country?

11. What dinosaur name means "fast thief"?

Science

Answers on page 375.

YOU BET!

What are the odds you can answer all of these questions?

1. In American casinos and online, what is the most widely played variation of poker?

2. What kind of mechanical animal is used as a lure in dog racing?

3. This Broadway musical and the 1955 movie based on it revolve around gamblers and illegal games of craps. Can you name it?

4. What does a blackjack player want when he asks for a "hit"?

5. Every year in Calaveras County, California, gamblers bet on a race that was made famous in a Mark Twain story. What animals are they putting their money on?

6. It was a popular music hall song written in 1892: "The Man Who Broke the Bank at..." what famous European casino?

7. In the movie *Rain Man*, Raymond helped his brother win a fortune at blackjack. What technique did Raymond use to beat the house?

8. Name the two German-American performers whose long-running Las Vegas magic act featuring white tigers was forced to close after one of them was mauled by one of the big cats.

9. The odds are nearly 650,000 to 1 that you'll end up holding the highest poker hand. What is it?

10. What is a bet on the first-, second-, and third-place winners in exact order called?

11. European roulette wheels have 37 pockets marked 0 to 36; American roulette wheels have 38 pockets. What is that extra pocket marked?

Answers on page 375.

AWARDS

If you get at least seven correct, you deserve a medal!

1. In what genre of literature is the Hugo awarded?

2. Although the official name of this statuette is the Academy Award of Merit, what is it better known as?

3. What military decoration was awarded to Sergeant First Class Randy Shughart and Master Sergeant Gary Gordon for defending a downed Black Hawk helicopter pilot and his crew during the 1993 Battle of Mogadishu?

4. In 1935, the Downtown Athletic Club of New York City began giving what annual award to the most outstanding college football player in the United States?

5. What is the oldest active international sports trophy, predating the modern Olympics (1894) by 43 years?

6. This heart-shaped medal with the profile of George Washington is given to those wounded or killed while serving with the military. Name it.

7. These awards are announced annually by the president of Columbia University and are named in honor of a famous American publisher of the *New York World* and the *St. Louis-Post Dispatch*. What are they?

8. A winged woman holding an atom is TV's equivalent of the Oscars. What is the statuette called?

9. The best Broadway productions receive Tonys, whereas the Off-Broadway and Off-Off–Broadway award winners receive what?

10. Each year, the American Library Association awards two medals: one to the author of the most distinguished contribution to American children's literature and another to the artist of the most distinguished American children's picture book. What are they called?

WE DIDN'T HAVE THAT (WHEN I WAS YOUR AGE)

Inventive inventions.

1. Introduced in 1953, what speedy Chevrolet was probably named after a class of small, fast, and powerful warships?

2. Originally created as wallpaper cleaner in 1956, what substance was reintroduced as a creative red, white, or blue children's toy in 24-ounce cans?

3. First installed in 1969 outside a Chemical Bank in New York, what invention (primarily known by its initials) was found in more than 160,000 locations by 1997?

4. What type of television introduced in 1954 cost $995, the same price tag as a car?

5. In 1951, 200 people paid $3 a year for the privilege of having what kind of paper (plastic came later) in their wallet?

6. What typist aid did Monkee Michael Nesmith's mother create in 1951 and sell to the Gillette Corporation for $47.5 million in 1979?

7. What did Bill Richards, the owner of a California surf shop, sell in 1958 as a pastime for surfers when the surf was flat?

8. The Oldsmobile Toronado was the first car to offer what safety feature in 1974?

9. In 1951, people started complaining about tripping over the cord of this device, named "Lazy Bones," invented by Zenith in 1950.

10. What popular pastime, invented by Willy Higinbotham in 1958, required relatively quick reflexes and an oscilloscope?

GAMES PEOPLE PLAY

New and classic board and table games.

1. What game—created over 50 years ago—do you try to win with pronouncements like "Colonel Mustard in the library with the rope"?

2. This children's board game includes 20 marbles that are gobbled up by four plastic animals named Henry, Harry, Homer, and Happy.

3. A part of most baby boomers' childhoods, what sweet board game consists of a winding track made up of 134 colored spaces and a deck of cards with corresponding colors?

4. Wooden playing pieces depict bombs, scouts, miners, captains, majors, and a flag in this war-themed board game introduced in 1961.

5. A four-player game developed more than 2,500 years ago is played with tiles containing suits called dots, bamboos, and characters. Name this ancient game.

6. Inspired by Rube Goldberg's works and introduced in 1963, what game has dozens of plastic pieces, including a bowling ball, bathtub, stop sign, and diving board?

7. Don't apologize if you don't know this 1934 Parker Bros. strategy and revenge game. It's not very nice because it allows players to send a competitor's piece back to the start.

8. If you are bent on world domination, you'll want to play this board game with dice, cards, and six sets of miniature armies.

9. What is the American version of the "Royal Game of India," where the goal is to get all four colored pawns to the center square?

10. It's all in the roll of the dice in this game, which resembles *senet*, played by the ancient Egyptians and possibly the oldest game in history.

Pop Culture

Answers on page 376.

"MAG"NIFICENT

Before there were Bathroom Readers, people read magazines in the bath.

1. Since the mid 1960s, what has been the most-circulated weekly magazine?

2. Nineteen percent of adult males in America read this periodical every week.

3. Bearing a four-word title, what is America's top-selling "household" magazine?

4. Known for its "Seal of Approval" on consumer products, what is the second-best–selling "household" magazine?

5. What monthly general-interest family magazine, with a circulation of more than 10 million, contains regular features such as "Word Power" and "That's Outrageous"?

6. What is the top-selling American weekly newsmagazine?

7. What is the top-selling magazine named after a single individual?

8. This publication was a family magazine for 79 years, but went in a whole new direction in 1965 when Helen Gurley Brown became its editor.

9. What magazine's first issue in December 1953 contained, among other things, a Sherlock Holmes story, a feature on desks for the modern office, and a photo spread of Marilyn Monroe?

10. Of the top 100 American consumer magazines, this is the only one with a two-word French title.

11. What automobile magazine enjoys the highest circulation in America?

Answers on page 376.

PLACE YOUR BETS

All about American casino gambling.

1. Name the casino, the first one to be established in Connecticut, that is also the world's largest.

2. Which Las Vegas casino is contained within a 350-foot-tall black glass pyramid?

3. What gambling town touts itself as "the Biggest Little City in the World"?

4. Although located in the middle of the desert, which Las Vegas casino has a man-made eight-acre lake on its premises?

5. What is the only South Dakota town where slot machines and table games such as poker and blackjack are legal?

6. On May 26, 1978, what was the first casino to open its doors in Atlantic City, New Jersey?

7. This Las Vegas casino boasts the highest observation tower (1,149 feet) in the United States.

8. Las Vegas became a major destination after Benjamin "Bugsy" Siegel opened what hotel/casino on the day after Christmas in 1946?

9. In what state can you find 10 casinos in the town of Tunica?

10. Massachusetts' sole gambling establishment, Horizon's Edge, is which type of casino?

11. Harrah's Cherokee Casino is the only gambling house in which eastern state?

Pop Culture

CAN YOU DIG IT?

Test your archaeological mettle with this quiz.

1. Name Indiana Jones's two professions.

2. Two movies based on a video game feature an adventurous "tomb raider" who collects artifacts from the ruins of temples, cities, and other sites. What's her name?

3. In 1930, at a dig site in the Middle East, the British archaeologist Max Mallowan met a mystery writer he married that same year. Who was she?

4. Famed archaeologist Louis Leakey gave these two women their first jobs as primate researchers in Africa.

5. When mild-mannered bank clerk Stanley Ipkiss finds a mask on the seashore, an archaeologist tells him the mask depicts Loki, the Norse god of tricks and deception. Who plays Stanley?

6. An artifact discovered in 1799 held the key to deciphering hieroglyphics. What was the artifact?

7. Archaeology studies the material remains of humankind. A related branch of academic study looks seriously at the trash we leave behind. What is that field called?

8. Who coined the phrase, "Man is a tool-making animal"?

9. Emile Gagnan and a colleague developed the Aqua Lung (similar to SCUBA gear) for underwater archaeology and exploring. Who was Gagnan's colleague?

10. Willard F. Libby was awarded the Nobel Prize in Chemistry in 1960 for his work on what procedure that revolutionized archaeology?

11. What name was given to the 9,300-year-old human remains found in Washington State in 1997?

Answers on page 376.

Pop Culture

DON'T BE A STRANGER

These "strangers" certainly made their mark.

1. A psychotic socialite, a famous tennis star, and a lot of double-crossing are the themes of what 1951 Hitchcock thriller?

2. This novel begins with the words "Mother died today. Or, maybe, yesterday; I can't be sure."

3. What TV game show ends with the words "Don't be a stranger"?

4. According to the Internet Movie Database, this was the only film directed by Orson Welles to show a profit on its initial release.

5. The 1977 album *The Stranger* was the breakthrough album for what singer/pianist/songwriter?

6. What dark-cloaked superhero, who briefly had his own DC Comics series in 1952, made his mark as an invaluable assistant to the Justice League?

7. The column "Savage Love" by Dan Savage appears in *The Stranger*, an alternative newspaper in what city?

8. What top-billed actor starred in the 2006 comedy/drama film *Stranger Than Fiction*, playing an IRS auditor?

9. Who played the homeless, possibly schizophrenic bag lady in the 1991 TV movie *Face of a Stranger*?

10. The 1966 James Garner movie *A Man Could Get Killed* introduced the music for what composition that later became a Sinatra standard?

11. This thriller starring Halle Berry and Bruce Willis was the first motion picture to be filmed at the 9/11 ground zero site in New York City. What's the film?

FANGS FOR THE MEMORIES

How well do you know the bloodsuckers who populate books and movies?

1. What 1897 novel was the basis for many vampire stories that followed in film and theater, and who was its Irish author?

2. Who played Buffy the Vampire Slayer in the first (1992) film with that title?

3. In the TV *Buffy* and its spinoff *Angel*, he's a vampire with a soul. In TV's *Bones*, he's the FBI's Special Agent Seeley Booth. Who is the actor?

4. In 1985's *Once Bitten*, Lauren Hutton plays a sexy vampire searching for a male virgin. Who's the male lead in this comedy/horror spoof?

5. What 1994 vampire movie starred Tom Cruise, Brad Pitt, Christian Slater, Antonio Banderas, and Kirsten Dunst?

6. Talisa Soto played a sexy vampiress in a skimpy costume in a 1996 film based on a comic book character. Who was the character, and what was the name of the movie?

7. In 1989's *Vampire's Kiss*, a publishing exec has an encounter with a neck-biter and thinks he's turning into a vampire. Who is the male star?

8. Bela Lugosi, the actor is most associated with playing Count Dracula, had a morbid fear of what?

9. Who played Count Dracula in the 1979 vampire spoof *Love at First Bite*?

10. What movie based on a Stephen King story about a vampire starred David Soul, James Mason, and Bonnie Bedelia?

HOCUS POCUS

Do you feel the magic in these questions?

1. Born Ehrich Weiss in 1874, he achieved fame as a "handcuff king" and escapologist. What stage name did he use?

2. This Hollywood landmark (and self-proclaimed "Academy of Magical Arts") is a Victorian mansion that's used as a performance venue by many magicians. What's it called?

3. He was born David Seth Kotkin in 1956, but what's this professional magician and illusionist's literary stage name?

4. This one-act musical appeared on Broadway in 1974. It starred magician Doug Henning, and its lyrics were composed by Stephen Schwartz, who also composed the music for 2003's *Wicked*.

5. Vaudeville magician Howard Thurston specialized in what?

6. *The Magic Mountain* was a 1924 novel by what author?

7. *Die Zauberflöte*, or *The Magic Flute*, is a 1791 opera in two acts by what composer?

8. In the Harry Potter books, humans who can perform magic are referred to as witches and wizards, in contrast to the nonmagical folk called what?

9. What do you call a square-shaped grid of numbers with identical row, column, and diagonal sums?

10. In 2006 two films about talented magicians came to mainstream theaters. Name the films and their stars.

Pop Culture

Answers on page 377.

ON THE RADIO

Time to tune in and pump up the volume.

1. Who "knows what evil lurks in the hearts of men"?

2. What "chatterbox" with "pretty auburn locks" has appeared in comics, on the radio, on Broadway, and in the movies? (Bonus: What company sponsored her radio show?)

3. What show—set in a fictional Minnesota town "where all the women are strong, all the men are good-looking, and all the children are above average"—premiered in 1974 and is still on the air today?

4. Shock Jock Howard Stern moved to satellite radio in 2006 to avoid having to adhere to FCC content restrictions. On what network can he now be heard?

5. What Tennessee-based radio program has aired continuously since 1925, making it the longest-running radio show in U.S. history?

6. Before Rachael Ray, Martha Stewart, and Julia Child, there was this (fictional) cooking queen, who got her own radio show in 1924.

7. What canine, who went on to become a movie star, first found fame on the radio? (He got his own half-hour show in 1930.)

8. Proctor & Gamble and Palmolive were two of the first sponsors of these radio dramas that began in the 1920s and are known today as what?

9. This radio program premiered in 1971 as the first news program on NPR. It remains one of the station's most popular shows today.

10. What engineer and "mad scientist" from Austria is credited with inventing the radio? (The U.S. Supreme Court as much as declared him so when it upheld his radio patent in 1943.)

Answers on page 377.

Pop Culture

WHEN THE CHIPS ARE DOWN

The poker world is full of crazy lingo, and there's a playing term in every answer. Are you all in?

1. Which TV sitcom that ran from 1987 to 1995 centers on three men and three children in San Francisco?

2. Which chess term is spoken after the opponent's king is placed in imminent danger?

3. This word can mean a cliff or a hill with a broad, steep face.

4. What's the four-word naval command ordering all able-bodied seamen to come together on the double?

5. On Broadway, what four-letter word is the antithesis of "smash hit"?

6. Often used outside the world of poker, what phrase describes a blank expression?

7. Which big-screen role played by Jack Nicholson in 1989 was first played by Cesar Romero in the 1960s on TV?

8. What position did Richie Cunningham, Gary Anderson, and Happy Feller play in the NFL?

9. What's the name of the camouflaged enclosure used by hunters or wildlife photographers to hide from their quarry?

10. It's a way to entice people to buy your product. But in poker, it means giving away your hand.

11. Roy G. Biv is a mnemonic device for the colors of this place where Leprachauns stash their gold. The hiding place is also a poker term.

Pop Culture

Answers on page 378.

IN THE NEIGHBORHOOD

You know the main characters, but who lives next door?

1. Who lives next door to Blondie and Dagwood?

2. Fred and Wilma Flintstone's neighbors and best friends are what blond and brunette couple?

3. What American poet said "good fences make good neighbors"? (Bonus: Name the poem this line is taken from.)

4. The 1981 movie *Neighbors*, based on the book by Thomas Berger, stars what two former SNL actors?

5. Fred and Ethel Mertz are neighbors to this Cuban bandleader and his redheaded wife.

6. Teri Hatcher, Felicity Huffman, Marcia Cross, Eva Longoria, and Nicollette Sheridan portray neighbors on *Desperate Housewives*. What street do they live on, and what characters do they play?

7. Who plays Matthew Modine and Melanie Griffith's scary neighbor in the 1990 movie *Pacific Heights*?

8. "Won't You Be My Neighbor?" is the theme song for what TV show?

9. Who and what does the Good Neighbor Award recognize?

10. Winnie Cooper is the prettiest girl in school and his neighbor in this television series of the late 1980s and early 1990s. Who's the main character, and what was his show?

11. On the 1990s WB college drama *Felicity*, the title character lived down the hall from her handsome resident advisor. What was his name?

Pop Culture

A PASSION FOR FASHION

Fashion in movies, TV, and life.

1. At the Grand Ole Opry or on *Hee Haw*, Minnie Pearl wore a straw hat with its price tag dangling down. What was the price?

2. What trademark apparel was Lt. Columbo always seen wearing on the police drama *Columbo*?

3. What was the signature outfit of the Fonz on *Happy Days*?

4. Laura Petrie (Mary Tyler Moore) on *The Dick Van Dyke Show* helped make what kind of pants a major trend in U.S. attire?

5. In the 2006 film *The Devil Wears Prada*, who plays Andrea "Andy" Sachs, the new assistant to the editor of a fashion magazine?

6. With appearances by Kate Moss, Naomi Campbell, and other supermodels, the 1995 fashion documentary *Unzipped* gave a behind-the-seams look at what designer?

7. Fred Rogers would come home and slip into what comfortable item of apparel on *Mr. Rogers' Neighborhood*?

8. On *Kung Fu*, David Carradine changed the color of his shirt from brown to saffron to commemorate the untimely 1973 death of what martial artist?

9. What is the national costume of Japan that's worn by men, women, and children?

10. On *Ally McBeal*, Ellen Vassal (Jane Krakowski) comes up with interesting inventions, including what useful item for joggers?

Pop Culture

TALES OF REVENGE

Take this quiz . . . or you'll be sorry.

1. Stephen King' sixth novel—but the first one to be published—was about a young girl with telekinetic powers who takes revenge on the classmates who taunted and bullied her. What's the book (and movie)?

2. Shakespeare's longest play is a revenge drama in which the title character and two other characters seek retribution for their fathers' deaths. What's the play?

3. Revenge is a major theme in what Herman Melville novel whose characters include Stubb, Pip, and Starbuck?

4. In a low-budget 1979 film, Mel Gibson plays a revenge-seeking character whose last name is Rockatansky. What's his better-known nickname?

5. Heathcliff's consuming desire for revenge is the main theme of this 1847 novel by "Ellis Bell." What is the novel?

6. What "epic-length revenge drama" by Quentin Tarantino stars Uma Thurman as the Bride and Lucy Liu as O-Ren Ishii?

7. Dustin Hoffman and Susan George starred in a 1971 film about a mathematician and his wife who move to England. Controversial for its violence and rape scene, what was the movie?

8. *Angel and the Badman* is a 1947 Western about a wounded outlaw obsessed with killing a man who murdered his foster father. Who plays the outlaw?

9. Liam Neeson plays a vengeful scientist who is disfigured and becomes a vigilante in what 1990 film that spawned two sequels?

10. John Travolta and Nicolas Cage each play two characters—one of them obsessed with revenge—in what 1997 John Woo film?

BEATLEMANIA

Trivia about Beatles songs . . . yeah, yeah, yeah.

1. One of the most covered and performed songs in pop music history, Paul McCartney's love ballad featured him accompanied only by a string quartet. What's the song written originally for *Help*?

2. George Harrison, the song's writer, did not perform the hard-driving guitar solo in "While My Guitar Gently Weeps." What legendary guitarist was the performer?

3. "Eleanor Rigby picks up the rice in a church where a wedding has been." Who is "writing the words of a sermon that no one will hear"?

4. Paul McCartney wrote what song as a show of sympathy to John Lennon's son, Julian, when Lennon was divorcing Julian's mother?

5. Desmond and Molly are the happily married subjects of what song that became the theme song for the 1980s TV drama *Life Goes On*?

6. "Get Back" is the only Beatles song with a co-credit—to the Beatles and this man, the band's sometime keyboard player.

7. Over 73 million people tuned in to see the Beatles on *The Ed Sullivan Show* in February 1964. They performed "All My Loving," "Till There Was You," "She Loves You," "I Saw Her Standing There," and what other song?

8. Which one of these was not sung by Ringo Starr: "Octopus's Garden," "Yellow Submarine," or "I Am the Walrus"?

9. John Lennon claimed that the song "Because" consists of the chord progression to what famous piece of classical music, played in reverse order?

10. Frank Sinatra called what Beatles song—written and sung by George Harrison—"the greatest love song ever written"?

Music

Answers on page 379.

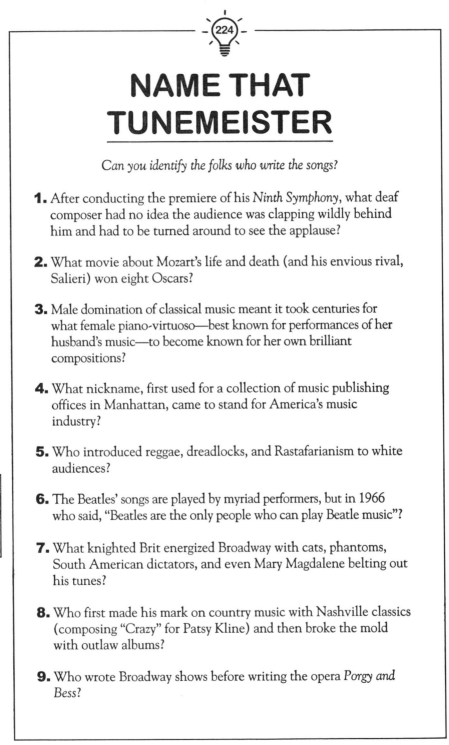

NAME THAT TUNEMEISTER

Can you identify the folks who write the songs?

1. After conducting the premiere of his *Ninth Symphony*, what deaf composer had no idea the audience was clapping wildly behind him and had to be turned around to see the applause?

2. What movie about Mozart's life and death (and his envious rival, Salieri) won eight Oscars?

3. Male domination of classical music meant it took centuries for what female piano-virtuoso—best known for performances of her husband's music—to become known for her own brilliant compositions?

4. What nickname, first used for a collection of music publishing offices in Manhattan, came to stand for America's music industry?

5. Who introduced reggae, dreadlocks, and Rastafarianism to white audiences?

6. The Beatles' songs are played by myriad performers, but in 1966 who said, "Beatles are the only people who can play Beatle music"?

7. What knighted Brit energized Broadway with cats, phantoms, South American dictators, and even Mary Magdalene belting out his tunes?

8. Who first made his mark on country music with Nashville classics (composing "Crazy" for Patsy Kline) and then broke the mold with outlaw albums?

9. Who wrote Broadway shows before writing the opera *Porgy and Bess*?

Answers on page 379.

Music

ONE-HIT WONDERS

Musical acts that had a single—but memorable—hit song.

1. When the German group Nena recorded their song "99 Luftballoons" in English, what was the song retitled?

2. What radio DJ became a one-hit wonder in the 1970s with the novelty song "Disco Duck"?

3. This pop group was "too sexy" for a shirt, a cat, and pretty much everything else.

4. David Soul, star of *Starsky and Hutch* went to #1 in 1977 with his ballad "Don't Give Up On Us." Was he Starsky or Hutch?

5. Bobby McFerrin sang—and provided the instrumental "backing"— in what ultrapositive, completely a capella hit from 1988?

6. The Starland Vocal Band had only one hit, but they still got a short-lived TV variety show out of it. Name the song.

7. Terry Jacks had joy. Terry Jacks had fun. Terry Jacks also had what?

8. "Rapper's Delight" is regarded as the first nationally popular rap song. The group that sang it, influential as they were, had only one hit. Name the group.

9. The 1960s garage rock classic "Double Shot of My Baby's Love" was performed by what band?

10. Devo wore flowerpots on their heads and sang like robots. What was their only hit?

11. The Tom Tom Club, who had one hit in 1982 with "Genius of Love" was a side project of two members from what mega-popular 1980s band?

Music

Answers on page 379.

CROONERS

If you need help, ask your grandma. Do-be-do-be-do.

1. This superb jazz pianist rode his smooth baritone to the top of the 1950s charts, becoming the first black artist to host his own TV show. Who was he?

2. Who's the baritone most remembered today for playing Daniel Boone's tomahawk-tossing sidekick on TV in the 1960s?

3. What was the nickname given to silky-voiced singer who also wrote one of the best-selling Christmas songs of all time?

4. Who was the singing barber whose laid-back style was parodied so wickedly by *Saturday Night Live*'s Phil Hartman?

5. This suave Italian was a straight man to one of the movies' great clowns, and he made a martini and a hiccup his signature.

6. This Englishman's name is Gerry Dorsey but his career didn't take off until he adopted the name of what 19th-century German composer?

7. A screen legend for his elegant dancing with a range of partners, who premiered more song classics, like "They Can't Take Away From Me" and "Night and Day," than any other performer?

8. In the 1920s, this ukulele-playing tenor scored big with hits like "Singin' in the Rain." He achieved immortality with what Oscar-winning song from a 1940 Disney cartoon feature about a puppet?

9. A singing sensation in the 1940s, this guy was washed up until he reinvented himself as a jazzy saloon singer in the 1950s and became the Chairman of the Board. Who is he?

10. Who was the mellow-voiced country crooner who knocked out hit after hit in the late 1950s and early 1960s until his career came to an abrupt end in a plane crash in 1964?

Answers on page 380.

COUNTRY CLASSICS

These folks pioneered country and western.

1. What "Man in Black" sold more than 50 million albums during his five-decade career?

2. Speaking of the "Man in Black," his second wife was part of one of the most famous families in country music. Name her and the group that her mother was a founding member of.

3. She may have sung about "The Pill," but this country music star married at 13, had her first child at 14, and was a grandmother by the time she was 29. What's her name?

4. What iconic country music singer/songwriter lived to be just 29 but during that time racked up 28 top ten hits? (Ten went to #1.)

5. She first appeared at the Grand Ole Opry at age 13, but it wasn't until she was 21 and joined Porter Wagoner's variety show that she found fame.

6. What "singing brakeman" was the genre's first real superstar and has been nicknamed the "Father of Country Music"?

7. Howdeee! Okay, she wasn't technically a singer, but what country comedian whose signature accessory was a straw hat with a dangling price tag became a Grand Ole Opry staple for almost three decades?

8. Now active in environmental causes—he started a company that makes biodiesel fuel from vegetable oil—for most of his career, he was best known as one of the pioneers of outlaw country.

9. Although she sang about standing by her man, this "First Lady of Country Music" was married five times.

10. What singer, who died in a plane crash at the age of 30, was voted the #1 greatest woman in country music in 2001?

Music

Answers on page 380.

NOVELTY SONGS

*These songs caught the public's imagination
and had them rocking and laughing.*

1. What dance did vampires and ghouls, and the *Crypt-Kicker Five* do in the lab late one night?

2. How did the miserable kid at Camp Grenada start his letter to his parents?

3. What did the man in the straitjacket sing when those nice young men in their clean white coats came to his door?

4. Can you describe the miniscule swimsuit was the girl wearing when she was afraid to come out of the water?

5. This famous Michael Jackson song was parodied by "Weird Al" Yankovic and became his first Top 20 hit in 1984.

6. Women gymnasts at the 1996 Summer Olympics turned this song by an obscure Spanish duet into an international dance craze. What was the song?

7. One of the founding fathers of rock 'n' roll had the biggest hit of his career with this risqué tune about a cute little toy with two bells dangling from a string?

8. What did the little Nash Rambler keep repeating to the Cadillac in the Playmates' 1958 ditty about an epic drag race?

9. What furry trio took the lines, "Christmas, Christmas time is here, time for toys and time for cheer" to the top of the charts in 1958?

10. What ran over Grandma in Elmo and Patsy's classic holiday song?

11. What's the name of the goofy guy with the "goo-goo-goo-ga-lly eyes"?

Music

Answers on page 380.

FICTIONAL BANDS

They may exist only in fiction, but these bands played on.

1. What two band leaders were sent "on a [fake] mission from God" to generate $5,000 to cover an orphanage's unpaid back taxes?

2. Over the years, "one of England's loudest bands" was known as The Originals, The New Originals, and The Thamesmen before settling on what name?

3. "Tragical History Tour," "Shabby Road," and "Let it Rot" were three of the albums by this fictional band that Eric Idle put together to spoof the Beatles.

4. What popular teenage time traveler was the lead guitarist in the garage rock band The Pinheads?

5. Speaking of time travel, if Bill and Ted hadn't gone on their excellent adventure, they would never have been able to launch what seminal rock band?

6. Rob Gordon's coworker Barry plays in the band Sonic Death Monkey when not working at the Championship Vinyl record store in what 2000 John Cusack romantic comedy?

7. What transsexual front woman's back-up band of Korean-born Army wives is called The Angry Inch?

8. What Hanna-Barbera cartoon band actually had a few hits: "Who's Your Baby?," "Bang-Shang-A-Lang," "Jingle Jangle," and the #1 hit "Sugar, Sugar?"

9. These prison escapee performers from *O Brother, Where Art Thou?* got their name after two of them were still wet after being baptized.

10. Stillwater, a band in this 1960s-themed film, was an amalgamation of real-life bands The Allman Brothers and Led Zeppelin.

Music

Answers on page 380.

MADE FOR A SONG

Hard to believe, but Hollywood based some movies on songs.

1. "Sex appeal in a bottle"— that's the theme of the 1992 movie that stars Tate Donovan and Sandra Bullock and was inspired by what popular doo-wop song?

2. A boy finally stands up for himself explosively after his girlfriend is assaulted in what movie based on a Kenny Rogers song?

3. What 1991 film directed by Sean Penn was based on a Bruce Springsteen song, "Highway Patrolman"?

4. Michael Landon starred in what 1959 Civil War movie based on a popular song, the tale of a Rebel soldier pursued by a lawman?

5. A pile of trash, a court hearing, and Thanksgiving dinner figure in what 1969 movie made from an Arlo Guthrie song?

6. Wow, this 1993 teen comedy has Matthew McConaughey, Philip Seymour Hoffman, Renée Zellweger, and Matthew Fox—as extras! It's a touching tale about a teenage boy who dies and comes back as a zombie. What's the movie based on a 1963 song by The Angels?

7. Robby Benson and Glynnis O'Connor star in what 1976 movie based on a huge Bobbie Gentry hit?

8. Redneck humor, barroom brawls, a little T&A—this movie's got it all! It's based very loosely on a Southern Gothic song performed by Vicki Lawrence, and later Reba McEntire. What's the film?

9. Johnny Paycheck did a famous cover of this song (about a disgruntled employee) that was so popular they made a movie out of it with Robert Hays, Art Carney, and Barbara Hershey. What's the song?

10. Oh no! The paradise of Pepperland is attacked by the music-hating Blue Meanies in what 1968 film based on a group's 13th single?

KEEP YOUR EYE ON THE BIRDIE

A whole flock of people with birdlike names.

1. What NBA team did Larry Bird go on to coach after leaving the Boston Celtics in 1997?

2. Nurse Florence Nightingale achieved fame serving in what war?

3. What did Captain Jack Sparrow of the *Pirates of the Caribbean* films rename the ship *Wicked Wench* after it was resurrected from the bottom of the sea?

4. Despite the nickname "Birdman of Alcatraz," inmate Robert Stroud only kept birds *before* being transferred to Alcatraz from what Kansas prison?

5. What famous Wild West legend did Martha Jane Canary grow up to be?

6. What radio personality is Howard Stern's longtime co-host?

7. What laws mandating "separate but equal" status for black Americans were named after a minstrel show character?

8. What fictional inmate is FBI trainee Clarice Starling assigned to in an Oscar-winning movie?

9. He flies through the air with the greatest of ease: Tony Hawk is a professional athlete in what sport?

10. Of homonym, homograph, or homophone, which describes Dan Quayle's surname in relation to the bird called a quail?

11. The TV show *The Partridge Family* was inspired by what real-life family of musicians?

People

Answers on page 381.

YOU'RE MY INSPIRATION

Famous fiction inspired by not-so-famous real people.

1. Sidney Reilly, a sophisticated playboy, was also Britain's most brilliant spy and the inspiration for what fictional secret agent?

2. Ten-year-old Alice Liddel asked a family friend to entertain her with stories. What famous children's classic did she inspire?

3. What castaway was based on Alex Selkirk, a Scottish sailor who deserted his ship to spend four years on an uninhabited island off Chile?

4. Jeff Dowd went to jail as a member of the Seattle Seven and is now a film producer and promoter. Jeff Bridges plays Dowd in which cult classic film?

5. What famous detective was based on Dr. Joseph Bell, an Edinburgh University professor of clinical surgery who dazzled his students with an uncanny ability to deduce information about his patients from seemingly unimportant details?

6. Fifteenth-century Romanian Prince Vlad Tepes was infamous for impaling his enemies as well as nailing their hats to their heads. Vlad's historic cruelty made him a natural as the evil "undead" character in which 19th century novel?

7. One of the first people in England to demonstrate how electricity could make dead frogs "jump" like live ones, Dr. James Lind may have been the inspiration for what Mary Shelley character?

8. After Dr. Sam Shepherd's wife was murdered, he was prosecuted for the crime despite his claim that a "bushy haired man" did it. Name the TV series and movie based on this case?

9. In 1934 William Coyne escaped prison and went on a killing spree that included cannibalism. According to a biographer, Thomas Harris used cannibal Coyne as the inspiration for who?

Answers on page 381.

DR. WHO?

Real and not-so-real doctors.

1. Which beverage, first manufactured in Waco, Texas, in 1885, is a combination of 23 fruit flavors?

2. Ray Conniff and the Singers' biggest hit "Somewhere My Love," aka "Lara's Theme," is from which 1965 classic film?

3. At the time of his death in 1991, which author had written and illustrated 44 books including *I Am NOT Going to Get Up Today* and *Ten Apples Up on Top*?

4. Which Illinois Medical School graduate went on to invent products such as the "Foot Eazer," "Zino-Pad," and "Rubberless" soft stockings?

5. Which 1970s rock group's first two hit singles were "Sylvia's Mother" and "The Cover of the *Rolling Stone*"?

6. What fictional character, who first appeared in print in 1886, is a well-respected physician who unwittingly discovers his dark side?

7. What is the popular "physician's" brand name for the children's one-piece footed pajamas made of a relatively thick, warm fabric?

8. Peter Sellers plays three characters in what 1964 war room movie generally acknowledged as the ultimate black comedy?

9. Which hour-long weekly medical drama starring Richard Chamberlain and Raymond Massey aired on NBC from September 1961 through August 1966?

10. What is the on-air name of Johnny Caravella, morning disk jockey at WKRP radio, 1530 on the AM dial?

11. Who wrote the 1946 book that became the second best-selling book in America with sales of over 50 million copies?

People

Answers on page 381.

COMIC PERSONAS

These comedians played some truly memorable characters.

1. This *Saturday Night Live* star is known for such roles as Beldar Conehead and impersonations of Julia Child and Jimmy Carter.

2. His characters included Rudy the Helpless Repairman, Pedro the Mexican, and a bus driver named Ralph Kramden.

3. This *Saturday Night Live* comic's personas included the Church Lady and Hans, who wants to "Pump… you up!"

4. He played Wanda the Ugly Woman ("I'm gonna rock your world!") on *In Living Color* before he went on to win a Best Actor Oscar for his portrayal of Ray Charles in *Ray*.

5. On SCTV, he was Bob McKenzie, co-host with brother Doug of "The Great White North," a talk show for Canadian hunters.

6. When she wasn't being bratty five-year-old Edith Ann, this *Laugh-In* regular might be doing Ernestine, the wisecracking telephone operator. ("Is this the party to whom I am speaking?")

7. Her many comic characters included South African golf pro Kiki Howard-Smith and Mrs. Noh Nang Ning, an Asian donut shop owner who manages to relate everything to the donut.

8. This comic's characters have included feisty old lady Maude Frickett, rural bumpkin Elwood P. Suggins, and Mearth, the baby boy of *Mork and Mindy*.

9. On *Laugh-In*, she played Gladys Ormphby, the crotchety old lady who sits on a park bench and slugs fresh guys over the head with her purse—especially Arte Johnson's "dirty old man."

10. What comic actor played the sassy black female Geraldine, Reverend Leroy, and the private eye Danny Danger?

People

THE MOTHER LODE

These mothers definitely know best.

1. Many people call her the "mother of the modern-day Civil Rights movement."

2. Peggy Wood played "Mother Abbess" in *The Sound of Music*. By what name was she most often called in the film?

3. What prominent American labor organizer now has a magazine named for her?

4. What small, long-winged seabird is sometimes called "Mother Carey's chicken"?

5. This is the title of a nursery rhyme . . . or the name for a long, loose-fitting dress?

6. What's the five-letter word for the natural, iridescent composite known as mother-of-pearl?

7. She's the archetypal woman of nursery rhymes . . . or the title of a 1971 song by Jethro Tull.

8. The 16th-century soothsayer and prophetess Ursula Southeil is better known by what nickname?

9. She wrote *A Vindication of the Rights of Women* in 1792 and has been called the "mother of feminism." She was also the mother of Mary Shelley, author of *Frankenstein*. Who is she?

10. What flowering plant is a common roadside weed and also a medicinal herb that may be used as a mild vasodilator, cardiac tonic, or a way to ease stomach cramps?

11. What Roman Catholic nun founded the Missionaries of Charity and won the Nobel Peace prize in 1979?

People

Answers on page 382.

WHAT A WAY TO GO

Strange deaths of famous people.

1. What English scientist known for experimenting with freezing me contracted pneumonia and then tried to extend his life by eating a frozen bird? (No such luck.)

2. What Russian revolutionary, who Stalin expelled from the communist party, was assassinated by an ice pick to the head?

3. What playwright of such Greek tragedies as *The Oresteia* and *Agamemnon* died when an eagle dropped a tortoise onto his head?

4. This man, who is credited with launching the American fitness revolution of the late 20th century, had a massive, fatal heart attack after his daily jog.

5. Name the Russian mystic who was shot three times, stabbed, poisoned, clubbed, and finally died by drowning.

6. What whiskey distiller got blood poisoning after he injured a toe while kicking his safe? (He couldn't remember the combination.)

7. This fearsome 5th century warrior died from a nosebleed he got on his wedding night—presumably caused from too much drinking and not enough time spent with his "hunny."

8. Columbian soccer player Andrés Escobar was murdered after accidentally scoring a goal for what nation (not his own)? The goal eventually lead to his team's elimination from the tournament.

9. What "Wild" West outlaw was inducted into the Poker Hall of Fame just for holding the "Dead Man's Hand" (two aces and two eights) when he was assassinated?

10. Where was scientist and French Revolutionary activist Jean Paul Marat when he was stabbed to death?

People

Answers on page 382.

FUNNY GUYS

These classic comedians did not need a laugh track.

1. Which violin-playing stand-up comic was forever linked with the four-word phrase, "Take my wife...please"?

2. Speaking of famous comic catchphrases, which actor and comedian owned the phrase, "I don't get no respect"?

3. This comedian maintained he was 39 years old up to the day he died in 1974—at the age of 80. Who was he?

4. Which comic actor had everyone in the country saying, "Well, excuuuse me!" during the 1970s?

5. What comedy team gained legendary status after their baseball routine "Who's on First?" appeared in the 1945 film *The Naughty Nineties*?

6. This legendary vaudevillian ended every show with the trademark sign-off, "Good night, Mrs. Calabash, wherever you are." Known worldwide as "Schnozzola," what was his real name?

7. The lines "Bang . . . Zoom!" and "One of these days . . . Pow, right in the kisser!" could only be delivered by which portly TV comic and screen actor?

8. Referred to sarcastically as "Mr. Warmth," this stand-up comic got big laughs calling audience members "hockey pucks." Who was this first insult-comedian ?

9. "Mom always liked you best" was a running gag of which comic team of the 1960s and 1970s?

10. Which comic actor's film roles included Otis B. Driftwood, Dr. Hugo Z. Hackenbush, Rufus T. Firefly, and Captain Geoffrey Spaulding?

People

Answers on page 382.

WOMB MATES

You shouldn't have double trouble with this quiz about twins!

1. Named after their grandmothers, name the first twins to occupy the White House?

2. What mythical twins—fathered by the god Mars but suckled by a she-wolf—were said to have founded Italy's capital city?

3. In the 1988 comedy *Twins*, what unlikely pair of actors played a set of twins reared apart?

4. The Minnesota Twins were the first professional baseball team to represent an entire state, not a city. What's the name of their home stadium?

5. In the 1960s, identical twin advertising icons Jayne and Joan Boyd starred in commercials for what brand of Wrigley gum?

6. Speaking of advertising spokestwins, what sort of product was advertised by the slogan, "Which twin has the Toni?"

7. CNN estimated that, on their 17th birthday, these blonde identical twin child actresses, producers, and clothing designers were worth $150 million each?

8. Born Esther Pauline Friedman and Pauline Esther Friedman on July 4, 1918, what identical twins ran competing advice columns for more than 30 years?

9. Furniture appraisers Leigh and Leslie Keno are so alike that they have been known to show up for work wearing identical custom-made outfits selected independently. They are stars on what popular PBS series?

10. What 16th century English playwright had twin children: a boy named Hamnet and a daughter named Judith? Sadly, Hamnet died of unknown causes at the age of 11.

People

COLORFUL CELEBS

Identify these entertainers by the color in their name.

1. What actor, whose alter ego is known as Tenacious D, played a masked Mexican lucha libre wrestler?

2. After dominating the 1970s with soulful hits like "Let's Stay Together" and "Tired of Being Alone," which singer quit the biz to become a preacher?

3. What's the stage name of singer Alecia Beth Moore, whose first album *Can't Take Me Home* went double platinum in the U.S.?

4. Which actor won a Tony and an Oscar for the same role in the Broadway and Hollywood versions of *Cabaret*?

5. Which Asian-American author is best known for her 1989 novel *The Joy Luck Club*?

6. Known as "The Godfather of Soul," and "The Hardest Working Man in Show Business," which legendary performer died on Christmas Day in 2006?

7. This hard-drinking Texan and member of the "Blue Collar Comedy Tour" often goes by the alias "Tater Salad." What's his real name?

8. Which trio of mute performers gets its name from the color of the head, face, and hands of each member?

9. Which type of radiation associated with sunlight is also the stage name of Isabelle Dufresne, a "superstar" in the early films of Andy Warhol's?

10. Star of his own TV variety show from 1951 to 1971 and creator of Klem Kadiddlehopper, which freckle-faced comedian always closed his show with a sincere, "God bless"?

People

POOR LITTLE RICH KIDS

Can you track these high-society tykes?

1. This Russian Emperor was called "Great," though his son Alexei (whom he tortured and killed) likely didn't find Dad so terrific.

2. In 1908, which country took two-year-old Emperor PuYi and isolated him for thirteen years in the "Forbidden City"?

3. What young star of *Stand By Me* and *The Lost Boys* described child-stardom as a "collision course with Hell"?

4. Woolworth heiress Barbara Hutton was called "the million dollar baby," but after mom's suicide, dad's desertion, and the abuse of several husbands, the media called her what?

5. This boy lost his parents to the guillotine and suffered harsh imprisonment that ended his life in 1795 at age 10. Who was he?

6. Who said, "One of the worst things in the world is being the child of a President. It's a terrible life they lead"?

7. In Shakespeare's *Richard III*, King Richard murders what youngsters in the the Tower of London?

8. Prince John, the uncle of Queen Elizabeth II, was isolated from society because of a learning disability. What ailment did he suffer from?

9. What movie about actress Joan Crawford features the famous line, "No more wire hangers ever"?

10. With amphetamines to raise her energy and tranquilizers to help her sleep, MGM made a prescription-drug addict out of this young actress who became a screen legend.

11. What six-year-old became Queen of Sweden in 1632 and had to sleep under a box containing the heart of her dead father?

People

Answers on page 383.

ROBBING THE CRADLE

. . . in movies, books, and real life.

1. On vacation in Jamaica, a 40-year-old San Francisco broker meets a 20-year-old hunk in what 1998 movie based on Terry McMillan's novel?

2. A near-seventy numbers runner falls for an oyster-bar waitress in her thirties in what film starring Burt Lancaster and Susan Sarandon?

3. At 40, Cher had a relationship with a 22-year-old bartender, Rob Camiletti. A previous job led the press to describe him by what nickname?

4. A young woman—played by Audrey Hepburn in 1954 and Julia Ormond in 1995—is romanced by an older man in what film?

5. He was 30 years older than her when they married in 1976. Three years later, she was a hit in the film *10*. Who was the couple?

6. In 2002, at age 68, the actress who played *Dynasty's* Alexis Colby married Percy Gibson, 36, a stage manager. It was her fifth marriage.

7. At age 75, the actor who played fussbudget Felix Unger in *The Odd Couple* married a woman 50 years younger, and they had two children before he died. Who was the actor?

8. He's been married twice but has five daughters and two sons by five different women. He married his current wife, Dina Ruiz, then 27, when he was 62. He has two Best Director Oscars. Who is he?

9. He was 54 and she had just turned 18 when they married in 1943. She was the daughter of a famous playwright, and he was one of the great comic actors of all time. Who are they?

10. Alfred Hitchcock's favorite actor was married five times, the last time to Barbara Harris when he was 77 and she 30. Who was he?

Answers on page 383.

WHO SAID IT?

We'll give you the quote; you name the speaker.

1. "There is no terror in the bang," said this master of suspense, "only in the anticipation of it."

2. "Power is the ultimate aphrodisiac," said what Nobel Peace Prize laureate and Secretary of State under two presidents?

3. "Happiness lies in the joy of achievement and the thrill of creative effort," said this Depression-era president.

4. "Genius is one percent inspiration and 99 percent perspiration." Who said it?

5. "Always do right. This will gratify some people and astonish the rest." What great American author and humorist said it?

6. What Irish playwright said, "A cynic knows the price of everything and the value of nothing"?

7. His remark, "It ain't over till it's over," is engraved on his plaque at Yankee Stadium. What baseball manager said it?

8. "Never in the field of human conflict was so much owed by so many to so few." Who said that, in a tribute to Allied fighter pilots?

9. "A little learning is a dangerous thing." Who wrote that, in his "Essay on Criticism"?

10. "What hath God wrought." Who saideth it?

11. "That government is best which governs least." Who wrote it?

12. "A little rebellion now and then is a good thing . . ." What American Founding Father said that?

People

Answers on page 384.

FIRST IMPRESSIONS

*How many of these famous
firsts do you know?*

1. Mae Jemison: what is she famous for?

2. Who became the world's first female president after her husband died in office?

3. Who was the first emperor of Ancient Rome?

4. Gertrude Ederle was the first woman to do what?

5. In 1994, he became the first black president of South Africa. Who is he?

6. What first is Tenzing Norgay famous for?

7. Who was the first person born in America in 1587 to English parents?

8. What was the first artificial satellite launched into orbit?

9. Who was the first U.S. president to die in office?

10. Who was the first Chief Justice of the United States?

11. What was the first novel whose manuscript was typewritten?

12. Who was the first American woman to win a Pulitzer Prize for fiction?

13. He was the first Catholic and youngest-ever president of the United States. Who was he?

14. The world's first nuclear submarine, the *Nautilus*, was built by which country?

People

Answers on page 384.

SILVER-SPOON SWEETIES

Heirs to wealth and royalty.

1. With this Fox reality show, Paris Hilton tried to expand her celebrity beyond starring in a naughty "home video" and being a socialite. What was the show's name?

2. Heiress to the Hearst newspaper fortune, Patty Hearst was kidnapped in 1974. A short while later, she helped her captors rob a bank. What was the "organization" she was a part of?

3. She's the second wife of Prince Charles and not of noble blood, but who still might be queen of England one day?

4. In the 1920s, Anna Anderson said she was Anastasia, the only survivor of the Russian royal family executed during the Bolshevik Revolution. What's the royal family she claimed to be heir to?

5. Donald Trump is making his daughter work for his billions, costarring on *The Apprentice* and speculating on real estate in the Middle East. What's her name?

6. Holly Branson's father owns an airline, commuter train, record store chain, and the Virgin music label. Who is he?

7. Who is better known for her tabloid-exploited relationships and attempts at a music career than for being princess of Monaco?

8. Prince Rainier III of Monaco made a princess out of what Hollywood legend when he married her in 1956?

9. When he died in 1992 and left his four children in charge of his retail empire, only one, Alice, decided not to take an active role. She makes billions each year anyway. What is the company?

10. Heir to a shipping fortune and stepdaughter to the ex-wife of a president, this young woman died at age 38 after four unsuccessful marriages. Who is she?

Answers on page 384.

People

MR. MOMS

Famous dads.

1. Can you name the star of *Midnight Cowboy* who is also the father of the actress who starred in *Lara Croft: Tomb Raider?*

2. Which star of *Apocalypse Now* is the father of the actor who starred in *Hot Shots!?*

3. This star of *That Championship Season* is also the father of the actress who starred in *Blue Velvet.* Can you identify him?

4. Which star of the 1952 film *Thunderbirds* is the father of the actress who starred in *50 First Dates?*

5. Name this star of 1958's *The Defiant Ones;* he's the father of the actress who starred in *True Lies.*

6. Which star of *Town Without Pity* is the father of the actor who starred in *Wall Street?*

7. This singer who appeared in *Butterfield 8* is the father of the actress who starred in *Star Wars.* Can you name him?

8. Which star of *Doctor Dracula* is the father of the actor who starred in TV's *Kung Fu?*

9. What director of *The Godfather* is the father of the director of *Marie Antoinette?*

10. Which star of TV's *Make Room for Daddy* is the father of the actress who starred in TV's *That Girl?*

11. Which star of the 2006 film *The Pursuit of Happyness* is the father of the other star of *The Pursuit of Happyness?*

People

Answers on page 385.

LADIES FIRST

The president's better half.

1. Who gained early 19th century fame as "hostess with the mostest?"

2. Barbara Bush has been both a First Lady and a First Mom, but who was the first?

3. After being fed up with his affairs, illegitimate children, and the Teapot Dome scandal, what first lady is rumored to have killed her husband on August 2, 1923?

4. Where did Mary Todd Lincoln's eldest son Robert send her after she suffered the deaths of her husband and sons Edward, Willie, and Tad?

5. though she later lived in "Camelot," who was the *first* First Lady to be born in a hospital?

6. Which First Lady married her cousin and was niece to a past president?

7. What did Ladybird Johnson call her plan for planting flowers along the country's highways and byways?

8. Where do many celebrities go when they suffer from alcohol or substance abuse?

9. What was the name of the TV program that gave many Americans their first peek ever inside the White House on February 14, 1962?

10. What was the name of the 1957 war movie that co-starred President Ronald Reagan and his soon-to-be first lady, Nancy Davis?

11. What was the name of the book Barbara Bush wrote with her English springer spaniel, giving a dog's view of the White House?

12. When Nancy Reagan heard about the drug and alcohol abuse among children and teens, what phrase did she coin to help kids resist the urge to abuse?

People

BIG-CITY FOLK

Personalities with the name of a big American city.

1. What is the ring name of the actor and professional wrestler, Steven James Anderson, born December 18, 1964?

2. Who held the starring role in the 2005 film comedy *The Ringer*?

3. From 1979 to 1986, she played the role of Edna Garrett on the TV sitcom *The Facts of Life*. Who is she?

4. Which legendary singer and cousin of Dionne Warwick starred in such hit movies as *Waiting to Exhale*, *The Preacher's Wife*, and *The Bodyguard*?

5. In the animated series *Family Guy*, what is the name of Peter Griffin's drinking buddy who owns a delicatessen?

6. Who was the first female attorney general of the United States?

7. What was the name of the character portrayed by Frank Sinatra in the 1955 film version of *Guys and Dolls*?

8. Who wrote "Annie's Song," arguably the most popular contemporary wedding song ever written, in less than 10 minutes while riding an Aspen ski lift?

9. Which actor, who starred in films such as *My Own Private Idaho* and *Sneakers*, died from a drug overdose outside the Hollywood nightclub, the Viper Room, in 1993?

10. Born Yvonne Vaughn, who hit country/western gold and a scored a Grammy in 1972 with "The Happiest Girl in the Whole USA"?

11. Which Canadian-born comic actor played Jim's Dad in the trilogy: *American Pie*, *American Pie 2*, and *American Wedding*?

People

DYNAMIC DUOS

Name these famous pairs.

1. What Biblical siblings were also famous for being the first victim and the first killer?

2. "The hills are alive with" the sound of these two composers of popular Broadway musicals. Who are they?

3. Who started their singing careers as "Caesar and Cleo," but got their big break (and their own TV show) only after they started using their real names?

4. The two-headed monster in the 1988 movie *Willow* was named "Eborsisk" after what dynamic duo who had been scaring moviemakers since 1975?

5. What comedy team of the 1940s and 1950s is known for a skit that plays continuously at the Baseball Hall of Fame?

6. This song made a splash twice on TV: in 1955, when it was sung by Frank Sinatra in a TV production of *Our Town*, and as the theme song for a 1980s sitcom.

7. The name of this comedy team comes from one partner's first name, and the "silent" partner's last name. Can you magically deduce what they call themselves on stage?

8. A sensational murder trial, fueled by anti-immigrant sentiment, sent these two Italian-American anarchists to the electric chair in 1927, though many people including their trial judge doubted their guilt.

9. The physical characteristics of what famous duo known to preschoolers everywhere are modeled after an orange and a banana?

10. What popular radio show was adapted as a TV show in the 1950s but is *never* shown in reruns because it's considered racially offensive?

KIDNAPPED!

In the United States, the FBI is called in to investigate kidnappings. See if you can solve these questions.

1. His skinflint relatives made billions in oil, but they bickered over the ransom amount, so kidnappers sent them a lock of his hair and his ear. What was his name?

2. What Scottish author wrote a book about the 18th-century Jacobite rebellion? The book's title shares this category's name.

3. What media sensation of the 1920s and 1930s founded the Foursquare Church and faked her own kidnapping in 1926?

4. During her captivity, messages from this wealthy heiress, who was abducted by the Symbionese Liberation Army, were issued under what pseudonym?

5. The Lindbergh baby kidnapping was "The Crime of the Century." What was the name of the German carpenter executed for the crime?

6. When Leopold and Loeb abducted a neighborhood boy in 1924 to see if they could get away with the perfect crime, one of them left behind an item that led police to them. What was this important clue?

7. Who was the five-time prime minister of Italy that was abducted by the Red Brigade in 1978 and killed after 54 days of captivity?

8. His son, Adam, was abducted from a Sears store in Florida, and in the aftermath of the child's death, this man became one of the world's best-known children's advocates and host of the TV show *America's Most Wanted*. Name him.

9. What did the media dub Jennifer Wilbanks, who falsely claimed she had been abducted in 2005? (She actually left town to avoid her upcoming nuptials.)

People

SEEING DOUBLE

These famous people share the same name

1. One is a baseball center fielder; another is an actress (of *Grace Under Fire* fame); and a third is a race car driver.

2. One is the founder and former CEO of Wendy's, and the other a Canadian actor.

3. This name belonged to a man of *Howdy Doody* fame and to a gravelly voiced disc jokey better known as Wolfman Jack.

4. One was a great British statesman, prime minister, and Nobel Prize winner; the other was a best-selling American novelist who wrote *Richard Carvel*, *The Crisis*, and *The Crossing*.

5. One man is a football analyst, a former coach, and an Ace Hardware spokesman. The other is the English director of the film *Shakespeare in Love*.

6. This name is shared by a folk singer (who partnered with Garfunkel) and a U.S. senator from Illinois who was known for wearing bow ties and heavy-rimmed glasses.

7. One is a Charles Dickens character; the other married Miss Vicky on *The Tonight Show* and sang "Tiptoe Through the Tulips."

8. This shared name involves another Dickens character (whose name is also the book's title) and the U.S. magician and illusionist.

9. One is an English philosopher and essayist whose most memorable aphorism is "Knowledge is power." Another is an Irish painter whose works often had grotesque or nightmarish themes.

10. One of these men is a Welsh singer with a powerful voice whose hits include "What's New Pussycat?" and the theme for *Thunderball*. The other is the foundling hero of a comic novel by Henry Fielding.

Answers on page 386.

ZZ TOPICS

All answers contain a word with two Zs.

1. In 1905, New York grocer Gennaro Lombardi was the first to sell this now-ubiquitous dish in the United States.

2. Which actor, who appeared in *A Bronx Tale* and *The Usual Suspects*, received an Academy Award nomination for his work in *Bullets over Broadway*?

3. To the chagrin of Bo and Luke, Sheriff Rosco Purvis Coltrane is the administrator of the law in which fictional "redneck" place?

4. During the 1950s and 1960s, what tablets turned water into a carbonated drink? (Flavors included root beer and blue razz.)

5. From 1952 to 1966, this idealized TV couple lived at 822 Sycamore Road in the fictional town of Hillsdale.

6. What automatically adds $7,700 to the base price of cars like the Ferrari 598 GTB and the Lamborghini Murcielago if they're sold in America?

7. This English stand-up comedian's memorable performances include *Glorious*, *Unrepeatable*, and *Dressed to Kill*.

8. What Carole King hit of 1974 contains the lyric "He can cry like a fallen angel when risin' time is near"?

9. What was the popular nickname for the Ford Model T coupes and sedans produced between 1908 and 1927?

10. In the mid 1930s, this small gadget was invented to remove the bubbles from a glass of sparkling wine; today, it performs a slightly different function.

11. In architecture, what's the name for a partial story that is not on the same level with the story of the main part of the building?

Word Play

Answers on page 386.

BOYS WILL BE BOYS

All answers contain the word "boy."

1. Hector Boiardi directed the catering at President Woodrow Wilson's second wedding, but he is better known by the name found on a line of food products.

2. A portrait of Jonathan Buttall, the son of a wealthy hardware merchant, is probably 18th-century painter Thomas Gainsborough's most famous painting. Name it.

3. The mascot of what American restaurant chain is a plump boy wearing red and white checked pants and holding a hamburger?

4. *Taboo* is a musical that premiered in 2002 and focuses in part on the life of George O'Dowd, better known by what name?

5. What was the code name of the atomic bomb that was dropped on Hiroshima on August 6, 1945?

6. What good-looking criminal of the 1930s earned his nickname from a witness's description of him after his first major robbery?

7. Joe and Frank appeared in print about 80 years ago, but they never grew older than 17 and 18. What is the name of the mystery series about the adventures of these two brothers?

8. What 1978 film based on an Ira Levin thriller starred Gregory Peck as Nazi Dr. Josef Mengele?

9. As of 2007, John Singleton is the youngest person to be nominated for a Best Director Academy Award—for what 1991 film?

10. According to long-held etiquette rules, what four-word phrase describes the optimal seating at a dinner party?

11. This sandwich, a variation of the submarine or hero, is popular in New Orleans.

Answers on page 386.

INITIAL IDEAS

G-strings, T-birds, and other stuff that starts with a single letter.

1. "B-girl" used to refer to a lady of easy virtue who hung out in bars or appeared in B-movies. These days, the term refers to a girl who's skilled at what kind of dancing?

2. "This Is Why I'm Hot" is the entrance music for superstar baseball player A-Rod, which is short for what?

3. FBI agents are also known as "G-men." What does the "G" stand for?

4. What comedienne and former cast member of *Suddenly Susan* is the star of the reality show subtitled *My Life on the D-List*?

5. If you are a G.I. and you've got some K-rations, what are you expected to do with them?

6. What color is the arcade game character Q*bert?

7. Its initial letter is widely believed to come from the word "violence," but its inventor says it was intended to stand for "viewer control." What is it?

8. *The Lone Gunmen* sounds like a Western but it was a spin-off of a popular sci-fi TV series of the 1990s and early 2000s. Name it.

9. What mechanical component was discovered to be the cause of the Space shuttle *Challenger* disaster in 1986?

10. Once worn only as underwear, its name most likely comes from the shape it makes when it's laid flat. What is it?

11. In 2004, a student magazine about sex called *H-Bomb* debuted amid controversy at what Ivy League university?

Word Play

LET'S DO "UNCH"

Let your brain feast on these questions.

1. If it's not quite breakfast and not quite lunch, it must be . . . what?

2. What 1969 Sam Peckinpah film starred Ernest Borgnine, William Holden, Ben Johnson, and Warren Oates as aging outlaws looking for one last score?

3. What Norwegian artist is best known for *The Scream*?

4. What fruit drink has a mascot named Sam?

5. What popular candy bar consists of milk chocolate over crisped rice?

6. What 1970s sitcom with Florence Henderson was about the misadventures of a large family that merged when two widowed people married?

7. What's a nine-letter word for a club used primarily by policemen?

8. What's a ten-letter word for a hired hand who tends cattle?

9. What American diplomat was the first African American to receive the Nobel Peace Prize and was undersecretary-general of the United Nations?

10. What 18th-century German baron joined the Russian military and later told outrageous tall tales about his adventures, such as riding cannonballs and traveling to the moon?

11. What nautical-themed breakfast cereal from Quaker Oats is popular with kids?

12. What was the name of Merv Griffin's first TV show?

Word Play

Answers on page 387.

CAN I GET BACK TO U?

How much do you know about these
words and phrases that end in U?

1. What is the capital and largest city of Nepal?

2. What two-word phrase can mean a blue ribbon, a distinguished chef, or a group of cooking schools teaching French cuisine?

3. What Hawaiian city's name means "sheltered bay"?

4. The TV series *Two and a Half Men*, *Gidget*, and *The Rockford Files* are, or were, all set in this California beachfront town. What is it?

5. What's the largest bird native to Australia and, after the ostrich, the second tallest bird in the world?

6. What comedic greeting was made popular by Robin Williams as Mork in *Mork & Mindy*?

7. This five-letter word for a swampy, sluggish stream, bigger than a creek but smaller than a river, is used especially in Louisiana.

8. This Italian dessert was the subject of a classic scene between Tom Hanks and Rob Reiner in *Sleepless in Seattle*. What were they talking about?

9. Japanese poetry that consists of three lines of 17 syllables in a 5-7-5 pattern is called what?

10. It's a famous pre-Columbian ruin in Peru, sometimes called "the Lost City of the Incas." What is it?

11. The killer whales at SeaWorld marine parks have individual names but also share a common stage name. What is it?

Word Play

Answers on page 387.

"X" MARKS THE SPOT

*Can you identify these objects
that all end in the letter X?*

1. When a story builds to a suspenseful point and then has a trivial or disappointing finale, it's said to have this kind of ending.

2. Who was Paul Bunyan's bovine companion?

3. Who was the star of TV's *Sanford and Son*?

4. In Joel Chandler Harris's *Uncle Remus* stories, the three main characters are Brer Rabbit, Brer Bear, and . . . who?

5. What's a ten-letter word for somebody who talks a lot, especially about unimportant things?

6. What is the largest of the U.S. Virgin Islands?

7. It's made by flying insects, used to make candles, and is part of the saying "Mind your own . . ." what?

8. What ten-letter word means unconventional, independent, or breaking with tradition?

9. What's the medical term for the end of the spinal column, commonly called the tailbone?

10. In Greek mythology, they are the twin sons of Leda, and the twins in the Gemini constellation. Who are they?

11. Before this became the leader of the *Lost* survivors, he played big brother to the orphans on *Party of Five*.

12. This fast-food chain originally had a clownlike character as its logo but blew it up in a commercial as part of a campaign to change its image.

Answers on page 387.

LEND ME YOUR "EAR"S

This quiz is quite an earful!

1. She was the first woman to fly solo across the Atlantic, but then disappeared somewhere in the Pacific in 1937. Who was she?

2. If you have unpaid debts or have fallen behind in your rent, you're said to be what?

3. Ramona Quimby lives on Klickitat Street in novels by what author?

4. He could be the title of a Kurt Vonnegut novel, or a monstrous fairy-tale villain who marries seven women and kills the first six for their disobedience. Who are we talking about?

5. Joe Rogan was the host of this NBC show in which contestants did extreme stunts and were also asked to eat something disgusting or swim through something revolting.

6. Which Shakespearean tragic hero was betrayed and mistreated by two of his scheming daughters?

7. Oops, she's performing again! What pop princess has sold more than 75 million albums?

8. If a man is clean-shaven, you could say he's what?

9. Henry Ford's hometown and the headquarters of the Ford Motor Company is in what city?

10. What critter is believed by some to have started the Great Chicago Fire?

11. The interval from January 1 to December 31 is known as a what?

12. "Honey," "Sweetie-pie," and "Babycakes" are possible examples of what ironically titled 1983 film?

Word Play

Answers on page 388.

FROM C
TO SHINING C

Do you "C" what we mean?

1. What's the word for a luxury car, a mountain in Maine, and the French founder of Detroit, Michigan?

2. What fine white linen or cotton cloth is used for linings, corset bodices, and as fabric for lace and needlework?

3. What's the name of the geologic era we are living in now?

4. What's the word for a group of languages, a kind of music, a type of knot, or a member of a Boston sports team?

5. What's a four-letter word for "stylish"?

6. What word means fanatically patriotic or convinced of the superiority of one's own gender?

7. What play by Edmond Rostand is about the hero's love for the beautiful Roxane?

8. Of what landlocked country is Prague the capital and largest city?

9. What's the name of an elegant, high-quality grape brandy produced in a region of western France?

10. Zydeco is a close relative of what emblematic musical genre of Louisiana?

11. What's the word for a dead-end street that's often circular at the end?

12. What word means easily angered or hot-tempered?

Answers on page 388.

Word Play

THE FIRST AND "L"AST

All the answers begin and end with the letter L.

1. This 16th James Bond film was the last to star Timothy Dalton as Bond. What's the film?

2. What two words might you hear before a bar closes for the night?

3. Speaking of bars, what citric garnish might you find next to the olives and toothpicks?

4. "Summer in the City" was a #1 hit by what pop-rock band of the 1960s (after "The")?

5. What was the key phrase in Olivia Newton-John's most famous tune that spent ten weeks at #1 in 1981–82?

6. What monument appears on the reverse of the U.S. penny and the back of the U.S. five-dollar bill?

7. Roberto Benigni won a Best Actor Oscar for what 1997 Italian-language film?

8. The Latin phrase *omnia vincit amor* appears in poems by Virgil. What's the English translation?

9. What 13-letter word means "lacking life, spirit, or zest; languid"?

10. What English city is associated with the origin of the Beatles?

11. What husky-voiced actress in *How to Marry a Millionaire* was born Betty Joan Perske?

12. What was the pen name of the author of the poem "Jabberwocky"?

Word Play

Answers on page 388.

GONE TO "POT"

You'll find a "pot" in all of the answers.

1. What popular face-changing toy debuted in 1952 and is based around a plastic tuber?

2. This optimum, desirable point on a tennis racket, bat, or golf club is just so . . . sugary. What's it called?

3. With the publication of the 1965 book *In Cold Blood*, this Southern author invented a new literary genre: the nonfiction novel. What was his name?

4. This nine-letter word describes an assortment of things (like this quiz) . . . or a mixture of dried flower petals, herbs, and spices.

5. In the old days, this 10-letter word described a pharmacist or chemist.

6. This English author of *The Tale of Jemima Puddle-Duck* grew up a lonely child, whose best friends were her pet animals: newts, frogs, a bat, dogs, and a pair of rabbits. What's her name?

7. They look a little like pigs, but these plant-eating African mammals are more closely related to whales and porpoises. Their name means "river horse." What are they?

8. What nine-letter word means "powerful one"? This person may be a monarch, dictator, autocrat, or tyrant.

9. The region between the Tigris and Euphrates rivers is now part of Iraq, but it used to be called what?

10. The side of a right triangle opposite the right angle is called what?

11. What's the name of a fake settlement that's erected to deceive someone?

Word Play

PEEKABOO!
I-C-U!

All answers contain "icu."
How many can you identify?

1. What's the word for a set of courses or course of study at an educational institution?

2. What's something you might get in a beauty salon?

3. What word describes a flourish, coil, squiggle, or fancifully curved figure?

4. What Polish astronomer's heliocentric theory (that planets orbit the sun) marked the beginning of the scientific revolution?

5. What's a word for a person with discriminating tastes in food and wine?

6. What's a fancy word for fighting or boxing?

7. What's a word for details, specific items, or alleged factual statements in a legal document?

8. This word means to make fun of, belittle, mock, or humiliate.

9. What word means a small portion, a bit, or token amount?

10. If something is marked by extreme attention to detail, it is what?

11. What's a 12-letter word for the science and art of cultivating plants?

12. What's the word for the genus that includes fig trees?

Word Play

Answers on page 389.

"LAND" HO!

All answers contain "land."

1. What is the state slogan of Illinois, seen on its license plates?

2. What 22nd and 24th president of the United States was once a county sheriff?

3. What camera inventor held 535 patents, second only to Thomas Edison's 1,097?

4. This eight-letter word describes the Taj Mahal, Big Ben, and the Washington Monument.

5. Where would you go to see Toontown, Critter Country, and Main Street USA?

6. What's another word for boonies, backwoods, or "out yonder"?

7. What London-born actress was married first to David McCallum and then to Charles Bronson?

8. What's the name of four theme parks that a toy company built in Denmark, Germany, England, and the United States?

9. What's the nine-letter adjective for art that depicts scenery, oceans, sky, etc.?

10. What's the common name of an antelope found in eastern and southern Africa?

11. What T. S. Eliot poem begins, "April is the cruellest month"?

12. What Hollywood singing star was born Frances Ethel Gumm?

M'M! M'M! GOOD!

*Test your familiarity with words and phrases
that begin and end with the letter M.*

1. Who was the Hawaii-based private investigator played by Tom Selleck from 1980 to 1988?

2. What's the name of *Li'l Abner*'s Dogpatch preacher who specialized in $2 weddings?

3. What's a six-letter word for chaos or severe disruption?

4. It's the third most plentiful element in seawater and has atomic number 12. What is it?

5. It's from the Greek phrase for "big world" and means the whole of a complex structure. What's the word?

6. She scored more goals in international soccer than any other player, male or female. Although she has a hyphenated name now, how do most people know her?

7. When you substitute a wrong word for the right one, as when Mike Tyson said he might just "fade into Bolivian" (instead of oblivion), what's that called?

8. In classic lingerie ads, a woman might say, "I dreamed I stopped traffic in" what kind of bra?

9. At what "happiest place on earth" would you find Space Mountain and Cinderella's Castle?

10. What's the 16-letter word for the political doctrine that says any means, however unscrupulous, may be used to achieve a ruler's desired end?

11. This white clay material is often used for pipe bowls.

Word Play

Answers on page 389.

"SIT"TING PRETTY

You'll find "sit" sitting somewhere in all of these answers.

1. What TV genre specializes in humorous half-hour series that feature recurring characters in everyday situations?

2. What's a word for an interesting or unusual phenomenon or person, or a thing that might be worth collecting?

3. What's the term for a really easy target or defenseless victim?

4. What phrase means that something or someone is traveling or being transported from one place to another?

5. What do you call a person who waffles or won't take a position on conflicting issues?

6. What's a ten-letter word for a leaning, inclination, or preference?

7. What Alaskan city is the largest city in the United States in terms of area, not population?

8. What English dame's best-known poem is "Still Falls the Rain," about the London blitz?

9. What's the name of the semisoft light yellow cheese from a Russian town now called Sovetsk?

10. What word means to pause, hold back, or waver?

11. What kind of phrase might begin with words such as under, before, across, above, or down?

12. What's a four-letter word for a type of therapeutic bath?

Word Play

WORDS THAT DON'T MEAN WHAT THEY SAY

Have these ever confused you?
(You're not the only one.)

1. The groundhog isn't a hog! What is it?

2. Catgut does not come from cats. It's from these animals.

3. Russia's October Revolution is celebrated in what month?

4. The Hundred Years' War lasted how long?

5. Panama hats originated where?

6. The koala bear isn't a bear. What kind of animal is it?

7. What part of a sperm whale does "sperm oil" come from?

8. The "white rhino" and the "black rhino" are actually what color?

9. Whalebone is not bone. It's this substance.

10. Cuttlefish are related to what marine creatures?

11. The Canary Islands were not named for canaries, but for these animals.

12. The "black box" in an airplane is what color?

DOUBLE DOT

*Don't connect the dots, but find the word with
consecutive dotted letters, like* jingle.

1. British explorer Captain James Cook charted much of the Pacific Ocean and was the first explorer to map Australia's coastline and to circumnavigate New Zealand. What Pacific island was he killed on in 1779?

2. What is a fine-toothed tool used for cutting curves, or a type of puzzle with lots of curved pieces?

3. These brown, medium-sized mushrooms native to Japan could only be grown locally until 1982, when worldwide commercial cultivation became possible. Grown on logs and traditionally added to miso soup, what is this fungus?

4. Both Sonny Bono and Michael Kennedy, one of Robert F. Kennedy's sons, were killed while participating in what sport?

5. Originally a term for a cut of grilled beef served on a tortilla, it has evolved to include a style of cooking. What is this Tex-Mex staple of marinated meats and vegetables?

6. Which volcano—that last erupted in 1708—is Japan's highest mountain peak?

7. Name the large (usually one-gallon), narrow-necked wine bottle often encased in wickerwork and popularly known in France as *dame-jeanne*, or "Lady Jane."

8. These dogs of African origin are known for being barkless. What is the breed?

9. What is an 11-letter synonym for a doohickey, whatchamacallit, or gizmo?

Word Play

TO COIN A PHRASE

Who said it first?

1. The term "cold war" may have been used first in 1945 by the author of *Animal Farm*. What's his name?

2. The Nobel physicist John Wheeler coined the two-word term to describe a region in space that nothing can escape from, not even light. What's the term?

3. This author first used the word "chortled" in his nonsense poem "Jabberwocky"?

4. This humorist who wrote *The Purple Cow* also invented the word "blurb," which he defined as "a flamboyant advertisement; an inspired testimonial," and as "self-praise: to make a noise like a publisher."

5. The poet who introduced the word "aesthetic" into the English language and coined the word "selfless" was also the person who wrote "The Rime of the Ancient Mariner." Who was he?

6. F. Scott Fitzgerald coined this phrase for the flamboyant, anything-goes era of the 1920s, known for its flapper culture and music. What was the phrase?

7. The term "robot" was first used by Karel Capek in what 1920 play?

8. In a 1798 paper, Edward Jenner pioneered and coined the term for this revolutionary medical procedure.

9. A *New York Times* sportswriter used this bridge term to refer to Don Budge's winning of four prestigious tennis tournaments— Wimbledon, the French Open, the U.S. Open, and the Australian Open. What was the phrase?

10. What U.S. president coined the term "lunatic fringe" to describe his extremist critics?

Word Play

Answers on page 390.

R & R

Both words of all answers start with the letter "R."

1. They include the Colosseum, the Forum, and Circus Maximus. In two words, what are they?

2. What "emotion" of drivers can get people killed?

3. What's the term for an exhausting routine or business rut that leaves no time for relaxation?

4. What was the name bestowed by newspapers on the 1st U.S. Volunteer Cavalry Regiment during the Spanish-American War?

5. What's the two-word term for the most potentially lethal game of "chicken"?

6. What actor has played the roles of Jay Gatsby, Waldo Pepper, Johnny Hooker, Roy Hobbs, Henry Brubaker, and Halsy Knox?

7. The very first cartoon characters from the Hanna-Barbera studio were a big, dumb dog and a small, smart cat. What were their names?

8. What's the term for a group tournament in which each player plays every other player an equal number of times?

9. As its name—"Hood to Coast"—implies, this 197-mile event covers a course from Mount Hood to the Oregon coast. What kind of event is it?

10. This sitcom star's movie roles have included Manny the Mammoth in *Ice Age* and Handy Harrison in *Welcome to Mooseport*. Who is he?

11. It's an acclaimed and "colorful" PBS series that leads kids to books. What is it?

Answers on page 390.

ROYAL FLUSH

You've been dealt a good hand. All the answers
contain a king, a queen, or a jack.

1. What fast-food franchise is known for soft-serve chocolate-dipped ice cream cones?

2. This term describes someone who's knowledgeable in a lot of different areas.

3. What was the only ABBA song to make it to the top of the Billboard Top 40 chart?

4. Speaking of chart toppers, which of Roger Miller's hits climbed the highest (#4) on the Billboard Top 40 chart?

5. What term goes back to a huge sum of money demanded by kidnappers to let someone go free, but now just means a whole lot of money?

6. Which NBC "giveaway show" of the 1950s and 1960s hosted by Jack Bailey was the forerunner of the contemporary reality show?

7. What boat, featured in the title of an Oscar-winning film, is permanently moored in Key Largo, where it's listed in the National Register of Historic Places?

8. What is the official state fish of Alaska?

9. What breed of dog is Eddie, Martin Crane's pet on the sitcom *Frasier*?

10. What was the full name of the character played by John Ritter on the TV sitcom *Three's Company*?

11. He was only an 18-inch puppet, but he made a big impression. Willis O'Brien created him and first displayed him in New York City on March 3, 1933. Who was he?

Word Play

Answers on page 391.

SON OF ALPHABET SOUP

URL, SRO, RSVP—what do all those initials mean?

1. Not to be confused with "rebar" (the steel rods used to reinforce concrete), what does FUBAR stand for?

2. A person protesting a development in his or her neighborhood carries a sign that says NIMBY. What does that mean?

3. We know what a wasp is, but what's a WASP?

4. In response to a funny e-mail, a person answers ROFLMAO. What's that mean?

5. In a moment of confusion, you order a QPC at KFC. What have you done?

6. Millions of people use URLs every day, but what exactly is it?

7. You see a sign in a Broadway box-office window for a show you want to attend that says SRO. Why are you disappointed?

8. A wedding invitation asks you to RSVP. Your friend tells you it is French for what you are supposed to do. What would that be?

9. Your neighbor looks askance at your SUV; he has an HEV. What's that?

10. What does the second "A" in NASA stand for?

11. Some people wince at the expression "ATM machine." Why?

12. You probably know what a bra is, but what's a BRI?

Answers on page 391.

TAKE A LETTER

*Sure, they're everyday acronyms—
but do you know what they mean?*

1. What does the "E" stand for in the name of the insurance company—GEICO?

2. What does the "S" stand for in the major sports association NASCAR?

3. In the military term for a blunder—SNAFU—what does the "N" stand for?

4. The "I" in the mnemonic for the rainbow spectrum—ROY G. BIV—represents what color?

5. In Jacques-Yves Cousteau's invention, SCUBA, what does the "B" stand for?

6. The "P" in the sports-intensive cable channel ESPN represents what?

7. "T" equals what in SWAT?

8. What does the "E" stand for in the name of the international organization—OPEC?

9. What does the middle "M" in the American corporation 3M stand for?

10. "H" means what in the recording video tape term VHS?

11. What does the "E" stand for in LASER?

12. "C" stands for what in the auto engine classification—DOHC?

Word Play

Answers on page 391.

"EX" MARKS THE SPOT

*All answers contain "ex"—some at the beginning,
some at the end, and a few in the middle.*

1. What do you call someone with an outgoing personality?

2. What's a 12-letter word for a lavish or spectacular entertainment?

3. There are two possible words for a theater with multiple screens. Can you name one? Both?

4. What company makes Cross Your Heart bras?

5. What's the name of the mythical sword of King Arthur?

6. This author of *Roots* ghostwrote *The Autobiography of Malcolm X*. What is his name?

7. Corning Glass Works introduced heat-resistant glass in 1915. What's the brand name they gave it?

8. What play by Sophocles did Aristotle consider the greatest tragedy ever written? (Hint: It is about a mother and son.)

9. What's a ten-letter synonym for rigid or unyielding?

10. What passenger train famed for luxury and intrigue now runs from Strasbourg to Vienna?

11. What book of the Old Testament includes the story of the parting of the Red Sea for the Israelites fleeing from the pursuing Egyptian army?

12. *The Scream* by Edvard Munch is considered one of the best examples of what genre of painting that depicts inner emotions?

IT'S HIGH TIME

If you sing out the answers in a "high" note, you will ace this quiz.

1. After he barely survives a lynching, Jed Cooper (Clint Eastwood) returns as a lawman determined to track down the vigilantes. What's the movie?

2. *Haute couture* means what in everyday English?

3. What North Carolina city is often called the "Furniture Capital of the World"?

4. An apartment building or condominium more than six stories in height could be called a what?

5. Someone who eats or lives this way is probably affluent and used to luxuries. What's the four-word expression?

6. Casinos love to see these "whales" come in. What's another phrase for them?

7. What's the word for a tall chest of drawers divided into two sections?

8. John Cusack, his sister Joan, and Jack Black were in the cast of what 2000 movie?

9. What late-afternoon or early evening meal is a British tradition that might include crumpets and scones, but also a meat or fish dish?

10. If you're in a helpless, difficult, or abandoned position, you've been left . . . what?

11. Javier Sotomayor is currently both the indoor and outdoor world record holder in what event with jumps of 8 feet (1989) and 8½ feet (1993), respectively?

Word Play

Answers on page 392.

DO I HAVE TO S-P-E-L-L IT OUT?

Can you solve these language "equations"?
(Example: "26 = L. of the A."
would mean 26 = Letters of the Alphabet.)

1. What is "4 = Q. in a G." short for?

2. Does "101 = D." bring a Disney movie to mind?

3. Forget "The OC"! What does "13 = O.C." stand for?

4. Good advice: "1 = D. at a T." What's it mean?

5. It helps to have "4 W. on a C." What's the translation?

6. Lawrence Sanders wrote mysteries about several of the "7 D. S." What are they?

7. If you saw *A Chorus Line*, you might have experienced "1 S. S." What's that?

8. "8 = S. on a S. S." What does that mean?

9. "Holey" types might know what "18 = H. on a G. C." means. What's your take?

10. Into English history? What's "6 = W. of H. the E" mean?

11. Can you translate (or reincarnate) "9 = L. of a C."?

12. Don't go postal on us, but what is "5 = D. in a Z. C."?

MY FAVORITE MARTIN

The answer to each question contains a "martin."

1. Why did George Burns say he would never take up jogging?

2. What Caribbean island is the home of the active volcano Mount Pelée?

3. What traditional Christian celebration begins on the eleventh hour of the eleventh day of the eleventh month?

4. What comedian authored *Shop Girl*?

5. This Czechoslovakian won the Wimbledon women's singles a record nine times. What is her name?

6. What president of the United States was nicknamed "Old Kinder-hook," or "OK"?

7. What was President Gerald Ford referring to when he said, "Where else can you get an earful, a bellyful, and a snootful at the same time?"

8. Who was the youngest man to receive the Nobel Peace prize?

9. What was 007's vehicle of choice in the 1964 film *Goldfinger*?

10. Musicians Johnny Cash, Eric Clapton, Paul Simon, Arlo Guthrie, and Neil Young have all been honored by a signature edition from this company. What is it?

11. What member of the "Rat Pack" started his public career as a prizefighter?

12. Who persisted for 37 years, 5 nominations, and more than 20 films before finally bringing home an Oscar for Best Director in 2007?

Word Play

Answers on page 392.

TAKE MY LEAVE

Each answer has the words "leaf" or "leave."

1. What objects, when properly swirled, are said to predict the future?

2. What product would you need if you were literally "gilding the lily"?

3. What collection of poems got Walt Whitman fired from his job at the Department of the Interior in 1865 for writing "dirty books"?

4. This federal law allows a person to take time off to care for a sick parent or a newborn.

5. What rhymed warning to hikers might prevent rash action?

6. This classic TV show debuted on October 4, 1957—the same day the Soviet Union launched *Sputnik 1*.

7. What professional sports team, one of the "Original Six" in its league, has sold out every game since 1946?

8. What begins accumulating at the start of a voyage, at the rate of 1 day for every 15 days served?

9. What 1945 hit melodrama starred Gene Tierney as an insanely jealous wife?

10. This "first couple" is said to have come up with the first fashion innovation. What did they wear?

11. In 2005, Joaquin Phoenix scored a hit with *Walk the Line*, but back in 1989, he was just a troubled kid in *Parenthood*. By what name was he listed in *Parenthood*'s credits?

BELOW SEE LEVEL

These questions are easy to see,
but their subjects aren't.

1. In the film *Harvey*, the character played by Jimmy Stewart befriends a large, invisible what?

2. Who wrote the novel that the 1933 Universal horror film *The Invisible Man* was based on?

3. What kind of garment does Harry Potter use to render himself invisible?

4. The superhero called Invisible Woman was the only female founding member of what team?

5. Who is the author of *Invisible Man*, a novel about an African American who considers himself socially invisible?

6. What 1977 Disney film features a live-action cast and an animated green dragon who can make himself invisible?

7. "Invisible Touch" was a hit song from in 1986 album by what band?

8. What onetime *Saturday Night Live* star portrayed the title character in the 1992 film *Memoirs of an Invisible Man*?

9. Especially known for *I Am the Cheese*, what author also wrote *Fade*, a book about a boy who can turn invisible?

10. She can fly all by herself now, but in comic books and on TV, what superhero flew on the Invisible Plane?

11. What theory, first postulated by Adam Smith, states that people pursuing private interests also benefit the economy as a whole?

Answers on page 393.

BIG RED

All answers contain the word "red."

1. This redheaded actor won an Academy Award for best supporting actor for his role as airman Joe Kelly in *Sayonara* and also had a memorable supporting role in *Hatari!*

2. What is the model of the Daisy BB gun model introduced in 1940 that became so popular its sales increased to over one million a year by 1949?

3. Which club founded by Sue Ellen Cooper for ladies over 50 requires members to wear formal purple outfits to club functions?

4. This dessert gets it signature red color from two ounces of food coloring.

5. This folk song contains the lyrics "Come and sit by my side if you love me. Do not hasten to bid me adieu."

6. Which well-known personality created the characters Sheriff Deadeye, Willie Lump Lump, and Gertrude & Heathcliffe?

7. Can you come up with a three-word phrase used to describe a particularly significant, usually very positive date?

8. What is the name of the 197,000-acre National Conservation Area located just 17 miles west of the Las Vegas Strip?

9. Which song by the pop group the Cyrkle climbed to the top of the *Billboard* charts in the summer of 1966?

10. What is the two-word designation for a star such as Proxima Centauri, that's cool, faint, and about one-tenth the size of the sun?

11. What does an official give a soccer player to remove him from a game?

Answers on page 393.

WHAT'S THE WORD FOR THAT?

See what kind of wordsmith you are.

1. How is a cranny different from a nook?

2. What is the warp and the weft in weaving?

3. What is the literary term when opposite words are combined like "jumbo shrimp"?

4. Explain the difference between an oenophile and a wino.

5. Explain the difference between a bibliophile and a biblopole.

6. Breakfast plus lunch creates what blended word? Motor plus hotel?

7. An ananym is a name formed by reversing letters of another name. Harpo is the ananym for this successful talk-show host's production company.

8. What do you call words that share the same spelling or pronunciation but have different meanings? Like "to" and "two"?

9. What do you call words that have opposite meanings, like love and hate or hot and cold?

10. A famous example of these phrases that read the same backward or forward is "A man, a plan, a canal—Panama." What is the term?

11. This type of wordplay requires that you rearrange one word or phrase to create another. For example, "astronomer" becomes "moon starer."

12. What's a phrase that compares two things using "like" or "as"?

Word Play

Answers on page 393.

WHAT'S IN A (NICK)NAME?

These items are better known as . . .

1. The U.S. State Department goes by what nickname?

2. The Mongol ruler Temujin is better known by what nickname?

3. The former Brazilian soccer player Edson Arantes do Nascimento is known to one and all as . . . what?

4. The American liberal political pundit and spinmeister James Carville is known by what nickname?

5. What nickname was bestowed on Napoleon I of France?

6. Baseball player George Herman "Babe" Ruth was often called what?

7. The American actress and pin-up girl Ann Sheridan was known by what bodacious nickname?

8. What smooth nickname was given to the pop-jazz singer Mel Tormé?

9. The acerbic critic John Simon is often called what?

10. What was the nickname for American singer Helen Kane, whose signature song was "I Wanna Be Loved by You"?

11. U.S. pool player Rudolph Wanderone Jr. was known by what nickname?

12. What folksy nickname was given to country singer Eddy Arnold?

Answers on page 393.

THERE'S A WORD FOR IT

Nicknames—of things, not people.

1. What is an "Arkansas toothpick"?

2. If someone offers you a "Colorado Kool-aid," what are you getting?

3. How wet do you get in an "Oklahoma rain"?

4. Care for a cup of "Texas tea"?

5. Well, how about a dish of "West Virginia coleslaw"?

6. Want some "Georgia ice cream" for breakfast?

7. If you saw someone in a "Full Cleveland," what would it look like?

8. In military slang, what does "fruit salad" mean?

9. What's a "Texas turkey"?

10. Would you want to eat a "Mississippi mud pie"?

11. Would you want a "short dog" as a pet?

12. Your uncle has decided to send you to "Camp Cupcake." Is that a good thing?

13. If you take in a show on the "Great White Way," where are you?

14. Grab your peanuts and Cracker Jacks and watch the "Bronx Bombers." Who are they?

15. Uncle John is on his way to "Beantown." Where is he going?

Word Play

YOU DON'T KNOW "JACK"

Words that either begin or end with "jack."

1. Which Johnny Knoxville–inspired MTV series was reformatted into a theatrical release in 2002 and again in 2006?

2. Sailor Jack and his dog Bingo are displayed on which classic snack food's package?

3. Which beverage is a type of brandy made by distilling hard cider?

4. If someone is "card counting" in Las Vegas, what game is he most likely playing?

5. The legendary jackelope is the cross between an antelope and what other beast?

6. What is the name for a professional who erects ladders or scaffolding high atop industrial chimneys, cooling towers, or clock towers?

7. Which word can mean the accidental folding of a big rig, a martial arts kick, or a basic dive off a diving board?

8. What is the name for a pneumatic drill that works as a power chisel to break up rock or pavement?

9. Sailing vessels like these still work the oyster beds of the Chesapeake Bay just as they did in the 1800s. What are they?

10. What is the name for a flat, fried cake of thin batter that ideally is crispy on the outside and chewy on the inside?

11. What is the name of the highest possible payout from a single slot machine?

Answers on page 394.

DEM BONES

*We worked our fingers to the bone
to bring you this quiz.*

1. In the song "Dry Bones," what's "connected to the head bone"?

2. The logo for the 1990 hardcover novel and 1993 film *Jurassic Park* features the skeleton of what kind of dinosaur?

3. In a 1957 song, who was "skinny as a stick of macaroni"?

4. What is two-word name for the iconic black-and-white skull-and-crossbones pirate flag?

5. On the TV show *Bones*, the investigator works for the fictitious Jeffersonian Institute, modeled after what real-life institute?

6. What is the common name for the bone that is officially known as the "patella"?

7. At what Ivy League university does the secret society Skull and Bones operate?

8. What best-selling 2002 novel by Alice Sebold is narrated by a girl in heaven?

9. Dominoes are also known as "bones." What do serious domino players call the pile of dominoes a player draws from?

10. In a signature sequence, the 1968 film *2001: A Space Odyssey* shows an apelike human toss a bone into the air, then cuts to a similarly shaped image of a what?

11. What was the full name of the *Star Trek* doctor nicknamed "Bones"?

12. What word from the Latin root for "bones" means a room or container that holds the bones of the dead?

One of a Kind

NEVER TICKLE A SLEEPING DRAGON

And other bits of wisdom
from the world of magic.

1. The first name of Harry Potter's archenemy at school is Latin for "dragon." Who is he?

2. The PBS animated series *Dragon Tales* regularly involves two languages: English and what?

3. The Crusaders brought back the story of a saint and the dragon he slew to save a princess in Libya. Name him.

4. In the Peter, Paul, and Mary hit "Puff, the Magic Dragon," what is the name of Puff's "little" friend?

5. In the Chinese calendar, a year of the Dragon began in 2000. In what year will the next one begin?

6. *Mazes and Monsters*, a 1982 made-for-TV-movie starring Tom Hanks, depicted a role-playing game modeled after what?

7. Called "one of the last great dragons of Middle-earth," Smaug was the antagonist in what 20th-century novel?

8. Found mainly far, far away in Indonesia (thank goodness!), what is the world's largest lizard species?

9. What 8th-century epic poem is named for a hero who dies as the result of a battle with a dragon?

10. First introduced as a character in the comic strip *Terry and the Pirates*, her name has come to refer to any powerful, intimidating woman. What would you call her?

B & W

*Do you see everything in black and
white? You will on this page.*

1. Black or white: Which is closest to the color of a zebra's skin?

2. Which black-and-white treat became the best-selling cookie of the
20th century?

3. At cocktail time, what ingredient makes all the difference between
a Black Russian and a White Russian?

4. What comic ruled Tuesday nights on the black-and-white boob
tube and earned the nickname "Mr. Television"?

5. Which contemporary Chinese leader philosophized: "No matter
if it is a white cat or a black cat; if it can catch mice, it is a good
cat"?

6. You probably see one every day: What kind of vehicle is also
known as a "black and white"?

7. What Paul McCartney/Stevie Wonder collaboration uses black-
and-white piano keys as a metaphor for racial harmony?

8. In 1878, Eadward Muybridge published a series of black-and-white
photos of a galloping horse to prove that it lifts how many hooves
off the ground at once?

9. What's black and white—and read all over the Big Apple—but
nicknamed "the Gray Lady"?

10. Which Dutch graphic artist created mathematically intricate litho-
graphs of black-and-white interlocking figures?

11. A black Scottish terrier and a white Westie terrier were the
canine models in ads for what Scotch whiskey?

One of a Kind

TO SUM THINGS UP . . .

All of the clues in each question add up to a single answer.

1. This mode of transportation, often found in shopping malls, is made up of treadboards, a comb, a skirt, a deckboard, and riding instructions.

2. What common gift for Father's Day includes a front apron, rear apron, slip-stitched seam, and shell?

3. Eureka! What illuminating household object has a support wire, mica disc, exhaust tube, ring contact, stem press, and base?

4. This small, everyday item is made up of a bow, shoulder, serrations, warding, and blade. (The kids in the Harry Potter series don't need one; they just command, "Alohomora!")

5. What digger has a blade, frog, socket, and handle?

6. Scotsmen know that this musical instrument contains mounts, tenor drones, a bass drone, a blowpipe, a chanter, and a tassel.

7. What winter item—made up of a crossbar, master cord, toe lacing, frame, toe hole, heel lacing, frame, and tail—will keep you from sinking?

8. You can overcome these in life or just know that they're made of a gate upright, gatebar, gate tube, base upright, base weight, and foot.

9. This common city structure consists of a bonnet, main cap, cap chain, steamer connection cap, barrel, and operating nut. (But likely, your dog doesn't care.)

10. Organized office workers keep tight hold of this item, made up of a base, rail, follow block, rear foot, hinge pin, metal cap, anvil, front foot, follow spring, and case assembly.

Answers on page 395.

GAME, SET, MATCH

All answers contain one or more of the three title words above.

1. What word has the highest number of definitions in the *Oxford English Dictionary* (464 definitions) and many other dictionaries?

2. What popular French magazine has long been known for its frequent use of paparazzi photos?

3. In mathematics, a collection of things is called a what?

4. What's a word for a certain kind of military training exercise or simulation?

5. What's a word for venison, wild turkey, pheasant, or rabbit?

6. What online site was recognized by the 2005 *Guinness Book of Records* as the largest online dating site in the world?

7. In Egyptian mythology, what ancient god was originally god of the desert?

8. What's the title of Hans Christian Andersen's fairy tale about a young girl who dies trying to sell her products during winter?

9. When a darts player wins three legs in a best-out-of-five-legs match, what has he won?

10. What was the nickname of Swedish industrialist Ivar Kreuger? (The companies he founded manufacture more than 66 percent of the fiery items in the nickname.)

11. Gene Rayburn was the longtime host of what American game show in which celebrities and contestants answered fill-in-the-blank questions?

12. What is geocaching?

One of a Kind

Answers on page 395.

GET OUTTA HERE

Which of the three choices does not belong?

1. Who was never a vice president of the United States: Thomas Jefferson, Theodore Roosevelt, or Dwight D. Eisenhower?

2. As of 2006, which of these has not been a flavor of Kellogg's Pop-Tarts: Strawberry Milkshake, Candy Cane, or Hot Fudge Sundae?

3. As of 2007, which of these has not been the name of a NASA space shuttle: *Atlantis, Endeavour,* or *Explorer*?

4. Which is not a bone in the human body: ventricle, sacrum, or clavicle?

5. Of locusts, earthquake, or darkness, which is not one of the ten plagues in the book of Exodus in the Bible?

6. As of 2006, which of these has not been a recurring character on *Sesame Street*: Buffalo Jill, Slimey, or Guy Smiley?

7. Of Quito, Arequipa, or Montevideo, which is not a capital of a South American country?

8. Which is not an animal of the Chinese zodiac: snake, bear, or ox?

9. Of Russian, Italian, or Arabic, which is not one of the six official languages of the United Nations?

10. As of 2007, which NFL team has not won back-to-back Super Bowls: the Miami Dolphins, Buffalo Bills, or Denver Broncos?

11. Which of the following is not a British dependent territory: Aruba, Bermuda, or the Falkland Islands?

12. Of the following, which is not a wedding expense traditionally paid for by the groom's family: clergy member's fees, rehearsal dinner, or music for the ceremony?

Answers on page 396.

SQUARESVILLE

Where there's a square everywhere.

1. After the *New York Times* moved to the neighborhood in 1904, Longacre Square was renamed what?

2. Paul Lynde, Joan Rivers, and Whoopi Goldberg were the "center" of attention on various incarnations of what game show?

3. What color are SpongeBob SquarePants's pants?

4. What country dance, very popular in Europe starting in the 18th century, is the official state dance of 19 U.S. states?

5. When someone has to start all over, what square are they said to go back to?

6. What is the mathematical relationship between 12 and 144?

7. In what square was a young man filmed facing down a column of tanks that had been sent to end the student protests there in 1989?

8. What NFL team sang backup on and appeared in the video for the 1986 Huey Lewis and the News hit "Hip to Be Square"?

9. What 1980s sitcom starred Sarah Jessica Parker as geeky teen Patty Greene?

10. What London square commemorates a British naval victory of the Napoleonic Wars?

11. In front of all those people! Where did Marilyn Monroe publicly sing "Happy Birthday, Mr. President" to John F. Kennedy?

12. Iconic Massachusetts newsstand Out of Town News is located in a kiosk in the center of what?

One of a Kind

SOME FOURS

"Four" (or "4") is somewhere in each answer.

1. Name of the spot where Utah, Colorado, New Mexico, and Arizona meet.

2. What's a slang term for 50 cents?

3. This complimentary popular epithet applied to the Beatles would not have worked if they had been a trio. What was it?

4. According to tradition, what plant can bring you good luck?

5. Small iced cakes or confections are also known as what?

6. Colin L. Powell and H. Norman Schwarzkopf are among the more than 200 Army officers who have held what rank?

7. After Mao Zedong's death, what group of Communist Chinese leaders were blamed for the events of the Cultural Revolution?

8. In this 1949 novel by George Orwell, people lead dehumanized and often fearful lives under the watchful eye of Big Brother. Set in the future, the book's title is the year the action occurs. What is it?

9. What common timber used in frame houses actually measures 1½ x 3½ inches?

10. One who bluffs, in poker or elsewhere, or makes false claims, is called a what?

11. What youth organization, administered by the USDA, is commonly associated with agriculture, summer camps, and county and state fairs?

12. Florida, Ohio State, Georgetown, and UCLA were the teams in what NCAA event in 2007?

Answers on page 396.

A "LITTLE" THIS & THAT

We'd like to thank all the little people . . .

1. What capital city in the U.S. is named for a natural landmark called *La Petite Roche*?

2. What Christmas song is also called "The Carol of the Drum" (pa-rum-pum-pum-pum)?

3. What were the Little Rascals called before they were syndicated for television in the mid-1950s?

4. What was Louisa May Alcott's follow-up novel to her 1868 book *Little Women*?

5. Name one of the four Native American tribes that fought Custer's troops at the Battle of Little Bighorn.

6. What kind of car can "do 140 with the top end floored," according to a 1963 Beach Boys song?

7. In what city's harbor is the statue called the *Little Mermaid*?

8. What off-Broadway play is based on a 1960 Roger Corman movie about a florist shop worker and a man-eating plant?

9. Rich Little or Little Richard—which of them was born Richard Wayne Penniman?

10. Tallulah Bankhead clashed with Lillian Hellman over politics while starring in Hellman's *The Little Foxes* on Broadway. In the movie, what Hollywood actress got Bankhead's role?

11. What pizza company's spokeperson is a cartoon guy in a toga?

Answers on page 396.

APPLES & ORANGES

One or the other, they're all in this juicy quiz.

1. What Oscar-winning actress named her daughter, born in the year 2004, Apple?

2. It's doubtful that the apple really fell on his head. But what British scientist was inspired to create a theory of gravity after (probably) seeing an apple fall from a tree?

3. What American college is named after England's William of Orange and his queen?

4. Contrary to urban legend, Osama bin Laden does not own what beverage brand that's named after its carbonated apple soda?

5. What kind of joke ends with "Orange you glad I didn't say banana?"

6. The iconic 1984 Super Bowl ad that Apple Computer ran to announce the Macintosh personal computer was based on what novel?

7. What famous theme park opened in 1955 in Orange County, California?

8. The Adam's apple is a protrusion of the human neck formed from what?

9. As of 2005, the U.S. government was paying compensation to 10,000 veterans of the Vietnam War who were affected by what defoliant?

10. What futuristic Anthony Burgess novel was made into a 1971 film starring Malcolm McDowell as a charming sociopath?

11. John Chapman was the given name of what legendary (but real) American nurseryman?

Answers on page 397.

TIME TRAVELERS

Take a bite out of time.

1. What troubled teenager used *The Philosophy of Time Travel* book to travel back in time 28 days to escape the end of the world (and the tormenting of a man-sized rabbit named Frank)?

2. Scientist Sam Beckett jumps from person to person to "put things right that once went wrong" in what Emmy-winning TV show?

3. Billy Pilgrim became "unstuck in time" in this 1969 Kurt Vonnegut classic, but the only things he "could not change were the past, the present, and the future," according to the narrator.

4. What British "Father of Science Fiction" wrote *The Time Machine*, a novella that popularized the time-travel genre but was intended to create debate about caste systems?

5. This American humorist wrote a story about entrepreneur Hank Morgan's visit to Camelot. Name the writer and the story.

6. Bill and Ted weren't the only people to use a telephone booth to travel time. What titular mystery man voyaged in a blue police callbox called a TARDIS?

7. TV Meteorologist Phil Connors got stuck in a time loop and was forced to relive the same 24 hours in what 1993 romantic comedy classic?

8. Kevin and six dwarves appear in what Terry Gilliam film with the tagline: "They didn't just make history, they stole it!"?

9. What unconventional 2004 Audrey Niffenegger love story is about artist Claire Abshire and her husband Henry DeTamble, who suffers from "Chrono-Impairment?"

10. John-Erik Hexum and Meeno Peluce starred in this 1980s TV show about time travelers whose mission is to "help history along."

Answers on page 397.

Potpourri

HAIR APPARENT

All about the hair up there.

1. In the comic strip *Peanuts*, Charlie Brown's father is in the hair business. What exactly does he do?

2. Before the handsome prince came along, who else climbed up Rapunzel's hair?

3. What's the name of the pigment that, when the hair stops producing it, makes human hair grow in gray?

4. What's the name of the long ponytail or braid that Chinese men were forced to wear—under pain of death—by their Manchu rulers in the 17th century?

5. Approximately how long does a head louse live on a human scalp?

6. The Native American tribe that originated the mohawk hairstyle was most likely not the Mohawks, but a tribe that one of the Great Lakes is named for. Who were they?

7. How many presidents featured on the Mount Rushmore National Memorial sport facial hair?

8. What hairstyle, a favorite of rockabilly artists like Elvis, is named for the mistress of France's King Louis XV?

9. Who tends to grow gray at a younger age: men or women?

10. What was Michael Jackson doing in 1984 when his hair caught fire?

11. What Oscar-winning actress made her Broadway debut in *Hair* in 1968?

12. Average number of hairs on a human head vary by hair color. Who has more: blondes, brunettes, or redheads?

Answers on page 397.

HATS OFF!

The truly well-attired person would never think of leaving home bareheaded.

1. What three-sided hat did Paul Revere wear on his famous midnight ride?

2. Often called a skimmer or a basher, what is the popular name for this straw hat worn by young men while boating on the Thames?

3. Hat makers Thomas and Bowler originally designed the bowler as a riding helmet. What's the other name for it?

4. What hat did Sherlock Holmes wear when tramping across the moors in the film, *The Hound of the Baskervilles*?

5. What felt hat with center dent was popularized by King Edward VII after he visited a spa in Germany?

6. Flappers in the roaring twenties cropped their hair and wore a hat that is the French word for bell. What is it?

7. When Fred Astaire "put on the Ritz," what hat would he wear with his white tie and tails?

8. Despite its name, this cowboy hat only holds 3 quarts of water. What is it?

9. It looks like a Jewish yarmulke but this white skullcap is worn by the Pope of the Catholic Church. What is it called?

10. What is the name for a person who makes hats for women? The name evolved from the traveling haberdashers from Milan, Italy.

11. What first lady wore a pink pillbox hat designed by Halston on the day her husband was assassinated?

12. Artists are often depicted in cartoons dressed in a painting smock, holding a painter's palette and wearing what kind of French hat?

Answers on page 397.

Potpourri

IT'S BIBLICAL, KIND OF

Every answer contains a book of the Bible.

1. Which band did drummer/singer Phil Collins walk away from in 1996 to focus on a solo career?

2. What is the only name found in the lyrics of Three Dog Night's "Joy to the World"?

3. What are the professions of TV personalities Judith Sheindlin, Joe Brown, Joseph Wapner, and Greg Mathis?

4. Which 1960 epic movie, starring Paul Newman, Eva Marie Saint, and Sal Mineo, tells the story of Israel's struggle for independence?

5. Which controversial TV sitcom of the 1950s centers around three Harlem residents who are members of the fictitious fraternal organization "Mystic Knights of the Sea"?

6. Which of the Baldwin brothers is the only one to fit this category?

7. Which luxury steakhouse chain founded in 1965 has become the largest, beating out The Palm and Morton's, with over 100 units across the U.S.?

8. Which 1940s Olympic swimmer went on to appear in 26 movies including starring roles in such watery epics as *Bathing Beauty* and *Million Dollar Mermaid*?

9. Which first name is shared by the authors of *Dubliners*, *Deliverance*, and *The Deerslayer*?

10. Who is the only athlete to win seven gold medals in a single Olympics—a feat accomplished in 1972?

11. Which charcter in the old TV sitcom *The Real McCoys* was played by Richard Crenna?

IT'LL REALLY MOVE YOU

When it comes to unique modes of transportation, this quiz gets around.

1. What cyan bovine measured "42 axe handles and a plug of chewing tobacco" between his horns?

2. This Royal Navy vessel was later adapted as a survey ship, and on its second voyage, a naturalist named Charles Darwin was aboard.

3. In Herman Wouk's Pulitzer Prize–winning 1951 novel, what's the name of the destroyer-minesweeper commanded by Lieutenant Commander Francis Queeg?

4. What is the name of the modified 1969 Dodge Charger that Bo and Luke Duke drive?

5. In Ian Fleming's third novel, it's a rocket, but for the 11th "official" James Bond movie it's made into a space shuttle. What's its lunar name?

6. Widowmaker is the name of the horse belonging what American cowboy of tall-tale legends?

7. This handy means of transport pops up in Russian folk tales, a Mark Twain story, and *1001 Arabian Nights*.

8. It's a polka dance and an amusement park ride, but mainly it's a ghost ship that is doomed to sail "the seven seas" forever. What is it?

9. This is a style of Caribbean folk music or the name of Jacques Cousteau's research vessel. What name are we referring to?

10. You need roads to get around. In the United States the main thoroughfare is often called "Main Street." What is it called in the United Kingdom?

Potpourri

Answers on page 398.

A LITTLE OF EVERYTHING

So many topics, so few pages. We were bound to have some extras.

1. What colonial American publisher used the pen name Richard Saunders?

2. What does Volkswagen mean in English?

3. What is "ROY G. BIV" a mnemonic device for?

4. What fictional New Hampshire town was the setting for Thornton Wilder's play *Our Town*?

5. In the TV sitcom *Three's Company*, Suzanne Somers played Chrissy Snow. What was "Chrissy" short for?

6. What does the first A in NASA stand for?

7. What kind of "fear" is arachibutyrophobia?

8. What was the name of the United States' first Earth satellite, launched in 1958?

9. In the United States, Inauguration Day is always held on what date?

10. Whose TV production company is called Worldwide Pants, Inc.?

11. What roadside attraction in Louisville, Kentucky, is 120 feet tall and weighs 34 tons?

12. Aretha Franklin is known as the Queen of Soul. Who was called Queen of the Blues?

13. Who is Graceland named after?

Potpourri

ON THE STREET WHERE YOU LIVE

Where every answer contains the word "street."

1. Nick Carter is a member of what clean-cut group that the *Guinness Book of Records* called "the biggest boy band in history"?

2. Big Bird, Snuffleupagus, and Oscar the Grouch live on what street?

3. In Sherlock Holmes stories, what was Holmes's gang of street urchins called?

4. Who was Perry Mason's secretary in Erle Stanley Gardner's stories?

5. It's a song in the musical *Annie*, a Charlie Chaplin movie, and the road a fat cat might be said to live on, metaphorically. What is it?

6. What portly actor appeared in nine films with Peter Lorre, including *Casablanca* and *The Maltese Falcon*, in which he played Kasper Gutman (aka "The Fat Man")?

7. The 1934 film *The Barretts of Wimpole Street* told the story of what pair of literary lovers?

8. A free-spirited young woman marries Will Kennicott, a doctor, in what satirical Sinclair Lewis novel set in Gopher Prairie, Minnesota?

9. What 1973 Martin Scorsese film starred Harvey Keitel and Robert De Niro?

10. This American skier won a silver medal in the downhill at the 1994 Winter Olympics and a gold medal in the "Super G" (Super Giant Slalom) in the 1998 Olympics.

Potpourri

Answers on page 399.

"FRANK"LY, MY DEAR

How many "franks" can you find in this quiz? Let's find out.

1. What member of the original "Rat Pack" went on to win an Oscar for Best Supporting Actor in 1953?

2. Long considered America's most prominent architect, who blurred the line between interior space and the surrounding terrain?

3. Franklin Delano Roosevelt was the author of what comprehensive set of programs designed to lift the U.S. out of the Depression?

4. Subtitled *The Modern Prometheus*, what 19th-century novel, called the first work of science fiction, warned against the excesses of scientific innovations?

5. What popular American snack is often associated with New York's Coney Island?

6. The Franks, an ancient barbarian tribe occupying most of what is today France, Belgium, Holland, and part of Germany, allied with the Romans to fight what other famous barbarian?

7. Name the practice, dating back to 17th-century England, which allows elected officials to send mail without paying for postage.

8. Who wrote *The Wizard of Oz* and its 13 sequels?

9. What metal-lined fireplace, named after its inventor, provides more heat and less smoke than ordinary fireplaces?

10. Name the company that began making and selling coins and medallions in 1964 but has since branched out into all aspects of the "collectibles" market.

11. Otto Frank arranged for the publication of her diary in 1947. What was the diary's title and who was its author?

LIVING IN THE MATERIAL WORLD

What are you wearing?

1. From the French word for velvet, what stretchy velvetlike fabric is used to make stage curtains, car seat covers, and track suits?

2. What versatile synthetic—now used in parachutes, guitar strings, and pantyhose—was first used for toothbrush bristles?

3. Also known as sack cloth, what coarse woven fabric is used more often to make bags than (extremely uncomfortable) clothing?

4. Which fabric, mostly used in shirts and pajamas, became a fashion statement in the 1990s when it became associated with grunge musicians?

5. What cotton fabric is named for Calicut, a seaport on India's coast?

6. The oldest form of fabric known isn't woven but pressed or matted into shape. You may have run across it on a pool table. What is it?

7. What luxurious material from the fleece of the Himalayan mountain goat is used to make Pashmina shawls?

8. First used in women's undergarments, it's now worn proudly on the outside. Its ability to stretch up to 600 percent is why its name is based on the word "expand." What is it?

9. Angora wool comes from the coat of the Angora rabbit, but which fabric is created from the fleece of the Angora goat?

10. More than half of it is produced by China (no surprise there!), the rest by India and Japan. What is it?

Potpourri

Answers on page 399.

IF THE SHOE FITS . . .

*So how much do you really know about that
most basic of fashion accessories—your shoes?*

1. What's the name of the dagger favored by assassins in the Italian Renaissance that inspired a popular heel shape in fashionable women's shoes?

2. This cheap shoe derived from a Japanese sandal can be found by showers and pools all over the world. What is its name?

3. What classic American shoe style was inspired by the slip-on shoes worn by Norwegian dairy farmers in the 1930s?

4. What colorful canvas sandals are named after the Catalan word for the tough, wiry Mediterranean grass used for making rope?

5. South Africans call them *takkies*. Aussies call them *sandshoes*. Brits call them *trainers*. What do Americans call them?

6. If the weather's bad you might be wearing a pair of *gumshoes* or *dickersons*. What's the more common term for these foul weather shoes?

7. David Bowie and other 1970s Glam Rockers spearheaded the short-lived return of what shoe fashion popular with actors in Ancient Greece?

8. Plimsolls were the name given to a landmark American shoe that was invented in the late 1800s. What made this shoe unique?

9. Italian shoes have long been considered the best in the world. Can you name two of the big three Italian shoe brands?

10. During the 1950s and '60s, young women often placed a coin in their penny loafers so that they would always have the money to call a cab if a date went bad. What was the coin?

Answers on page 399.

OOH! THAT STINGS!

Movies and books on stings, cons, grifters, and swindlers—real and fictional.

1. This 1973 Best Picture starring Paul Newman and Robert Redford didn't have to swindle anyone to win six other Oscars, including Best Director. What's the film?

2. John Cusack, Anjelica Huston, and Annette Bening are all con artists in what 1990 movie?

3. Tom Hanks is an FBI agent chasing Frank Abagnale, Jr., a real-life impostor, forger, and con artist, in 2002's *Catch Me If You Can*. Who plays Abagnale?

4. Olivia d'Abo plays Nicole Wallace, a sociopathic thief and con artist, in a recurring role on what successful crime drama from creator Dick Wolf?

5. There are at least three known con artists on the TV series *Lost*. Who's the most obvious one?

6. What impostor and murderer appears in five of Patricia Highsmith's novels, each of which has the character's name in the title?

7. *The Phil Silvers Show* of the 1950s starred Silvers as a master sergeant who spent most of his time trying to make money through get-rich-quick scams. In reruns, the show is sometimes titled what?

8. Foulfellow Fox and Gideon the Cat are confidence tricksters in what 1940 Disney film?

9. In the 1967 movie, *The Flim-Flam Man*, Mordecai C. Jones is a drifting con artist who makes his living playing tricks on people in the South. Who plays him?

10. One of the characters on TV's *Green Acres* was a local salesman and con man portrayed by veteran character actor Pat Buttram. What was his character's name?

Potpourri

Answers on page 400.

FLOWERY WRITING

A rose is a rose, but that's not always the right answer.

1. In Shakespeare's *Hamlet*, what flower does Ophelia say is "for remembrance?"

2. What Scottish poet penned, "My love is like a red, red rose"?

3. When philosopher Socrates was condemned to death in 399 B.C., what poisonous plant's nectar did he drink?

4. In the movie *Little Shop of Horrors*, the man-eating plant is a cross between butterwort and what kind of plant?

5. Wordsworth began this poem about yellow flowers with these words, "I wandered lonely as a cloud." What is the title of the poem?

6. Singer Marty Robbins was all dressed up for the dance wearing a white sport coat and what kind of flower?

7. What famous actress declared, "The calla lilies are in bloom again," in the 1937 movie classic, *Stage Door*?

8. The Wicked Witch of the West puts Dorothy and her friends in Oz to sleep with the juice of what flowers?

9. F. Scott Fitzgerald named his famous heroine in *The Great Gatsby* after this perky bloom. What is her name?

10. What is the name of Peter Pan's Indian friend in Never Never Land?

11. In the classic movie, Citizen Kane, the newspaper magnate dies whispering, "Rosebud." What is Rosebud?

12. What is the name of the movie that centers on the lives of Southern women at a hairdressing salon and starred Shirley MacLaine, Dolly Parton, and Julia Roberts?

Potpourri

WHEELS OF FORTUNE

These top-of-the-line cars are pricy,
fast, and oh, so sexy!

1. Which luxury ride is the darling of the diplomatic corps, and comes in C, E, and S classes?

2. Silver Cloud, Silver Spur, and Silver Shadow are former models of which legendary motorcar?

3. James Bond made what sports car synonymous with speed and glamour in the films *Goldfinger*, *Thunderball*, *GoldenEye*, and *Casino Royale*?

4. "The Ultimate Driving Machine" is the slogan for which German car company?

5. What classic American muscle car has been the Indy 500 Pace Car since 2003?

6. The $63,000 diesel V-10 Touareg is a recent entry into the "Super SUV" category from what unlikely European carmaker?

7. The Murcielago and Gallardo are two models available in the U.S. from which supercar manufacturer?

8. It's called the XLR-V. It's a convertible. It costs $100,000, and it's all-American. Who builds it?

9. Which carmaker created the 2006 Veyron 16.4, the fastest, most powerful, and most expensive production car ever built?

10. The $695,000 Koenigsegg CCX, an 806-horsepower street-car capable of speeds over 245 mph, is produced in which country?

11. What line of luxury vehicles is made in Japan by the world's largest automaker?

Answers on page 400.

Potpourri

CLOSE ENOUGH

Any answer within 50 is close enough.

1. How many days a year does the temperature dip below 32°F in Flagstaff, Arizona?

2. At the height of its popularity, *Baywatch* was on TV in how many countries?

3. How many Starbuck's coffee houses are listed in the 2007 Seattle *Yellow Pages*?

4. While Ronald Reagan was in the White House, how much did First Lady Nancy spend for a haircut?

5. How many feet high is the average Old Faithful eruption?

6. How many bullets were fired at Bonnie Parker and Clyde Barrow during their final showdown?

7. What was the price of the most expensive console radio from Sears, Roebuck in 1951?

8. What was the highest combined score ever amassed in an NBA game?

9. How many prime numbers are found between 1 and 1,000?

10. How many chests of tea were thrown overboard during the 1773 Boston Tea Party?

11. In which year was the American Automobile Association (AAA) established?

12. How many calories are in a Denny's "All American Slam" breakfast?

Potpourri

SOUNDS A BIT LIKE BOWLING TO ME

In each answer there is a bowling term.

1. What's it called when the president fails to sign a bill presented to him within ten days?

2. James is the first name of which villainous character in J. M. Barrie's *Peter Pan*?

3. Who starred as Max Bialystock in both the Broadway version and the 2005 film remake of *The Producers*?

4. What is the three-word nickname for the area around Manhattan's East 14th Street near Third Avenue, often cited as the birthplace of American popular music?

5. What 1932 Great Depression anthem asks the question "Why should I be standing in line, just waiting for bread"?

6. What turn-of-the-century dance with a bird in its name is performed with the feet well apart to fast ragtime music?

7. What six-word American idiom means to take action immediately in order to have a better chance at success?

8. Jackie Robinson broke professional baseball's "color barrier" when he joined which team in 1947?

9. Antique Royal, Shadow Box, American Renaissance, and Prestige are all styles of which household wall accessory?

10. What is the generic name given to condos and apartments that are created from former large industrial buildings and warehouses?

11. Featuring Mark Adkins as lead singer and Scott Sheldon on guitar, this California punk band's first album is entitled *Full Length*.

Answers on page 401.

Potpourri

AS GOOD AS GOLD

Thar's gold in them thar hills—and in most of these answers.

1. Because people mistook it for the real thing, this became another name for iron pyrite. What is the other name?

2. Before it became independent from Britain in 1957, what was the African nation of Ghana previously called?

3. Pro golfer Jack Nicklaus got this nickname from his high school alma mater's team name. What is it?

4. Ian Fleming wrote his first James Bond novel, *Casino Royale*, at his home in Jamaica in 1952. What was the home called?

5. Considered one of the greatest hockey players ever and perhaps the greatest left winger ever, his slap shot was once clocked at 118.3 mph. What was the nickname of Canadian hall-of-famer Bobby Hull?

6. The precision parachuting team of the U.S. Army is called what?

7. Golden Rule was the original name of a dry goods and clothing store founded in 1902 in Kemmerer, Wyoming, by the namesake of what what large retail chain?

8. The organization of World War II airmen who have been rescued from the sea after being shot down is known as what?

9. Who is the pro football hall-of-famer known as The Golden Boy?

10. The Gold Hill School was the name of the orphanage run by the title character played by Merlin Olsen in what TV series?

11. What Arizona senator who ran for president in 1964 used the symbols of two elements on his campaign buttons?

Answers on page 401.

FOR CRYING OUT LOUD!

Who knew that crying could be so much fun?

1. Tears produced by hypocritical or insincere weeping are called what?

2. The shortest verse in English bibles is found in the Gospel of John 11:35. What does it say?

3. Besides "tear gland," what's the more technical term for the gland that produces tears?

4. "To weep is to make less the depth of grief." Who wrote that?

5. She may be clued in crossword puzzles as "daughter of Tantalus" or "weeper of myth." Who is she?

6. "Weep no more my lady" is a line from what Stephen Foster song?

7. This governor of Maine withdrew from the 1972 presidential race after he was vilified for weeping in public after a verbal attack on his wife. Who was he?

8. What punny character in *Alice in Wonderland* was always weeping, and also showed Alice how to dance the Lobster Quadrille?

9. "You take somebody that cries their goddam eyes out over phony stuff in the movies, and nine times out of ten they're mean bastards at heart." What character said it, in what book?

10. What's the title of Thomas Pynchon's shortest novel, published in 1966?

11. The Incas referred to what precious metal as "tears of the moon"?

Potpourri

Answers on page 401.

WE'RE NUMBER TWO!

If something's the best, there usually is a runner-up.

1. Mount Everest is the tallest mountain in the world. What other Himalayan peak is number two?

2. The Marabou stork's 13-foot wingspan is the longest in the bird world. What species, cited in "The Rime of the Ancient Mariner," has the next longest wingspan?

3. The Nile is the world's longest river. Can you name the river that's only 145 miles shorter and occupies the number-two spot?

4. *Titanic* and *Ben-Hur* top the Academy Awards' list with 11 wins each. This 1961 film with Natalie Wood and Rita Moreno won 10 Oscars and sits alone in second place.

5. Jupiter is the largest planet in the solar system. What planet, boasting the most moons, is the number-two giant?

6. Texas has more farms than any other state. This state, the birthplace of Harry Truman, has the second-highest number of farms.

7. Between 1955 and 2000, The Beatles had 20 number-one singles on the Billboard Top-40 charts. Who came in second with 18 chart toppers?

8. Brazil is the largest South American country. What country is that continent's second largest?

9. With more than 1.3 billion residents, China is the world's most populous country. What is the only other country to break the 1 billion mark?

10. Georgia is the largest U.S. state east of the Mississippi River. What state, that borders four of the five Great Lakes, is the second largest in the East?

Answers on page 401.

Potpourri

IT'S GREEK TO ME

*Be careful—these are questions about
the Greek (not Roman) gods.*

1. What god shares a name with his domain, also called "the underworld"?

2. The most important and powerful of the Greek gods were said to live where?

3. Gods need to eat—but they don't have a lot of variety. What's the name of the magical substance that the gods eat for strength?

4. Contrary to popular belief, this figure was condemned to hold up the heavens, not the earth. What's his name?

5. What goddess of war lent her name to a major Greek city?

6. In Roman mythology, he's Neptune, god of the sea. What's his equivalent in Greek mythology?

7. Who is the god of love? (Hint: it's not Cupid.)

8. Artemis was the goddess of the hunt and what other god's twin sister?

9. In Greek mythology, who's Mother Earth and one of the creators of the world?

10. When Prometheus stole fire from the gods and gave it to humans, in what kind of plant did he smuggle it?

11. Ancient Greeks worshiped the pantheon of gods at the what?

12. Zeus's wife is also his older sister. What's her name?

Potpourri

Answers on page 402.

IT'S NOT EASY BEING GREEN

Green, green, green—sometimes it's in the question and sometimes it's in the answer.

1. Someone who is skillful or "lucky" with plants is said to possess what?

2. According to legend, his publisher bet him that he couldn't write a book with only 50 different words. The author won the bet (and 49 of the words were even monosyllabic). What is the name of this famous children's book and who is its author?

3. Can you name the football team that won the first two Super Bowls in 1967 and 1968?

4. What does the green flag mean in an auto race?

5. In what U.S. state is the grass so rich that it appears to be blue?

6. What environmental organization was founded in Vancouver in 1971?

7. Othello was overcome by this "green-eyed monster"?

8. What's a "green room," even if it isn't painted green?

9. Water vapor, carbon dioxide, methane, nitrous oxide, and ozone are known as what kind of gases, environmentally?

10. An inexperienced person or tenderfoot might be called a what?

11. What country's flag consists of a plain green field with no other marks or symbols?

12. What relative of kale is a staple of soul food?

Potpourri

Answers on page 402.

ANIMALS ON THE ROAD

No, not roadkill—domestic and foregin car models with animal names.

1. What luxury car company, a British institution for more than 50 years, was bought by Ford in 1989?

2. Studebaker didn't just make Larks. What more aggressive bird can be placed after "Golden," "Sky," and "Silver" to name three of their models of the 1950s?

3. Named for an African antelope and introduced in 1959, what was the first Chevrolet model to be given an animal name?

4. Which super-hot Fords that bear the same name as SMU footballers were referred to as a "1964 ½" models because they were introduced in April instead of September?

5. It may have been named for a strong male animal, but what Dodge pickup name also means to "crash into"?

6. What 1964 Plymouth muscle car came equipped with a 383-cubic-inch V-8 and a unique "meep-meep" horn?

7. After a series of rear-end collisions and resulting explosions, what infamous Ford compact became known as "the barbecue that seats four"?

8. What was the model name change of the Volkswagen Golfs exported to the U.S.A.?

9. Introduced by Fiat in 1980 as a city car, what now-extensive line of vehicles were named for a bear that's native to China?

10. Which car model did Carroll Shelby create in 1961 when he stuffed a big Ford V-8 into a little English AC Ace?

11. Which Rambler model with a "fishy name" was created in 1965 as an attempt to cash in on the current fastback craze?

IT'S LIKE POULTRY IN MOTION

Chickens, ducks, geese, and other quackers.

1. According to an old fable, who thought the sky was falling after an acorn dropped on her head?

2. Who wrote the classic tale of *The Ugly Duckling*?

3. Young female chickens are called what?

4. What Ibsen play has poultry in the title?

5. In American sports, what's a slang term for a score of zero?

6. What does rattlesnake meat taste like?

7. Cary Grant and Leslie Caron starred in what 1964 romantic comedy?

8. The rooster appears in the zodiac of what calendar?

9. What was the nickname for the Hughes H-4 Hercules, dubbed "The Edsel of Aviation," that was built by Howard Hughes' aircraft company?

10. In *Rebel Without a Cause*, James Dean and Corey Allen race their cars towards a cliff in a "game" called what?

11. Maurice Ravel wrote the piano duet *Ma Mère l'Oye*, about what nursery-rhyme matron?

12. In his famous "Freedom from Want" painting (one of his *Four Freedoms* series), Norman Rockwell featured what animal as a symbol of prosperity?

SMELLS GOOD

*Bacon, cinnamon, flowers—all of these
are olfactory turn-ons for most people.*

1. Shalimar, Joy, and Bay Rhum are three examples of what kind of stuff that's meant to smell good?

2. "Stir-fried noodles" is the literal meaning of what two-word Asian food that smells good?

3. When life hands you these, make a refreshing beverage! What fragrant hybrid fruits are we talking about?

4. Good luck trying to ignore the aroma of a shop that's selling what toroidal products?

5. Drive through Gilroy, California, for a whiff of what aromatic member of the lily family?

6. The anther, stigma, ovary, bract, and sepal are some of the parts of what things that often smell good?

7. Shepherd's, pecan, custard, pumpkin, cutie, and humble are words that might precede what word with aromatic connotations?

8. Tartine, ciabatta, ziti, risotto, calamari, mortadella—what kind of restaurant serves this great-smelling food?

9. The cooking herbs basil, rosemary, sage, and oregano are part of what family of aromatic plants?

10. If your beverage of choice is an aromatic tisane or rose hips with hibiscus, what are you drinking?

11. Commonly spoken of as a root, it's actually the rhizome of the monocotyledonous perennial plant *Zingiber officinale*. You might find some with your sushi. What popular spice are we referring to?

Potpourri

BOX IT

Put a "box" in every answer and you'll do fine.

1. What's the nickname for a forerunner of the blog—a makeshift stage that speechmakers once stood on while they regaled listeners with their opinions?

2. Even though he never hopped a freight train in his life, this musician was best known for "hobo music." What was his name?

3. What British holiday is traditionally celebrated on December 26th?

4. In a 1994 hit movie, what did a former flying nun tell her simple-minded (but ping-pong savvy) son about life?

5. What TV network became the first to broadcast via satellite in 1975, with a telecast of the "Thrilla in Manila" bout between Muhammad Ali and Joe Frazier?

6. In an emergency, it's a primary source of information for investigators. And, contrary to popular belief, it's usually bright orange. What is it?

7. What two-word term is used to describe how much money a movie takes in?

8. What mechanical device triggers a riot in the 1989 film *Do the Right Thing*?

9. What becomes superfluous if your resting foundation is a futon?

10. If you're lucky (and you don't strike out), your trip originating here may bring you home. What is it?

11. What 1978 instrumental hit by Frank Mills is now a popular theme song for ice-cream trucks everywhere?

Answers on page 403.

IT'S A NUMBERS GAME

It's not a math quiz, but numbers are required. Calculators optional.

1. What catchphrase was made famous by astronomer Carl Sagan, even though he never actually said it on his TV series, *Cosmos*?

2. In Lewis Carroll's *Through the Looking Glass*, how many impossible things could the White Queen imagine before breakfast?

3. What are the seven numbers between 0 and 100 that look the same when written upside down?

4. According to the hypercomputer known as Deep Thought in *The Hitchhiker's Guide to the Galaxy*, what is the answer to "the ultimate question about life, the universe, and everything"?

5. What is the phrase (and title of a novel) that describes being caught in a no-win situation?

6. What was the telephone number in Tommy Tutone's 1982 hit single "Jenny"?

7. According to a sailors' song in Robert Louis Stevenson's novel *Treasure Island*, how many men are on a dead man's chest?

8. What is the sum of "four score and seven"?

9. How many days are in a fortnight?

10. What telephone prefix will always give you a wrong number?

11. If you just bought a gross of eggs, how many did you get?

12. A horse's height is measured in hands. How many inches are in a hand?

Potpourri

Answers on page 403.

TUNNEL VISION

All about tunnels of one kind or the other.

1. In 1944, 76 Allied prisoners made a bid for freedom from a German POW camp by escaping through a hand-dug tunnel nicknamed "Harry." Nineteen years later, what Oscar-nominated movie dramatized their efforts?

2. If you're at a traditional carnival with your sweetheart, where do you go to make out?

3. What is the significance of the 13th pillar of the Pont de l'Alma tunnel in Paris?

4. What 1966–67 television show followed the adventures of two scientists who are lost in history—and sometimes in the future?

5. This link between Great Britain and France is considered one of the Seven Wonders of the Modern World. What is it called?

6. In the early 1900s, sailors in Portland, Oregon, were often drugged, kidnapped, and "recruited" onto ships via a labyrinth of tunnels. What was the name of this underground network?

7. Before computer modeling, what did scientists use to test an object's aerodynamics?

8. What are the names of the tunnels that link Manhattan with New Jersey?

9. The "Big Dig," widely regarded as the most expensive highway project in American history, brought an underground roadway system to what city?

10. What Virginia tunnel complex features two mile-long tunnels, two bridges, four manmade islands, and its own police department?

WHERE'S THE REMOTE?, page 1

1. Cleveland, OH
2. Milwaukee, WI
3. Las Vegas, NV
4. Dodge City, KS
5. Baltimore, MD
6. Washington, D.C.
7. Nantucket, MA
8. Phoenix, AZ
9. Virginia City, NV
10. Chicago, IL

A QUIZ ABOUT NOTHING, page 2

1. *The Today Show*
2. Seven (Mantle's number)
3. Their wedding invitation envelopes
4. Festivus
5. Elaine
6. Cosmo
7. Coffee tables
8. It writes upside down.
9. Jon Voight
10. It was ugly.
11. Burma (Myanmar)
12. *Tropic of Cancer*

THE FACTORY FACTOR, page 3

1. A textile mill
2. *Schindler's List*
3. *Charlie and the Chocolate Factory*
4. *The Terminator*
5. Auto plant
6. Factory worker on an assembly line
7. *Gung Ho*
8. Boxes
9. A sheet-metal factory
10. A fish-processing factory

YOU CAN QUOTE ME, page 4

1. Norman Bates, in *Psycho* (1960)
2. *Return of the Jedi* (1983)
3. Randle P. McMurphy (Jack Nicholson), in *One Flew Over the Cuckoo's Nest* (1975)
4. *Rocky* (1976)
5. *The Sound of Music* (1965)
6. *Dead Poets Society* (1989)
7. Humphrey Bogart, in *The African Queen* (1951)
8. *High Noon* (1952); Gary Cooper is Will Kane
9. *Scent of a Woman* (1992)
10. *Rear Window* (1954)

POPCORN PLEASURES, page 5

1. *Sideways*
2. *Eat Drink Man Woman (Yin shi nan nu)*
3. *The Spitfire Grill*
4. *Soylent Green*
5. *The Godfather*
6. *Chocolat*
7. *Babette's Feast*
8. *Tom Jones*
9. *Felicia's Journey*
10. *Mambo Café*

ALPHABET SOUP, page 6

1. Chief Petty Officer
2. Annual Net Usage Statistics and Weekly Estimated Net Usage Statistics
3. President of the United States
4. Alien Life Form
5. Judge Advocate General
6. John Ross
7. Beyond Body Odor
8. Glorious Ladies of Wrestling
9. Surgical (Mobile Army Surgical Hospital)
10. Bad Attitude
11. Impossible Missions Force

PRIMETIME PHOBIAS, page 7

1. Animals
2. Erin Moran
3. Her toothbrush
4. A beer bottle cap
5. Sigmund Freud
6. Flying
7. Clowns
8. Alan Shore (James Spader)
9. Monk (Tony Shalhoub)
10. Bowling

TELENOVELS, page 8

1. *Gilligan's Island* (1964–67)
2. *Magnum, P.I.* (1980–88)
3. *Mister Ed* (1961–66)
4. *Knots Landing* (1979–83)
5. *The Rosie O'Donnell Show* (1996–2002)
6. *Night Court* (1984–92)
7. *The Addams Family* (1964–66)
8. *Everybody Loves Raymond* (1996–2005)
9. *The X-Files* (1993–2002)
10. *The Munsters* (1964–66)
11. *Charmed* (1998–2006)

Answers

TV "CAT"ALOG, page 9

1. *Ren and Stimpy*
2. Heathcliff
3. Garfield
4. Smelly Cat
5. Fancy Feast
6. *Charmed*

7. A lion
8. Lucky
9. *The Simpsons*
10. *Eek! the Cat*
11. Koolio

TV OPENERS, page 10

1. *Charlie's Angels* (1976–81)
2. *Law and Order* (1990–)
3. *Unsolved Mysteries* (1988–99)
4. *The Pretender* (1996–2000)
5. *Fame* (1982–87)
6. *Xena: Warrior Princess* (1995–2001)

7. *Sheena* (2000–02)
8. *Alias* (2001–06)
9. *The People's Court* (1981–93)
10. *Quincy, M.E.* (1976–83)
11. *JAG* (1995–2005)

OLD WINE IN NEW BOTTLES, page 11

1. *Clueless*
2. *Scrooged*
3. *The Taming of the Shrew*
4. Gwyneth Paltrow
5. *Twisted*
6. *Romeo and Juliet*

7. Henry James
8. Michael Crichton
9. Cain and Abel
10. *Beauty and the Beast*
11. *The Princess and the Pea*

CULTURE CLASH, page 12

1. *Witness*
2. *Shogun*
3. *The Sheltering Sky*
4. *Deliverance*
5. *Gorillas in the Mist*

6. *The Emerald Forest*
7. *Moscow on the Hudson*
8. *Lawrence of Arabia*
9. *Mississippi Masala*
10. *A Passage to India*

HOME SWEET HOME, page 13

1. *The Beverly Hillbillies*
2. The Ewings' Southfork ranch of *Dallas*
3. The Bundy house of *Married…with Children*
4. *Gilmore Girls*
5. *The Simpsons*
6. Jim Rockford, of *The Rockford Files*
7. *Falcon Crest*
8. *Fantasy Island*
9. M*A*S*H
10. *Designing Women*

IT'S ALIVE!, page 14

1. *Godzilla*
2. *Alien*
3. *Rodan*
4. *Jurassic Park*
5. *King Kong*
6. *The Blob*
7. *The Thing (from Another World)*
8. *Pitch Black*
9. *Tremors*
10. *Them!*
11. *Anaconda*

COLORFUL CHARACTERS, page 15

1. Murphy Brown
2. Perry White
3. Ron Burgundy
4. Bonnie Blue Butler
5. Silver
6. *The Blue Lagoon*
7. The Green Lantern
8. Olive Oyl
9. Red Ryder
10. The Scarlet Pimpernel
11. Sapphire

B-LIST ACTORS, page 16

1. Marlon Brando
2. Sandra Bullock
3 Annette Bening
4. Humphrey Bogart
5. Lisa Bonet
6. Richard Burton
7. Lorraine Bracco
8. Ernest Borgnine
9. Peter Boyle
10. Kevin Bacon

Answers

THE FUGITIVES, page 17

1. *Bonnie and Clyde*
2. *The Fugitive*
3. *Wild at Heart*
4. *The Big Fix*
5. *The Sugarland Express*
6. *Thelma and Louise*
7. *Butch Cassidy and the Sundance Kid*
8. *It Happened One Night*
9. *Rabbit-Proof Fence*
10. *Roman Holiday*

WHO ARE YOU?, page 18

1. Charlie Chaplin
2. *Monty Python's Life of Brian*
3. *Dave*
4. *Being There*
5. Jack Lemmon
6. *North by Northwest*
7. *The Sopranos*
8. *The Third Man*
9. *The Big Lebowski*
10. *Sister Act*

DON'T MIND IF I DO, page 19

1. *Desperate Housewives*
2. Cheyenne Hart, Reba's married daughter, played by Joanna Garcia
3. John Spencer
4. Barney Gumble
5. Otis Campbell, played by Hal Smith
6. Capt. Frank Furillo
7. Sue Ellen
8. George Wendt
9. The Betty Ford Clinic
10. Scott Wolf

SCHWING!, page 20

1. *Rowan and Martin's Laugh-In*
2. *The Beverly Hillbillies*
3. *Beavis and Butt-head*
4. Conan O'Brien
5. Steve Allen
6. *Laverne and Shirley*
7. Stephen Colbert on *The Colbert Report*
8. "Wayne's World"
9. *Perfect Strangers*
10. Andy Kaufman

SOUNDS, SMELLS, & LOOKS LIKE TEEN SPIRIT, page 21

1. *Joan of Arcadia*
2. *The Notebook*
3. Thora Birch
4. *American Graffiti*; Suzanne Somers
5. Katherine Heigl
6. *Mystic Pizza*
7. *Fast Times at Ridgemont High*
8. *Ferris Bueller's Day Off*
9. *Say Anything*
10. *The Legend of Billie Jean*

WILD AND CRAZY FLICKS, page 22

1. *Planes, Trains and Automobiles*
2. *The Jerk*
3. *Sgt. Bilko*
4. *Three Amigos*
5. *L.A. Story*
6. *Dirty Rotten Scoundrels*
7. *The Out-of-Towners*
8. *All of Me*
9. *Leap of Faith*
10. *Sgt. Pepper's Lonely Hearts Club Band*

"BLACK" & "WHITE" MOVIES, page 23

1. *Black Widow*
2. *White Fang*
3. *White Lightning*
4. *Black Sunday*
5. *The Black Hole*
6. *White Heat*
7. *White Men Can't Jump*
8. *Black Hawk Down*
9. *White Chicks*
10. *Black Beauty*

TV MOMS, page 24

1. June Lockhart
2. Alice
3. June Cleaver
4. Bouvier
5. Clair Huxtable
6. *Family Ties*
7. *One Day at a Time*
8. Cunningham
9. Michael Learned
10. *The Fresh Prince of Bel-Air*
11. Roseanne Conner of *Roseanne*

YOU LOOKIN' AT ME?, page 25

1. *Goodfellas*
2. *Frankenstein*
3. *Jurassic Park*
4. *Full Metal Jacket*
5. *Airplane!*
6. *Mommie Dearest*
7. *A League of Their Own*
8. *Ed Wood*
9. *Raising Arizona*
10. *To Have and Have Not*

HOLLYWOOD SHORTS, page 26

1. *Elf*
2. *Hulk*
3. *Hook*
4. *Big*
5. *Troy*
6. *xXx*
7. *Heat*
8. *Jaws*
9. *300*
10. *X-Men*

HOMER ALONE, page 27

1. Moe's Tavern
2. Springfield dog track
3. A pink shirt
4. Mel Gibson
5. Hammock
6. Blowfish (sushi)
7. Bill Gates
8. Marijuana
9. Jay
10. Evergreen Terrace
11. The Frying Dutchman
12. Abraham
13. Duff Beer

JINGLES ALL THE WAY, page 28

1. Chiffon
2. Wisk
3. Texaco
4. Pepsodent
5. Hamm's
6. Ken-L Ration
7. Schaefer
8. Chock Full O' Nuts
9. Brylcreem
10. Crest
11. Esso (later Exxon)
12. Timex

MARVELOUS MUPPETS, page 29

1. Kermit the Frog
2. Barbara Billingsley (from *Leave It to Beaver*)
3. Charles Durning
4. Marionette and puppet
5. *The Muppet Show*
6. Washington, D.C.
7. Fozzie Bear
8. Waldorf and Statler
9. Frank Oz
10. Jim Henson's Creature Shop

WHAT'S MY LINE?, page 30

1. She's the owner of an antiques store called "Same As It Never Was."
2. She's a forensic anthropologist and a best-selling novelist.
3. Newspaper columnist; her column is called—guess what? —"Sex and the City."
4. Exotic dancer
5. He was a former waste management consultant for Barone Sanitation, a part owner of Satriale's Meat Market, and part owner of the Bada Bing Strip Club. (Get credit for any of these.)
6. Egg farmers
7. *The Pretender*
8. Fourteen
9. *The Larry Sanders Show*
10. He has a heating and air-conditioning business.
11. A Hollywood stunt man who moonlighted as a bounty hunter

CULT FAVORITES, page 31

1. *The Princess Bride*
2. *Twin Peaks*
3. *Monty Python's Flying Circus*
4. *This Is Spinal Tap*
5. *American Graffiti*
6. *Beautiful Girls*
7. *Mystery Science Theater 3000*
8. *The Prisoner*
9. *Doctor Who*
10. *The Professional*

CREATURE FEATURES, page 32

1. Mary Shelley
2. *Arachnophobia*
3. A gigantic mutant dinosaur
4. *Tremors*
5. A man-eating crocodile
6. Bodega Bay, California
7. *The Creature from the Black Lagoon*
8. Bigfoot, Sasquatch, Yeti, or the Abominable Snowman
9. Naomi Watts
10. *Anaconda*
11. *Frankenweenie*

ARE WE HAVING FUN YET?, page 33

1. The Fonz, who else?
2. Ed Asner
3. *Friends*
4. Chuckles the Clown
5. *Seinfeld*
6. Bronson Pinchot
7. The Cookie Monster on *Sesame Street*
8. Al Bundy of *Married . . . with Children*
9. Lucy Liu, on *Ally McBeal*
10. Tootie Ramsey

COOL CATS, page 34

1. Krazy Kat
2. Garfield
3. T. S. Eliot
4. The Cheshire Cat in *Alice in Wonderland*
5. Mary Tyler Moore (MTM Productions)
6. Morris
7. Sylvester
8. White gloves
9. B. Kliban
10. Mrs. Norris
11. Socks
12. Cloned cat

O.K. ANIMALS, page 35

1. Opossum
2. Komodo dragon
3. The otter
4. An ocelot
5. Orangutan (then called Ourang-Outang)
6. Koala
7. Owls
8. Octopus
9. Ostrich
10. Kookaburra
11. King cobra
12. Katydid

ANIMALS AT LARGE, page 36

1. Big Bird
2. A caterpillar
3. Clifford the Big Red Dog
4. Rabbit
5. Gorilla
6. A roc
7. Foghorn Leghorn
8. A seahorse
9. Ants
10. "Here, kitty, kitty."
11. Crows

DON'T GO NEAR THE WATER!, page 37

1. A zombie
2. South America
3. A stingray
4. Barracuda
5. *Shark Tale*
6. Orcas
7. Florida
8. True
9. Portuguese Man O' War
10. Havana, Cuba

GREAT APES, page 38

1. Ronald Reagan
2. Orbit the Earth in a space capsule.
3. Koko
4. Dr. Jane Goodall
5. Orangutan
6. Swinging from one hold to another by the arms
7. Dian Fossey
8. The Man in the Yellow Hat
9. Cheetah
10. Jambo the Gorilla
11. King Kong
12. The Nairobi Trio

DOG DISH, page 39

1. Poodles
2. Chesapeake Bay Retriever
3. A Cocker Spaniel and a Pomeranian
4. Bulldogs
5. Airedale
6. Bloodhound
7. Irish Setter
8. Saint Bernard
9. Boston Terrier
10. Lhasa Apso
11. Greyhound

FOR THE BIRDS, page 40

1. Albatross
2. Wild Turkey
3. Grouse
4. Meadowlark Lemon
5. Cuckoo clocks
6. *The Firebird*
7. "Blackbird"
8. Dove
9. Eagle
10. Jonathan Swift

GOOD MOUSEKEEPING, page 41

1. Speedy Gonzales
2. Stuart Little
3. Walt Disney
4. Tom and Jerry; Jerry is the mouse
5. *Of Mice and Men*
6. *Flowers for Algernon*
7. Reepicheep
8. DangerMouse
9. Itchy
10. Basil

THIS LITTLE PIGGY, page 42

1. Miss Piggy
2. To buy a fat pig
3. Piglet
4. Piggly Wiggly
5. Petunia Pig
6. Sir Oinksalot
7. Napoleon
8. *Razorback*
9. Arnold Ziffel
10. Babe
11. Empress of Blandings
12. Wilbur

IT TAKES ALL KINDS, page 43

1. Red
2. Peacock
3. The turkey vulture
4. Dolly was cloned.
5. The flamingo
6. Snake flatulence
7. Australian marsupial mouse
8. Butterflies
9. Sleep
10. The flea
11. Eyelids
12. The elephant

4-LETTER BIRDS, page 44

1. Coot
2. Rook
3. Loon
4. Hawk
5. Duck
6. Crow (singer is Sheryl Crow)
7. Tern
8. Lark
9. Wren
10. Kite
11. Dove (band is Devo)

OUT OF AFRICA, page 45

1. Zebra
2. Giraffe
3. Cheetah
4. Rhinoceros
5. Wildebeest
6. Leopard
7. Hippopotamus
8. Hyena
9. Lion
10. Elephant

WOOF!, page 46

1. Labrador retriever
2. The Westminster Kennel Club Dog Show
3. Fang
4. Laika
5. Edinburgh
6. Purina Dog Chow
7. Scooby Doo
8. "(How Much Is) That Doggie in the Window?"
9. Groucho Marx
10. Lassie
11. $300
12. Spuds McKenzie

WHERE ARE HUE?, page 47

1. England
2. The Emerald Isle
3. Huang He
4. California
5. Black Forest
6. Lebanon
7. Blue Ridge Mountains
8. Erik the Red
9. French
10. The Golden Gate Bridge
11. Los Angeles

A CAPITAL IDEA, page 48

1. Irving Berlin (Germany)
2. Jack London (England)
3. Brussels sprouts (Belgium)
4. Stockholm Syndrome (Sweden)
5. Tokyo Rose (Japan)
6. Vienna sausage (Austria)
7. Sofia Coppola (Bulgaria)
8. Jerusalem artichoke (Israel)
9. Santiago (Chile)
10. Beef Wellington (New Zealand)

HIDDEN CITIES, page 49

1. Oslo
2. Lima
3. Rome
4. Athens
5. Turin
6. Berlin
7. Milan
8. Mobile
9. Nome
10. Mesa
11. Leon
12. Nice
13. Agra
14. Paris
15. Ulm
16. Reno
17. Riga

ISLAND HOPPING, page 50

1. Bali
2. Paul Gauguin
3. Madagascar
4. Sicily
5. Fantasy Island
6. Easter Island
7. *The Island of Dr. Moreau*
8. Mediterranean Sea
9. Hawaii (the "Big Island")
10. Borneo, in Southeast Asia
11. Amity Island
12. Cuba
13. Cyprus, Sicily, or Sardinia

WELL STATED, page 51

1. "Sweet Home Alabama"
2. "Washington Post March"
3. "Rocky Top" (Tennessee)
4. "Oklahoma!"
5. "My Old Kentucky Home"
6. "California Dreamin'"
7. "Deep in the Heart of Texas"
8. *Blue Hawaii*
9. "Massachusetts"
10. "New York State of Mind"
11. "O-Hi-O" (also called "Round on the End and High in the Middle")
12. "Montana Anna"

WHERE AM I?, page 52

1. The Taj Mahal
2. CN Tower, in Toronto, Canada
3. The Serengeti migration of some 2 million animals (and thousands of predators).
4. The Great Wall of China
5. The Galápagos Islands
6. Hadrian's Wall
7. The Gateway Arch in St. Louis, Missouri
8. In and around Hong Kong
9. Fiji
10. The Rock of Gibraltar

BABY, IT'S COLD OUTSIDE, page 53

1. Siberia
2. The South Pole
3. Minnesota
4. California
5. Greenland
6. Lapland
7. The Yukon
8. Point Barrow, Alaska
9. Chile
10. Nunavut

BAY WATCH, page 54

1. Acapulco Bay
2. Green Bay
3. Bay of Pigs
4. Canada
5. Tampa Bay
6. Chesapeake Bay
7. Hudson Bay Company
8. Bay of Biscay
9. Greenland
10. Monterey Bay
11. Botany Bay
12. Cape Cod Bay

HOT ROCKS, page 55

1. The Rock of Gibraltar
2. Ayers Rock
3. The Stone of Scone
4. Alcatraz
5. Devils Tower
6. The Blarney Stone
7. Plymouth Rock
8. The Rosetta Stone
9. El Capitan
10. Independence Rock
11. A meteorite

"G"EOGRAPHY, page 56

1. Gibraltar
2. Greeley
3. Guatemala
4. Galilee
5. Genoa
6. Gouda
7. Glasgow
8. Gdansk
9. Gettysburg
10. Guadalajara
11. Geneva
12. Georgetown

BIG, BIGGER, BIGGEST, page 57

1. Russia is nearly twice as big as Canada, the next largest.
2. Vatican City, at less than one-fifth of a square mile.
3. Asia, with Mount Everest at 29,035 feet.
4. Asia, with 3.6 billion people.
5. The United States, with 269 billionaires.
6. Asia, at 17.2 million square miles.
7. The Pacific Ocean, at about 64 million square miles.
8. The Caspian Sea, at 143,244 square miles.
9. Africa, with 53 countries.
10. Africa's Sahara measures 3,500,000 square miles.
11. The Pacific Ocean's Mariana Trench is 35,827 feet deep.
12. The Dead Sea in the Middle East (between Israel and Jordan) is 1,369 feet below sea level.

NEW NAME, SAME PLACE, page 58

1. Sri Lanka
2. Istanbul
3. Madagascar
4. Mali
5. Tanzania
6. Czech Republic and Slovakia
7. Canaan
8. Zambia and Zimbabwe
9. Botswana
10. Burkina Faso
11. Vanuatu
12. Thailand
13. East Pakistan

TITLE TOWNS, page 59

1. "I Left My Heart in San Francisco"
2. "The Little Old Lady from Pasadena"
3. Clarksville, Tennessee ("Last Train to Clarksville")
4. Phoenix ("By the Time I Get to Phoenix")
5. "Chicago"
6. "New York, New York"
7. "Viva Las Vegas"
8. "Philadelphia Freedom"
9. "The Battle of New Orleans"
10. Kansas City
11. El Paso
12. "The Night Chicago Died"

WHERE IN THE WORLD?, page 60

1. Egypt (the Great Pyramid)
2. China (Three Gorges Dam)
3. South America (Aconcagua in Argentina)
4. Bahamas (San Salvador)
5. Indonesia (Krakatoa and Tambora)
6. Venezuela (Angel Falls)
7. Chile
8. Asia (China's Taklamakan Desert)
9. Africa
10. Russia (Lake Bikal)
11. United Arab Emirates (the Burj Dubai in Dubai)
12. India

Answers

LIFE'S A BEACH, page 61

1. South Beach
2. Myrtle Beach
3. Daytona Beach
4. Laguna Beach
5. Miami Beach
6. Cocoa Beach
7. Malibu
8. Muscle Beach
9. Brighton Beach
10. Pebble Beach
11. Virginia Beach

BLESSED CITIES, page 62

1. San Juan Capistrano
2. San Diego Padres
3. San Andreas
4. St. Augustine, Florida
5. St. Petersburg
6. "St. Louis Blues"
7. San Clemente
8. San Simeon
9. San Antonio, Texas
10. San Francisco
11. St. Joseph

VIVE LA FRANCE!, page 63

1. Julienned
2. Coco Chanel
3. Francois Truffaut
4. The Statue of Liberty
5. "Dominique"
6. The Coneheads
7. Vermouth (It's German, although dry vermouth is sometimes called "French vermouth.")
8. St. Louis, Missouri
9. *Amélie*
10. Mayonnaise

HIT THE ROAD, page 64

1. The Autobahn
2. Rodeo Drive
3. Downing Street
4. Baker Street
5. Beale Street
6. Route 66
7. Fleet Street
8. Massachusetts Avenue
9. The Ginza
10. The "Alcan Highway"

PRESERVING PARKS, page 65

1. Yosemite
2. Banff (Canada)
3. Alligator Alley (Interstate 75)
4. The Great Barrier Reef
5. Serengeti National Park
6. The Alps
7. The Grand Canyon
8. Queen Elizabeth II
9. Edinburgh
10. Kilauea and Mauna Loa

UNREAL ESTATE, page 66

1. Bedrock
2. Brigadoon
3. South Park, CO
4. Skull Island
5. Atlantis
6. Lanford, IL
7. Lilliput
8. Utopia
9. Metropolis
10. Shangri-La
11. Castle Rock

UNCLE JOHN, page 67

1. Uncle Remus
2. John Deere
3. Uncle Sam
4. John Cusack
5. "Uncle!"
6. John Doe
7. *The Man from U.N.C.L.E.*
8. "Sloop John B"
9. Uncle Ben's
10. John Goodman
11. *Uncle Vanya*

THE SCOOP ON POOP, page 68

1. Queen Elizabeth I
2. Thomas Jefferson
3. Chicken droppings
4. Giant Swallowtail
5. Bat guano
6. Just one year
7. The scarab
8. Elephant dung
9. Camel dung
10. Bilirubin
11. Eating it
12. Kopi Luwak

GO WITH THE FLOW, page 69

1. *Mayflower*
2. Afterglow
3. Cauliflower
4. Feather pillow
5. Eiffel Tower
6. Fall off the wagon
7. Flavor of the week
8. *Cactus Flower*
9. Longfellow
10. Full-grown
11. Bedfellows
12. Buffalo, New York

THE STRAIGHT POOP, page 70

1. Reese Witherspoon
2. Winnie the Pooh
3. Harpooner
4. "Gag me with a spoon!"
5. Cesspool
6. Poodle
7. Spoonerism
8. Party pooper
9. *Harvard Lampoon*
10. Whiffenpoof
11. Poop sheet
12. Liverpool

THE THRONE ROOM, page 71

1. A baby alligator
2. Carroll O'Connor
3. *Ally McBeal*
4. *Babylon 5*
5. *Pulp Fiction*
6. You guessed it—it was flushed (though not with pride).
7. Old-fashioned pull-chain mechanism for the toilet.
8. *Psycho*
9. *Married . . . with Children*
10. Dick Solomon played by John Lithgow on *3rd Rock from the Sun*.

CLOSE ENCOUNTERS OF THE TURD KIND, page 72

1. Toto
2. SaTURDay!
3. American Standard
4. "Where is the bathroom?"
5. Fart
6. 119
7. Scott Paper Company
8. Johnny Carson
9. Toilet paper
10. Charmin

PORCELAIN SWAN SONGS, page 73

1. 1977
2. Evelyn Waugh
3. Heroin
4. Agamemnon
5. He gets eaten by a Tyrannosaurus rex.
6. He was Edmund "the Ironsides"
7. Vivien Leigh
8. The French Revolution
9. Tycho Brahe

PATRIOT GAME, page 74

1. Thomas Jefferson
2. Alexander Hamilton
3. James Monroe
4. John Hancock
5. John Quincy Adams
6. Benjamin Franklin
7. Jefferson & Madison
8. Samuel Adams
9. John Adams
10. James Madison
11. Thomas Paine

THE WINDY CITY, page 75

1. Blues and jazz
2. The West Side
3. The Sears Tower, completed in 1974
4. The Cubs, White Sox, Bears, Bulls, and Blackhawks
5. Al Capone
6. The Great Chicago Fire
7. The Second City
8. *ER*
9. Shel Silverstein
10. The 1968 Democratic Convention

AS AMERICAN AS . . ., page 76

1. Casey Jones
2. *American Gothic*
3. Barbed wire
4. The diner; *Diner*
5. The 37-foot-high left field wall is made of iron.
6. Route 66
7. Burma-Shave
8. Norman Rockwell
9. "Casey at the Bat"
10. The Gunfight at the O.K. Corral

CALIFORNIA DREAMIN', page 77

1. Grizzly bear
2. San Diego
3. Mount Whitney
4. Yosemite National Park and Kings Canyon and Sequoia National Parks (the latter two parks are adjacent and administered as one unit)
5. "Snowy range"
6. Huntington Beach
7. Death Valley National Park
8. Nevada, Arizona, and Oregon
9. Los Angeles County
10. San Francisco
11. The University of California
12. Hearst Castle

THE STATE ON YOUR PLATE, page 78

1. Hawaii
2. Kentucky
3. Arkansas
4. Wyoming
5. Maine
6. Alabama
7. Mississippi
8. Missouri
9. New Mexico
10. South Dakota
11. South Carolina
12. Virginia

ALL ABOUT ALASKA, page 79

1. 1959
2. Canada's Yukon Territory and British Columbia
3. *Exxon Valdez*
4. The Bering Strait
5. Jewel Kilcher
6. Anchorage
7. The Trans-Alaska Pipeline System; it carries oil.
8. Mount McKinley
9. Caribou, or reindeer
10. Diptheria

WE LOVE NEW YORK, page 80

1. Manhattan, Brooklyn, the Bronx, Queens, Staten Island
2. Henry Hudson
3. Harlem (The Harlem Renaissance)
4. A mandatory draft imposed by the U.S. Congress to conscript soldiers into the Union Army during the Civil War.
5. Joe DiMaggio
6. Radio City Music Hall
7. In the 17th century, Wall Street was a 12-foot-high defensive wall. It formed the northern boundary of New Amsterdam.
8. *Rent*
9. Fashion Week
10. Ed Koch

STATES OF THE UNION, page 81

1. West Virginia
2. Kentucky
3. Nevada
4. Pennsylvania
5. Hawaii
6. Missouri (Gateway Arch)
7. North Dakota
8. Virginia
9. South Dakota
10. New Jersey
11. New Mexico
12. Wyoming

WHAT'S IN A PRESIDENT'S NAME?, page 82

1. Walker (George Herbert Walker Bush and George Walker Bush)
2. Rudolph
3. F. Scott Fitzgerald
4. Richard Milhous Nixon and Milhouse Van Houten
5. William Howard Taft
6. Quincy (John Quincy Adams)
7. Knox
8. (James Earl) Carter & Ray
9. David (Henry David Thoreau and Dwight David Eisenhower)
10. William Jefferson Clinton and Thomas Jefferson
11. President William Henry Harrison and American Revolutionary hero Patrick Henry

ALOHA!, page 83

1. Captain James Cook from Great Britain
2. He called them the Sandwich Islands in honor of the noble who had financed his expedition, the Earl of Sandwich.
3. There are eight islands: Oahu, Hawaii (the Big Island), Kauai, Maui, Molokai, Nihau, Kahoolawe, and Lanai.
4. Don Ho
5. Queen Lili'uokalani
6. Duke Kahanamoku
7. Hawaiian Pidgin (also called Hawaii Creole English)
8. Pearl Harbor
9. King Kamehameha the Great (or King Kamehameha I)
10. Bonzai Pipeline

PARTICULARLY PENNSYLVANIA, page 84

1. Erie
2. Hershey
3. Phil (the Groundhog)
4. Philadelphia
5. Johnstown
6. The Atlantic Ocean
7. Rocky Balboa
8. Pittsburgh
9. York
10. Slinky
11. Delaware River
12. Delaware

MADE IN AMERICA, page 85

1. Samuel Colt developed the Colt revolver, or "six-shooter."
2. Benjamin Franklin
3. The television
4. DuPont
5. Nuclear submarine
6. Windshield wipers
7. Air conditioner
8. Dry cleaning. It was invented (accidentally) in 1855. Blue jeans were patented in 1873.
9. The safety pin
10. Skyscraper; the building was 10 stories tall.
11. The laser

GEORGIA ON MY MIND, page 86

1. Georgia, the country on the Black Sea
2. The Harlem Globetrotters
3. Georgia Gibbs; "Her Nibs, Miss Gibbs"
4. Georgia O'Keeffe
5. Florida
6. Strait of George, aka the Gulf of Georgia
7. "Georgia On My Mind"
8. Alice Walker
9. Ty Pennington
10. Okefenokee Swamp
11. A soul

THE PRESIDENT'S INN, page 87

1. John Quincy Adams
2. British soldiers
3. Abigail Adams
4. 35
5. The clothes closet off the presidential office
6. Abraham Lincoln
7. Harry S. Truman
8. Benjamin Harrison
9. Theodore Roosevelt
10. *Dave*
11. George Washington
12. Rosalynn Carter

DON'T MESS WITH TEXAS, page 88

1. Mexico
2. Oil
3. Stephen F. Austin
4. Houston (more than 16,000 seats)
5. "The Yellow Rose of Texas"
6. Dallas
7. Big Tex
8. The Alamo
9. Jack Johnson
10. Bonnie Parker and Clyde Barrow

STAR-SPANGLED PAST, page 89

1. The Smithsonian Institution
2. *The Feminine Mystique*
3. Moonshine, or home-distilled alcohol
4. Pocahontas
5. Haight-Ashbury, or "The Haight"
6. Missouri
7. Matthew Brady
8. Kansas
9. Wounded Knee Massacre
10. The Whiskey Rebellion
11. Yellowstone
12. Theodore Roosevelt and Woodrow Wilson

BORN IN THE USA, page 90

1. Bob Dylan
2. Grandma Moses
3. Chuckwagon
4. "The Raven"
5. Pony Express
6. Rodeo
7. Zippo lighter
8. *The Grapes of Wrath*
9. Pop art
10. Mark Twain
11. Harriet Tubman

COWBOY STATE OF MIND, page 91

1. Yellowstone National Park
2. Devils Tower National Monument, featured prominently in Steven Spielberg's *Close Encounters of the Third Kind*
3. E. Annie Proulx
4. J.C. Penney
5. It's the largest coal producer in the U.S.
6. Bucking bronco
7. Dick Cheney
8. Well . . . Cody, Wyoming!
9. It was the first state to allow women the right to vote.
10. A jackalope
11. Wyomingites
12. Matthew Fox (plays Dr. Jack Shephard)
13. The bison

THE SUNSHINE STATE, page 92

1. Juan Ponce de León
2. Everglades National Park, Dry Tortugas National Park, and Biscayne National Park
3. John F. Kennedy; the site is the Kennedy Space Center.
4. Key West
5. The University of Florida and Florida State University
6. Vice President Al Gore
7. Walt Disney World
8. Little Havana
9. Snow
10. Hollywood

TEED OFF, page 93

1. A caddy
2. The fairway
3. Ko'olau Golf Course
4. Eldrick "Tiger" Woods
5. 80 mph; 84 mph is the average
6. "Babe Didrikson" Zaharias
7. They both have dimples.
8. Jack Nicklaus
9. Arnold Palmer (Arnie's army)
10. A golf club
11. Crocodiles

FEELING PUCKISH?, page 94

1. The USA and the USSR
2. Falling on it.
3. Wayne Gretzky
4. *Slapshot*
5. *Morrie*
6. The Montreal Canadiens
7. The New York Rangers
8. She was the first woman to play for the NHL.
9. Three
10. A fight
11. The penalty box
12. Finland

BASES LOADED, page 95

1. Hoboken
2. Yankee Stadium
3. Ty Cobb
4. Yogi Berra
5. Japan
6. Lou Gehrig
7. The Montreal Royals
8. Felipe
9. Tommie
10. The New York Giants
11. The 1994 baseball strike

IT'S HALL IN THE GAME, page 96

1. Canton, OH
2. Ice hockey
3. The International Boxing Hall of Fame
4. Baseball and soccer
5. Bicycling
6. NASCAR
7. Golf
8. Swimming
9. Pro wrestling
10. Volleyball

WOMEN ARE GOOD SPORTS, page 97

1. Mildred "Babe" Didrikson Zaharias
2. Susan B. Anthony
3. Soar in a hot air balloon
4. Venus and Serena Williams
5. Women's World Cup in soccer
6. Annette Kellerman
7. Gymnastics
8. Jackie Joyner-Kersee
9. Women's figure skating
10. Hayley Wickenheiser

ALL ABOARD!, page 98

1. Surfboards
2. Snowboarding
3. The Boogie Board
4. Windsurfing (or sailboarding)
5. Skateboarding
6. A wakeboard
7. Skateboarding
8. Windsurf board or sailboard
9. Surfing
10. Snowboarding

HOOPLA, page 99

1. Michael Jordan
2. March
3. Wilt Chamberlain
4. Dr. James Naismath
5. *Hoosiers*
6. Earvin "Magic" Johnson (Michigan State) and Larry Bird (Indiana State)
7. John Wooden
8. Dennis Rodman
9. *Hoop Dreams*
10. Boston Celtics

SPORTIN' LIFE, page 100

1. New York Yankees
2. Athens, Greece
3. Boarding
4. Quarterback
5. The Belmont Stakes
6. Yogi Berra
7. Hank Aaron's
8. Football
9. Traveling
10. "Tiger" Woods
11. Roger Federer

SPORTS TALK, page 101

1. Soccer
2. Boxing
3. Ice hockey
4. Tennis
5. Golf
6. Polo

7. Volleyball
8. Basketball
9. Rugby
10. Horse racing
11. Lacrosse

OFF TO THE RACES, page 102

1. The bugle
2. W. C. Fields
3. King Charles II of England
4. Eclipse
5. The steeplechase
6. Dick Francis

7. Secretariat
8. George Washington
9. Julie Krone
10. Quarter horse
11. *Seabiscuit*
12. Dubai

MORE SPORTIN' LIFE, page 103

1. Soccer
2. Tour de France
3. Plato
4. Rugby
5. Tennis
6. Soccer

7. *Alice In Wonderland*
8. Fencing
9. Notre Dame
10. Judo
11. "We Are the Champions"
12. The Philadelphia Phillies

VICTORY WITH DE FEET, page 104

1. The World Cup
2. Ronaldo Luis Nazário de Lima, or Ronaldo
3. Cambridge
4. Charles Goodyear
5. Pelé

6. Brazil
7. Iraq
8. David Beckham
9. Mia Hamm
10. Robocup

WHAT A RACKET!, page 105

1. Play!
2. King Henry VIII
3. The Wimbledon Championships
4. Zero points
5. Billie Jean King
6. Caravaggio
7. Pete Sampras
8. Arthur Ashe
9. The Davis Cup
10. John McEnroe
11. Katherine Hepburn
12. The French Open

TACKLE THIS, page 106

1. Harvard
2. Baseball
3. Theodore Roosevelt
4. Odessa, Texas
5. Jerry Rice
6. Joe Namath
7. Bud Wilkinson
8. Walter Payton
9. *Remember the Titans*
10. The Rose Bowl
11. John Madden

EENY, MEENY, MINY, MOE!, page 107

1. Hide-and-Seek
2. Red Rover
3. Hopscotch
4. Marco Polo
5. Tag
6. Kickball
7. Dodgeball
8. Four Square
9. Red Light, Green Light
10. Marbles

IT'S BOXING DAY, page 108

1. Rome
2. James Figg
3. Marquess (or Marquis) of Queensberry Rules
4. Four
5. Jack Dempsy
6. Max Schmeling
7. In Zaire, now known as the Democratic Rep. of the Congo
8. Joe Louis
9. Sugar Ray Robinson
10. Robert De Niro
11. 110 rounds
12. Sumya Anani

GOLD FEVER, page 109

1. Greece
2. Clothes
3. Baron Pierre de Coubertin
4. Women
5. Jesse Owens
6. Giant hornet stomach juice
7. Mark Spitz
8. Muhammad Ali
9. 18
10. Finland
11. *Chariots of Fire*

AAARGH!, page 110

1. "Bloody Red" or red
2. Cape Cod
3. Disneyland and Disney World
4. Mark Twain
5. She was a woman.
6. *The Pirates of Penzance*
7. Blackbeard, or Edward Teach
8. Captain Kidd, or William Kidd
9. *Treasure Island*
10. Henry Morgan
11. St. Augustine's harbor
12. *Seabourn Spirit*

IT HAPPENED IN 1800, page 111

1. Philadelphia
2. Charles Goodyear
3. Volt
4. France
5. Library of Congress
6. Smallpox
7. Napoléon Bonaparte
8. John Adams
9. They were hanged.
10. Ottawa

WAR! WHAT IS IT GOOD FOR?, page 112

1. Man O'War
2. "War is hell."
3. Warts
4. Warren Zevon
5. Warlock
6. Anwar al Sadat
7. The War Room
8. Warren Buffett
9. John Warner
10. Portuguese Man O' War
11. Daddy Warbucks

1900s: BY THE DECADE, page 113

1. Hawaii
2. Jim Thorpe
3. Dorothy Parker
4. 1939
5. Dwight D. Eisenhower
6. The Warsaw Pact
7. Jean Louise "Scout" Finch
8. The first successful test tube (in vitro) baby
9. The space shuttle *Challenger* explosion (January 28, 1986) and the launch of the Soviet space station *Mir* (February 19, 1986)
10. Madeleine Albright

THE WORLD'S WORST, page 114

1. None—this was its first voyage.
2. *The Unsinkable Molly Brown*
3. A zeppelin
4. The U-Boat attacks. Between January and the summer of 1942, they sank 82 ships and half a million tons of cargo.
5. The *Edmund Fitzgerald*
6. 87
7. Japan Airlines
8. A tsunami
9. Casey Jones
10. *Airplane!*

CURSES!, page 115

1. Sleeping Beauty
2. The darkness
3. The Boston Red Sox
4. King Tut or Tutankhamun
5. *Macbeth*
6. Marie Antoinette
7. China
8. James Dean
9. The Bermuda Triangle
10. The evil eye

HEADACHES, page 116

1. David
2. The Queen of Hearts and *Alice in Wonderland*
3. Richard III
4. Salome
5. Judith
6. Dr. Joseph Ignace Guillotin (the guillotine)
7. Adolf Hitler
8. *The Legend of Sleepy Hollow*
9. Henry VIII
10. Sir Walter Raleigh

DOING BATTLE, page 117

1. Gettysburg
2. Waterloo
3. William the Bastard
4. "The Charge of the Light Brigade"
5. Bunker Hill
6. The marathon
7. Iwo Jima
8. The Battle of the Somme
9. The French
10. The Lunar New Year

A ROYAL MESS, page 118

1. Queen Mary
2. Prince Rainer
3. A passenger elevator
4. *The Affair of the Necklace*
5. King Charles II
6. The Bahamas
7. Agrippina
8. Mary Queen of Scots
9. Prince Albert
10. Sarah Ferguson

BANKS AND ROBBERS, page 119

1. Wall Street
2. The Confederacy
3. Charles Arthur Floyd or Pretty Boy Floyd
4. Clyde Barrow of Bonnie and Clyde
5. "Ma" Barker or Kate Barker
6. The Central Bank of Iraq
7. Frank James
8. *The Lavender Hill Mob*
9. Ronnie Leibowitz returned the stolen money.
10. From the sewers

LET'S PLAY FAMILY FEUD!, page 120

1. The Hatfields and the McCoys
2. Joseph
3. Joan Fontaine and Olivia De Haviland
4. Lennon
5. The Campbells
6. The Taj Mahal
7. Thomas Jefferson
8. California wine
9. The throne of England
10. Celtic mythology

HISTORY'S MYSTERIES, page 121

1. Atlantis
2. Jack the Ripper
3. Anastasia
4. Christopher Columbus
5. *The Man in the Iron Mask*
6. The *Mary Celeste*
7. Nessie or the Loch Ness Monster
8. In Kenya
9. Jimmy Hoffa
10. Sir Francis Drake

LOST!, page 122

1. India
2. Amelia Earhart
3. From New York to California
4. Hansel and Gretel
5. The Nile
6. Oceanic 815
7. The Northwest Passage
8. China
9. New Jersey
10. George Mallory
11. Antoine de Saint-Exupery

HOW DARE THEY?, page 123

1. Watergate
2. Bob Woodward and Carl Bernstein
3. Alexander Hamilton
4. Aaron Burr
5. Mark Twain
6. Rome
7. Imelda Marcos
8. Nancy Reagan
9. His mother
10. Great Britain

THAT'S NO LADY, page 124

1. The Borgias
2. Pirate
3. Witchcraft
4. Lizzie Borden
5. Velma Barfield
6. Rob a stagecoach
7. *Basic Instinct*
8. Tokyo Rose
9. Retaining her youth and beauty
10. Myra Maybelle Shirley (Belle Star)

WHERE IS IT?, page 125

1. Erwin Rommel
2. Mark Twain
3. Captain Kidd
4. The money pit or the treasure pit
5. A hurricane
6. The Confederate States of America
7. *Raiders of the Lost Ark* and *The Last Crusade*
8. The Declaration of Independence
9. The Incas
10. Rare books or manuscripts

ON TRIAL, page 126

1. The Nuremberg Trials
2. Perry Mason
3. The Black Sox Trial
4. The theory of evolution
5. Nelson Mandela
6. *The Verdict*
7. Integration
8. Socrates
9. Anna Nicole Smith
10. Gloria Vanderbilt

REMEMBRANCE OF THINGS PAST, page 127

1. Boston Tea Party
2. Franklin D. Roosevelt
3. Rosa Parks
4. The Korean War
5. West
6. The Mediterranean Sea
7. Ponce de León
8. The Red Cross
9. Democracy
10. Crispus Attucks
11. Kemal Atatürk
12. Appomattox Courthouse

PETER, PAUL, AND MERRY, page 128

1. (Saint) Peter
2. Merry-go-round
3. Paul Cézanne
4. Peter the Great (aka Peter I)
5. Merry Men
6. Les Paul
7. Lord Peter Wimsey
8. The Merry Monarch (from the liveliness and hedonism of his court)
9. Peter Paul Rubens
10. The Peter and Paul Fortress
11. The Merry Pranksters
12. Jean-Paul Sartre

RANDOM ACTS OF HISTORY, page 129

1. March 15
2. Iraq
3. The Berlin Wall
4. Marie Antoinette
5. The Great Fire of London
6. Paul Klee
7. She was the first woman to swim the English Channel.
8. Africa
9. Leonardo da Vinci
10. Estonia, Latvia, and Lithuania
11. The Holy Roman Empire

FIRST LADIES, page 130

1. Lucy, the oldest known hominid
2. Pandora
3. The Amazons
4. Nefertiti
5. Penelope
6. Japan
7. Sappho
8. Jezebel
9. Vietnam
10. Lysistrata

THE USUAL SUSPECTS, page 131

1. *The Manchurian Candidate*
2. The Joker (*Batman*)
3. The Wicked Witch of the West (*The Wizard of Oz*)
4. Hannibal Lector (*The Silence of the Lambs*)
5. Lex Luthor (*Superman*)
6. Cruella de Vil (*101 Dalmations*)
7. Professor Moriarty (*Sherlock Holmes*)
8. Dr. Fu Manchu
9. Dolores Umbridge (*Harry Potter*)
10. *Die Hard*

WHAT'S HER NAME?, page 132

1. *Exxon Valdez*
2. *Santa Maria*
3. *Andrea Doria*
4. *Kon Tiki*
5. USS *Arizona*
6. HMAV *Bounty*
7. USS *Maine*
8. *Queen Mary*
9. HMS *Britannic*
10. The *Clermont*

QUARTER BACKS, page 133

1. "The First State"
2. A racehorse
3. New Jersey
4. Pennsylvania
5. Tennessee
6. Louisiana
7. Kansas
8. Maine
9. Orville & Wilbur Wright
10. Utah
11. Founding of Jamestown
12. Alabama
13. Arkansas

TO ERR IS DIVINE, page 134

1. The Post-it Note
2. The Slinky
3. Coca-Cola
4. Hard pretzels
5. Ivory soap
6. Silly Putty
7. Velcro
8. Frisbee
9. The X-ray
10. Potato chips

NATIVE SONS, page 135

1. Pontiac
2. Sitting Bull
3. Squanto
4. Sequoias
5. Geronimo
6. Chief Joseph
7. Cochise
8. Jim Thorpe
9. Jay Silverheels
10. Hiawatha

KEEP THE FAITH!, page 136

1. Thor, the god of thunder and war
2. *The Kitchen God's Wife*
3. Islam
4. Christianity (Islam is second, at 20.28%)
5. Hare Krishna
6. Kokopelli
7. Mezuzah
8. Martin Luther
9. Rastafarianism
10. Angels
11. Jehovah's Witnesses

THAT'S SO FIVE CENTURIES AGO!, page 137

1. Nothing!
2. White lead
3. In Ancient Rome
4. Benjamin Franklin
5. Pantaloons
6. Belladonna
7. Kilts
8. The bustle
9. To hide a scar on her neck
10. Plato
11. To powder their wigs

CURSED KING HENRY, page 138

1. Ferdinand and Isabella
2. Anne Boleyn
3. Anne of Cleves
4. Having an affair
5. Gout
6. Childbirth
7. Anne Boleyn
8. Bloody Mary
9. Elizabeth I
10. Thomas Cromwell

THEY RULED!, page 139

1. Mikhail Gorbachev
2. Anwar Al Sadat (Egypt) and Menachem Begin (Israel)
3. Francisco Franco
4. Indira Ghandi
5. Winston Churchill
6. Emperor Showa Hirohito
7. Margaret Thatcher
8. Golda Meir
9. Fidel Castro
10. Charles de Gaulle

BATTLE CRY, page 140

1. The Battle of Britain
2. The First Battle of Bull Run
3. *All Quiet on the Western Front* by Erich Maria Remarque
4. "Nuts!"
5. Kurt Vonnegut
6. Trafalgar Square
7. Attila the Hun
8. William Henry Harrison
9. Hannibal

OH, MUMMY, page 141

1. Pearls
2. The heart
3. It's the only one still standing.
4. A lion
5. The Alexandria lighthouse
6. George Herbert
7. A broken leg
8. Queen Nefertiti
9. A pregnancy test
10. The Mediterranean Sea

THE CRUSADES, page 142

1. The Turks or Seljuk Turks
2. Pope Urban II
3. Peter the Hermit
4. Hungary
5. Heaven
6. Muslims and Jews
7. Eleanor of Aquitaine
8. Constantinople
9. Thoroughbreds
10. Richard I or Richard the Lionhearted

FOUND!, page 143

1. Lucy
2. Controversy surrounds the authenticity of The Shroud of Turin—whether it's an actual burial cloth or a manmade forgery—and if it is authentic, whose image is depicted.
3. Elizabeth Smart
4. *The Mona Lisa.* When it was stolen, one of the persons brought in for questioning was Pablo Picasso.
5. She was a woman.
6. The Dead Sea Scrolls
7. The Rosetta Stone
8. Author Roald Dahl based the character of the grand-mother in his story "The Witches" on his mother as a tribute to her.
9. Polio
10. *The Merrimack*

WHAT'S THIS QUIZ ABOUT, EH?, page 144

1. Lillehammer, Norway
2. Bethlehem
3. Beehive
4. Nehemiah
5. Behemoth
6. Mehitabel
7. Moosehead Breweries Limited
8. Hedgehog
9. *Heehaw*
10. "Auf wiedersehen!"

UP NORTH, page 145

1. Canada's "Nessie" is called the Ogopogo monster, a large serpentlike creature that reportedly lives in Okanagan Lake, near Kelowna, in British Columbia.
2. The TV series was *Dawson's Creek*; the Canadian city is Dawson Creek. No relation.
3. At the Dynamic Earth science museum in Greater Sudbury, Ontario. It's a 30-foot replica of a 1951 Canadian nickel.
4. Cavendish, where author Lucy Maud Montgomery grew up. Her Green Gables farmhouse is a popular tourist attraction.
5. Timmins, Ontario
6. The Bay of Fundy, and Ungava Bay
7. The Washington Nationals
8. Victoria, British Columbia, one of the province's sunniest cities
9. Moose Javians
10. Winnipeg, the capital of Manitoba. The windy intersection is the corner of Portage and Main.
11. Ottawa, Canada's capital
12. The beaver

O CANADA!, page 146

1. English and French
2. One—Ottawa
3. "Canada"
4. Red and white
5. "From sea to sea"
6. "God Save the Queen"
7. Oil
8. Lacrosse
9. Boston Pizza
10. Halifax
11. Tim Hortons
12. Three territories—Yukon, Northwest Territories, and Nunavut

IN THE PROVINCES AND THE TERRITORIES, page 147

1. Alberta
2. Manitoba, Saskatchewan, and Alberta
3. Quebec
4. Ontario, Quebec, New Brunswick, and Nova Scotia
5. Ontario
6. Yukon Territory
7. Mackenzie River, in Northwest Territories.
8. New Brunswick, at Moncton.
9. Newfoundland and Labrador
10. Prince Edward Island
11. Iqaluit
12. Alberta

NORTH STARS, page 148

1. Canadian cultural icon Don Cherry, hockey commentator, former coach, sometime curmudgeon and general superstar
2. Samuel Bronfman
3. Cirque du Soleil
4. James Cameron, *Titanic*
5. Tim Horton
6. Gordon Lightfoot
7. Evangeline Lilly
8. Steve Christie
9. Jack Warner (cofounder of Warner Bros.)
10. Fur trading
11. Jack Kent Cooke

O CANADIANS, page 149

1. Wayne Gretzky
2. Kenneth Thomson, worth about U.S. $19 billion
3. Frank Gehry
4. Karsh was a noted portrait photographer, especially known for his photo of Winston Churchill.
5. Speed skating
6. A neurologist, Bondar is also an astronaut, the first Canadian woman in space.
7. They were all born in Ontario.
8. Morley Safer, born in Toronto
9. Margaret Atwood
10. Bat Masterson
11. The Nobel Peace Prize, for his intervention in the Suez Crisis.
12. Lord Beaverbrook

NORTHERN HIGHLIGHTS, page 150

1. Three—Pacific, Atlantic, and Arctic
2. Whitehorse (Yukon Territory) and Yellowknife (Northwest Territories)
3. MB
4. The British monarch—as this is written, Queen Elizabeth II
5. Four—the Conservative Party, Liberal Party, New Democratic Party, and *Bloc Québécois*
6. Toronto (5.5 million) and Montreal (3.6 million)
7. Yonge Street, a whopping 1,178 miles from Toronto to Rainy River, Ontario, at the Minnesota border
8. Nunavut
9. In winter, a section of Canada's Rideau Canal in central Ottawa becomes officially the world's largest skating rink, equal to 90 Olympic hockey rinks.
10. Yonge Street
11. Nunavut, the newest territory as of 1999, is primarily tundra except for the far southwestern corner, but still has much beautiful scenery and wildlife.
12. The governor general
13. Mount Robson
14. Niagara Falls
15. Size

CHOCOLATE-COVERED QUIZ, page 151

1. Food of the gods
2. The Olmecs
3. Hernán Cortés
4. *Psycho*
5. Forrest Gump
6. The heart
7. The dog
8. Chocolate-chip cookies; the reasturant was the Toll House Inn.
9. Hawaii
10. Switzerland

THEM'S DRINKIN' WORDS, page 152

1. Vodka
2. Cognac
3. Rum and Coke
4. Gin
5. A worm
6. Ouzo
7. Scotch whiskey
8. Cranberry juice
9. Canadian whiskey
10. Tennessee
11. Gin, orange juice, vermouth
12. Gibson

SWEET TALK, page 153

1. Good & Plenty
2. M&M's
3. 5th Avenue
4. Jelly Belly
5. Cherry, lemon, lime, orange, licorice
6. Sky Bar
7. 3 Musketeers
8. Snickers
9. Cinnamon
10. 100 Grand
11. A Junior Mint

TV DINNERS, page 154

1. *The Addams Family*
2. *The Drew Carey Show*
3. The Fonz
4. Lieutenant Columbo
5. Laverne De Fazio on *Laverne & Shirley*
6. *The Beverly Hillbillies*
7. *Green Acres*
8. Homer Simpson
9. *Babylon 5*
10. *Home Improvement*

SAY CHEESE, page 155

1. Velveeta
2. Ray Romano
3. Stilton
4. Edam ("Made" spelled backward)
5. String cheese
6. Swiss cheese
7. Sheep
8. California
9. Feta
10. Norway
11. Parmesan
12. Cheddar

OUR DAILY BREAD, page 156

1. Tortilla
2. Corn bread
3. Challah
4. Sourdough
5. Bagels
6. Irish soda bread
7. Hush puppies
8. Boston brown bread
9. Stollen
10. Pumpernickel
11. Pita

TIME TO SPICE THINGS UP, page 157

1. Garlic
2. The vanilla bean
3. Yale
4. The Spice Islands
5. Salt
6. Anise
7. Sage
8. Cinnamon
9. Saffron
10. Hungary
11. India
12. Turmeric

HAIL TO THE CHEF, page 158

1. Shrimp on the barbie
2. "Skewer of meat" (in Persian)
3. Julia Child
4. Sous chef
5. Ho Chi Minh
6. *Who Is Killing the Great Chefs of Europe?*
7. Pastry chef
8. Surf and turf
9. White kidney beans
10. Dolphinfish (It's a fish, not a dolphin.)
11. Stuffed with ham and cheese

COUNTER INTELLIGENCE, page 159

1. Poached eggs on toast
2. A Dr Pepper with ice
3. Spaghetti
4. Salt and pepper
5. American cheese
6. Coffee with doughnuts
7. Beef stew
8. A banana split (with chocolate syrup)
9. The cook is backed up with too many orders.
10. A rare hamburger with onions and fries
11. Franks and beans
12. Spareribs (Eve was made from Adam's rib), a potato, and a salad on the side

BOOZE CLUES, page 160

1. Kahlúa
2. Frangelico
3. Drambuie
4. Absinthe
5. Jägermeister
6. Grand Marnier
7. Sambuca
8. Chambord Royale
9. Chartreuse
10. Goldschlager

JUNK FOOD FOR THOUGHT, page 161

1. Subway
2. Ruby Tuesday
3. Starbucks
4. Wendy's
5. In-N-Out Burger (1948), Burger King (1954), McDonald's (1955)
6. White Castle
7. Taco Bell
8. 11
9. *The Jungle*
10. In-N-Out Burger

WHAT'S FOR DINNER?, page 162

1. Macaroni and cheese
2. A plum
3. Clarence Birdseye
4. Spam
5. Jell-O
6. Fish sticks
7. 57 Varieties
8. They're types of Pepperidge Farm cookies.
9. I Can't Believe It's Not Butter!
10. The Twinkie defense

BEER BLAST, page 163

1. Corona
2. Heineken
3. Boston Beer Company
4. Schlitz
5. Foster's
6. St. Pauli Girl
7. Stroh's (shorts)
8. Guinness Stout
9. Yuengling
10. Rolling Rock
11. A brewster

Answers

EATING ABROAD, page 164

1. Scotland
2. Russia
3. Mole
4. Korea (North and South)
5. Moussaka
6. Pierogi
7. Germany
8. Austria
9. Ireland
10. Foie gras
11. Vegemite

POP QUIZ, page 165

1. Pepsi Cola
2. Diet Rite
3. Mello Yello
4. A&W
5. Royal Crown
6. Dr Pepper
7. Jolt
8. Alcohol
9. Mug
10. Moxie
11. Vernor's Ginger Ale

MANGEZ-VOUS FRANÇAIS?, page 166

1. Vinaigrette
2. French toast
3. Salt and pepper
4. Spinach
5. Butcher shop
6. Zinfandel; originally from Italy
7. The liver
8. Baguette
9. Crescent
10. Snails, steak with french fries, and ice cream
11. Cheese

THE COOKIE JAR, page 167

1. S'more
2. Lion, tiger, bear, elephant
3. Newton, referring to Fig Newtons
4. Twice-cooked, which is why biscotti are so nice and crisp.
5. Famous Chocolate Wafers
6. Biscuits
7. Molasses
8. Thin Mints
9. False; fortune cookies are an American invention.
10. Graham crackers
11. Oreos

EAT YOUR VEGGIES, page 168

1. Broccoli
2. Beets, rutabagas, turnips, radishes, parsnips
3. Cabbage
4. Arugula
5. Avocado
6. Potatoes, eggplant, tomatoes, sweet and hot peppers, tomatillos
7. Corn
8. Zucchini
9. Asparagus
10. Celery; the soda is called Cel-Ray.
11. Carrot

LADIES IN THE KITCHEN, page 169

1. Sara Lee
2. Mrs. Fields
3. Mrs. Butterworth
4. Tootsie Roll
5. False; she was invented in 1921 to "sign" the letters sent to consumers who participated in a Gold Medal Flour promotion.
6. Aunt Jemima
7. A&P (The Great Atlantic & Pacific Tea Company)
8. Pillsbury
9. Marie Callender
10. Margaret "Maggie" Rudkin

SUSHI, ANYONE?, page 170

1. Soybeans
2. Sake
3. Dried seaweed
4. Noodles
5. Dashi
6. Sushi is paired with vinegared rice; sashimi is raw fish without the rice.
7. Tempura
8. Teriyaki
9. Sumo wrestling
10. Mushrooms

BEYOND APPLES AND ORANGES, page 171

1. Breadfruit
2. Passion fruit
3. Kiwifruit
4. Kumquat
5. Carambola
6. False; they look slightly similar, and in some places people call papayas by the name "pawpaw," but the two fruits are botanically unrelated.
7. Durian
8. Lychee (or litchee, litchi, or leechee).
9. Pomegranate
10. Guava

OH, NUTS!, page 172

1. Pecans
2. Kola nuts
3. Pistachios
4. Chestnuts
5. Macadamia nuts
6. Pine nuts
7. Cashews
8. Hazelnuts
9. Almonds
10. Walnuts
11. Brazil nuts
12. Peanuts

NO MUGGLES HERE, page 173

1. A Squib
2. They are dentists.
3. Tom Marvolo Riddle
4. Parents: Molly and Arthur, Kids: Bill, Charlie, Percy, Fred, George, and Ginny
5. Norberta
6. Vincent Crabbe and Gregory Goyle
7. The Dementors
8. Bellatrix Lestrange was the torturer; the hospital is St. Mungo's Hospital for Magical Maladies and Injuries.
9. Gryffindor: Professor McGonagall
Hufflepuff: Professor Sprout
Ravenclaw: Professor Flitwick
Slytherin: Professor Snape
10. The Society for the Promotion of Elfish Welfare
11. He uses a fire spell to repell the Inferi, and they retreat into the lake.

STORYBOOK ROMANCE, page 174

1. *Gone with the Wind*
2. Count Dracula
3. Heathcliff (*Wuthering Heights*)
4. Darcy is pride, and Elizabeth is prejudice.
5. Becky Thatcher
6. Lady Chatterley
7. Spenser (of the Robert B. Parker series)
8. Edward Rochester
9. Pongo and Missis (of *101 Dalmatians*) are the only dalmatians in the quiz.
10. A dog (Macon's dog Edward)

FRAMED, page 175

1. *Mona Lisa*
2. James McNeill Whistler
3. Campbell soup cans
4. He was an inveterate thumb sucker, and his left thumb was discolored.
5. Jackson Pollock
6. Rembrandt
7. *Guernica*
8. Claude Monet
9. *Home Alone*
10. Moulin Rouge

DANCING MACHINES, page 176

1. Mikhail Baryshnikov
2. Savion Glover
3. Martha Graham
4. Arthur Murray
5. Debbie Allen
6. Gelsey Kirkland
7. Mata Hari
8. Gregory Hines
9. Rudolf Nureyev and Margot Fonteyn
10. Alvin Ailey (The company is the Alvin Ailey American Dance Theater.)

BANNED BOOKS, page 177

1. *Alice's Adventures in Wonderland*
2. *American Heritage Dictionary*
3. *Fahrenheit 451*
4. *Where the Sidewalk Ends*
5. *The Age of Reason*
6. *The Call of The Wild*
7. William Shakespeare
8. *Where's Waldo?*
9. *As I Lay Dying*
10. *The Lorax*

DANCING WITH THE STARS, page 178

1. Jerry (the mouse, as in *Tom and Jerry*)
2. Courtney Cox
3. A vacuum cleaner
4. "Opposites Attract"
5. *The Cosby Show*
6. "Cheek to Cheek"
7. John Travolta
8. "Twist and Shout"
9. "Aquarius/Let the Sunshine In"
10. Drew Barrymore

BUILDING BLOCKS, page 179

1. Fallingwater
2. Function
3. Classical Greek orders, or column types
4. Thomas Jefferson
5. I. M. Pei
6. Bauhaus
7. Ludwig Mies van der Rohe
8. Sir Christopher Wren
9. Maya Lin
10. Frank Gehry
11. Ziggurat

CULTURE VULTURES, page 180

1. St. Peter's Basilica (Vatican City)
2. Classical music
3. Marcel Duchamp
4. Madrid
5. Matthew Arnold
6. Auguste Rodin
7. Edgar Degas
8. Alliteration
9. William Shakespeare
10. Deconstruction
11. The Parthenon
12. Classical ballet

JUST ONE BOOK, page 181

1. Harper Lee, *To Kill a Mockingbird*
2. *A Confederacy of Dunces*
3. Margaret Mitchell
4. *The Picture of Dorian Gray*
5. *Contact*
6. Zelda Fitzgerald
7. Marcel Proust
8. *Black Beauty*
9. Emily
10. Karl Marx

PICTURE THIS, page 182

1. *National Geographic*
2. Demi Moore
3. Ansel Adams
4. Alfred Eisenstadt
5. O. J. Simpson
6. The Black Power salute
7. The U.S. Marine Corp Memorial, which depicts the raising of the American flag at Iwo Jima.
8. He was never identified.
9. Anne Geddes
10. Annie Leibovitz
11. Henri Cartier-Bresson

FAMOUS FIRST LINES, page 183

1. *Moby Dick*, Herman Melville
2. *A Tale of Two Cities*, Charles Dickens
3. *Anna Karenina*, Leo Tolstoy
4. *Fahrenheit 451*, Ray Bradbury
5. *One Flew Over the Cuckoo's Nest*, Ken Kesey
6. *Peter Pan*, J. M. Barrie
7. *The Metamorphosis*, Franz Kafka
8. *Watership Down*, Richard Adams
9. *The Stranger*, Albert Camus
10. *The Divine Comedy, Inferno*, Dante Alighieri
11. *Slaughterhouse-Five*, Kurt Vonnegut
12. *Waiting for Godot*, Samuel Beckett
13. *Notes From the Underground*, Fyodor Dostoevsky
14. *Pride and Prejudice*, Jane Austen
15. *Cat's Cradle*, Kurt Vonnegut

FIRST REJECTED—NOW COLLECTED, page 184

1. *Harry Potter and the Philosopher's Stone*
2. Agatha Christie
3. *The Day of the Jackal*
4. *The Fountainhead*
5. Dr. Seuss
6. *Zen and the Art of Motorcycle Maintenance*
7. *The Hunt for Red October*
8. James Patterson
9. John Grisham
10. *Lust for Life*

WRIGHT STUFF, page 185

1. The carport
2. Lincoln Logs
3. The Prairie Houses are credited as the first examples of an "open floor plan."
4. *The Fountainhead*
5. Taliesin I, II, III, and Taliesin West were Wright's personal homes, and Taliesin was an early Welsh poet.
6. The Usonian houses were single-story homes that used radiant floor heat and had no basements or garages.
7. Organic Architecture
8. Fallingwater
9. SC Johnson Building in Racine, Wisconsin
10. The Guggenheim Museum

DOUBLE TROUBLE, page 186

1. Agent 86 (Maxwell Smart) and Agent 99 (whose real name was never revealed)
2. Frank and Joe Hardy
3. Lieutenant Joe Leaphorn and Officer Jim Chi
4. Magnum, P. I. and Higgins
5. Nick and Nora Charles, *The Thin Man*
6. Hercule Poirot
7. Inspector Lynley
8. Nero Wolfe and Archie Goodwin
9. Stephanie Plum
10. Charlie Chan and Number One Son

THE PLAY'S THE THING, page 187

1. *The Producers*
2. *Cabaret*
3. *Mamma Mia!*
4. *My Fair Lady*
5. *Oklahoma!*
6. *A Chorus Line*
7. *The Sunshine Boys*
8. *Spamalot*
9. *Wicked*
10. *Hair*
11. *Spring Awakening*

LITERARY BRAIN TEASERS, page 188

1. Alexander Graham Bell
2. Rosinante (horse), Dapple (donkey)
3. Being an Axis collaborator; he made broadcasts for the enemy from Italy.
4. Liza Minelli
5. "Have a son"
6. J.D. Salinger. The book is *Catcher in the Rye.*
7. Carlo Collodi
8. A dog named Spot and a cat named Puff.
9. They were silver.
10. *Uncle Tom's Cabin* by Harriet Beecher Stow

BOOK LEARNIN', page 189

1. A heffalump (Heffalumps make their appearance later, though, in Pooh movies.)
2. *Paradise Lost* (John Milton)
3. Woodcutter
4. *Lost Horizon*
5. Beatrice
6. Goethe
7. Nancy Drew
8. Lord Byron; it's the first line of his 1814 poem, "She Walks in Beauty."
9. *The Leatherstocking Tales*
10. Washington Irving
11. Cervantes' *Don Quixote*
12. Samuel Taylor Coleridge

PLAY RIGHTS, page 190

1. Oedipus
2. *Death of a Salesman*
3. *Our Town*
4. *Pygmalion*
5. Prostitute
6. 12
7. Faust
8. *Taming of the Shrew*
9. *The Glass Menagerie*
10. Cyrano de Bergerac

WRITE ON, page 191

1. The Dewey Decimal Classification System
2. A Latin Bible
3. *Epic of Gilgamesh*
4. *Tale of Genji*
5. The Bible
6. *Casino Royale*
7. Sumerians
8. He wrote his English dictionary that, while not the first, was the most meticulously researched, and the most comprehensive to date.
9. The Library of Congress
10. Endpapers or endsheets

TEST YOUR METAL, page 192

1. Copper
2. Zinc
3. Silver Screen
4. A bullet
5. Shakespeare
6. Stick to it
7. Mercury
8. Platinum
9. Copper
10. Gold
11. Aluminum

WHAT'S UP, DOC?, page 193

1. Aspirin
2. India
3. High blood pressure
4. Chloroform
5. Insulin
6. Ulcers
7. Penicillin
8. Handwashing
9. Birth-control pill
10. It was the first successful heart transplant.

SUBSTANCE ABUSE, page 194

1. Plato
2. Oxygen
3. Half-life
4. Helium
5. Carbon
6. Gold
7. Silver
8. The bends (decompression sickness)
9. Platinum
10. Lead

BODY LANGUAGE, page 195

1. Neck
2. Finger
3. Elbow
4. Hip
5. Sole
6. Heel
7. Back
8. Chest
9. Head
10. Toe
11. Shoulder
12. Foot
13. Knee

GETTING BETTER ALL THE TIME, page 196

1. Harriet the Galápagos tortoise
2. "Lucy in the Sky with Diamonds"
3. Richard Owen
4. Canadian Arctic
5. Intelligent design
6. Louis Leaky
7. Geico
8. *The Origin of Species*
9. William Jennings Bryan
10. Birds
11. Gregor Mendel

KEYS TO THE GEEKDOM, page 197

1. The Internet
2. *2001: A Space Odyssey*
3. Chess
4. Flying toasters (a screensaver)
5. Issac Asimov
6. The Furby
7. Apple Computers
8. *The Return of the King*
9. Nintendo
10. *The Matrix*
11. Video game

MOTHER NATURE GETS TOUGH, page 198

1. An earthquake
2. Mt. St. Helens
3. An asteroid
4. An earthquake
5. It becomes a tornado.
6. Volcanic eruptions
7. Spanish influenza
8. An avalanche
9. *The Perfect Storm*
10. The Hwang Ho or Yellow River

STARRY, STARRY QUIZ, page 199

1. Pegasus
2. Sirius, or Dog Star
3. Vincent Van Gogh
4. Venus
5. Milky Way
6. Betelgeuse
7. *Star Wars*

8. Oscar Wilde
9. In the Earth's atmosphere
10. 5 billion
11. Red
12. Jiminy Cricket
13. 1969

MEDICAL EXAM, page 200

1. In your gut
2. The vagus nerve
3. 206
4. Stem cells
5. Elbow
6. The foot
7. Pancreas

8. Circadian rhythm
9. Synovial fluid
10. Outside the body—it's the skin.
11. Muscles
12. The teeth

TIN MEN AND WOMEN, page 201

1. Housekeeper
2. Vacuuming
3. Gauri Nanda
4. Mars
5. *The Terminator*
6. Leonardo da Vinci

7. A dog
8. Automobiles
9. Adam Smith
10. A humanoid or android
11. Czech
12. Conducted it

ELEMENTARY, MY DEAR WATSON, page 202

1. Blood
2. Forensic entomologists
3. G. K. Chesterton
4. The FBI
5. Archimedes

6. DNA evidence
7. *CSI* Effect or *CSI* Syndrome
8. Fingerprints
9. Bruno Maglis
10. Bite marks

ALL ABOUT ANATOMY, page 203

1. The femur, or thighbone
2. Kneecap
3. Veins
4. Carotid
5. The sole of the foot
6. Adam's apple
7. Tissue
8. Endocrine system
9. The epiglottis
10. Dr. Alfred Kinsey
11. Radius and ulna
12. In the ear

AT THE SCIENCE FAIR, page 204

1. Backbone (or spine)
2. Nothing—it's darkened.
3. Metamorphosis
4. Molars
5. Viruses
6. Heavier on the earth, which is larger, so the force of gravity is stronger.
7. Lever (It provides leverage.)
8. Fossil fuels
9. Omnivore
10. Newtons (All forces are measured in newtons, or N for short.)
11. Chemistry
12. Humus
13. 12; there are 6 on each side of mouth.

THAT'S MY INVENTION, page 205

1. (Ferdinand Von) Zeppelin
2. (Richard J.) Gatling
3. (King C.) Gillette
4. (Rudolf) Diesel
5. (Adolphe) Sax
6. (Robert) Moog
7. (Earl) Tupper
8. (Frank J.) Zamboni
9. (Hans) Geiger
10. (Robert) Bunsen

IT'S ELEMENTARY, page 206

1. Hydrogen
2. Copper
3. Uranium
4. Titanium
5. Krypton
6. Carbon
7. Nobelium
8. Cobalt
9. Silicon
10. Aluminum

IT'S REIGNING DINOSAURS, page 207

1. Dragon bones
2. Birds
3. Care for their young
4. Whether they were warm- or cold-blooded
5. Michael Crichton
6. The Sauroposeidon
7. Tyrannosaurus rex
8. Robert T. Baker
9. Albertosaurus
10. England
11. Velociraptor

YOU BET!, page 208

1. Texas Hold 'em
2. Rabbit or hare
3. *Guys and Dolls*
4. Another card
5. Frogs
6. Monte Carlo
7. Counting cards
8. Siegfried and Roy
9. Royal flush
10. Trifecta
11. 00

AWARDS, page 209

1. Science fiction
2. The Oscar
3. The Medal of Honor
4. The Heisman Memorial Trophy Award
5. The America's Cup, 1851
6. The Purple Heart
7. The Pulitzer Prize
8. The Emmy
9. The Obie
10. The Newbery and the Caldecott

WE DIDN'T HAVE THAT (WHEN I WAS YOUR AGE), page 210

1. Corvette
2. PlayDoh
3. Automated teller machine (ATM)
4. Color TV
5. Credit card
6. Liquid Paper
7. Skateboard
8. Air bag
9. TV remote control
10. Video games

GAMES PEOPLE PLAY, page 211

1. Clue
2. Hungry Hungry Hippos
3. Candy Land
4. Stratego
5. Mah-jongg
6. Mouse Trap
7. Sorry!
8. Risk
9. Parcheesi
10. Backgammon

"MAG"NIFICENT, page 212

1. *TV Guide*
2. *Sports Illustrated*
3. *Better Homes and Gardens*
4. *Good Housekeeping*
5. *Reader's Digest*
6. *Time*
7. *O, the Oprah Magazine*
8. *Cosmopolitan*
9. *Playboy*
10. *Bon Appétit*
11. *Car and Driver*

PLACE YOUR BETS, page 213

1. Foxwoods
2. Luxor
3. Reno, Nevada
4. Bellagio
5. Deadwood
6. Resorts Atlantic City
7. Stratosphere
8. Flamingo
9. Mississippi
10. Casino boat
11. North Carolina

CAN YOU DIG IT?, page 214

1. Archaeologist and professor
2. Lara Croft
3. Agatha Christie
4. Jane Goodall and Dian Fossey
5. Jim Carrey, in *The Mask* (1994)
6. The Rosetta Stone
7. Garbology
8. Benjamin Franklin
9. Jacques Cousteau
10. Carbon-14 dating
11. Kennewick Man

DON'T BE A STRANGER, page 215

1. *Strangers on a Train*
2. Albert Camus' *The Stranger*
3. *Identity*. The words are spoken by host Penn Gillette.
4. *The Stranger* (1946)
5. Billy Joel
6. The Phantom Stranger
7. Seattle
8. Will Ferrell
9. Gena Rowlands
10. "Strangers in the Night"
11. *Perfect Stranger*

FANGS FOR THE MEMORIES, page 216

1. *Dracula* by Bram Stoker
2. Kristy Swanson
3. David Boreanaz
4. Jim Carrey
5. Anne Rice's *Interview with the Vampire*
6. Vampirella
7. Nicolas Cage
8. Blood
9. George Hamilton
10. *Salem's Lot*

HOCUS POCUS, page 217

1. Harry Houdini
2. The Magic Castle
3. David Copperfield
4. *The Magic Show*
5. Card manipulation
6. Thomas Mann
7. Wolfgang Amadeus Mozart
8. Muggles
9. Magic square
10. *The Prestige* (Hugh Jackman and Christian Bale) and *The Illusionist* (Edward Norton)

ON THE RADIO, page 218

1. The Shadow
2. Little Orphan Annie (Ovaltine was the show's sponsor.)
3. *A Prairie Home Companion*
4. Sirius (Howard 100 and Howard 101)
5. *The Grand Ole Opry*
6. Betty Crocker
7. Rin Tin Tin
8. Soap Operas
9. *All Things Considered*
10. Nikola Tesla

Answers

WHEN THE CHIPS ARE DOWN, page 219

1. *Full House*
2. Check
3. Bluff
4. "All hands on deck"
5. Flop
6. Poker face
7. The Joker
8. Kicker
9. Blind
10. Advertising
11. Rainbow

IN THE NEIGHBORHOOD, page 220

1. Herb and Tootsie Woodley
2. Barney and Betty Rubble
3. Robert Frost's "The Mending Wall"
4. John Belushi and Dan Aykroyd
5. Desi and Lucy
6. On Wisteria Lane, you'll find Hatcher (Susan Mayer), Huffman (Lynette Scavo), Cross (Bree Van De Kamp), Longoria (Gabrielle Solis). and Sheridan (Edie Britt).
7. Michael Keaton
8. *Mister Rogers' Neighborhood*
9. Realtors who have made an extraordinary commitment to improving the quality of life in their communities through volunteer work.
10. Kevin Arnold (played by Fred Savage), *The Wonder Years*
11. Noel Crane

A PASSION FOR FASHION, page 221

1. $1.98
2. A rumpled raincoat
3. A leather jacket
4. Capri pants
5. Anne Hathaway
6. Isaac Mizrahi
7. A zip-front cardigan sweater
8. Bruce Lee
9. Kimono
10. A "face bra," to help prevent wrinkles from all that bouncing and stretching

TALES OF REVENGE, page 222

1. *Carrie*
2. *Hamlet*
3. *Moby Dick*
4. "Mad Max"
5. *Wuthering Heights* ("Ellis Bell" was Emily Brontë's pseudonym.)
6. *Kill Bill*
7. *Straw Dogs*
8. John Wayne
9. *Darkman*
10. *Face/Off*

BEATLEMANIA, page 223

1. "Yesterday"
2. Eric Clapton
3. Father McKenzie
4. "Hey Jude"
5. "Ob-La-Di, Ob-La-Da"
6. Billy Preston
7. "I Want To Hold Your Hand"
8. "I Am the Walrus"
9. Beethoven's "Moonlight Sonata"
10. "Something"

NAME THAT TUNEMEISTER, page 224

1. Ludwig van Beethoven
2. *Amadeus*
3. Clara Schumann
4. Tin Pan Alley
5. Bob Marley
6. John Lennon
7. Andrew Lloyd Webber
8. Willie Nelson
9. George Gershwin

ONE-HIT WONDERS, page 225

1. "99 Red Balloons"
2. Rick Dees
3. Right Said Fred
4. Hutch
5. "Don't Worry Be Happy"
6. "Afternoon Delight"
7. He had "Seasons in the Sun"
8. The Sugarhill Gang
9. The Swinging Medallions
10. "Whip It"
11. Talking Heads

CROONERS, page 226

1. Nat King Cole
2. Ed Ames
3. "The Velvet Fog" Mel Tormé
4. Perry Como
5. Dean Martin
6. Engelbert Humperdinck
7. Fred Astaire
8. "When You Wish Upon a Star" (Cliff Edwards)
9. Frank Sinatra
10. Jim Reeves

COUNTRY CLASSICS, page 227

1. Johnny Cash
2. The Carter Family (June Carter Cash was Johnny Cash's wife.)
3. Loretta Lynn
4. Hank Williams
5. Dolly Parton
6. Jimmy Rodgers
7. Minnie Pearl
8. Willie Nelson
9. Tammy Wynnette
10. Patsy Cline

NOVELTY SONGS, page 228

1. The Monster Mash (Bobby "Boris" Pickett and the Krypt-Kickers)
2. "Hello Muddah, Hello Faddah" (Allen Sherman)
3. "They're Coming to Take Me Away Ha-Ha" (Napoleon XIV)
4. An itsy bitsy teenie weenie yellow polka dot bikini. (Brian Hyland)
5. "Beat It" ("Eat It")
6. "The Macarena" (Los Del Rio)
7. Chuck Berry ("My Ding-a-Ling")
8. "Beep Beep!"
9. The Chipmunks
10. A reindeer
11. Barney Google

FICTIONAL BANDS, page 229

1. The Blues Brothers
2. Spinal Tap
3. The Rutles
4. Marty McFly
5. Wyld Stallyns
6. *High Fidelity*
7. Hedwig Robinson
8. The Archies
9. Soggy Bottom Boys
10. *Almost Famous*

MADE FOR A SONG, page 230

1. "Love Potion No. 9"
2. "Coward of the County"
3. *The Indian Runner*
4. *The Legend of Tom Dooley*
5. *Alice's Restaurant*
6. *My Boyfriend's Back*
7. *Ode to Billy Joe*
8. *The Night the Lights Went Out in Georgia*
9. "Take This Job and Shove It"
10. *Yellow Submarine*

KEEP YOUR EYE ON THE BIRDIE, page 231

1. Indiana Pacers
2. Crimean War
3. Black Pearl
4. Leavenworth Federal Penitentiary
5. Calamity Jane
6. Robin Quivers
7. Jim Crow laws
8. Hannibal Lecter
9. Skateboarding
10. Homophone
11. The Cowsills

YOU'RE MY INSPIRATION, page 232

1. James Bond
2. *Alice in Wonderland*
3. Robinson Crusoe
4. *The Big Lebowski*
5. Sherlock Holmes
6. *Dracula*
7. Victor Frankenstein
8. *The Fugitive*
9. Hannibal Lecter

DR. WHO?, page 233

1. Dr Pepper
2. *Dr. Zhivago*
3. Dr. Seuss
4. Dr. Scholl
5. Dr. Hook and the Medicine Show
6. Dr. Jekyll
7. Dr. Denton's
8. *Dr. Strangelove*
9. *Dr. Kildare*
10. Dr. Johnny Fever
11. Dr. (Benjamin) Spock

COMIC PERSONAS, page 234

1. Dan Aykroyd
2. Jackie Gleason
3. Dana Carvey
4. Jamie Foxx
5. Rick Moranis

6. Lily Tomlin
7. Tracey Ullman
8. Jonathan Winters
9. Ruth Buzzi
10. Flip Wilson

THE MOTHER LODE, page 235

1. Rosa Parks
2. Mother Superior
3. Mary Harris Jones, known as Mother Jones
4. The storm petrel, which early sailors thought was a sign of oncoming storms.

5. Mother Hubbard
6. Nacre
7. Mother Goose
8. Mother Shipton
9. Mary Wollstonecraft
10. Motherwort
11. Mother Teresa

WHAT A WAY TO GO, page 236

1. Sir Francis Bacon
2. Leon Trotsky
3. Aeschlyus
4. Jim Fixx
5. Grigori Rasputin

6. Jack Daniels
7. Attila the Hun
8. The United States
9. Wild Bill Hickok
10. In his bathtub

FUNNY GUYS, page 237

1. Henny Youngman
2. Rodney Dangerfield
3. Jack Benny
4. Steve Martin
5. Abbott & Costello

6. Jimmy Durante
7. Jackie Gleason
8. Don Rickles
9. The Smothers Brothers
10. Groucho Marx

WOMB MATES, page 238

1. Barbara and Jenna Bush
2. Romulus and Remus
3. Arnold Schwarzenegger and Danny DeVito
4. Metrodome
5. Doublemint
6. Home permanent kits
7. Mary-Kate and Ashley Olsen
8. Ann Landers and Abigail Van Buren
9. *Antiques Roadshow*
10. William Shakespeare

COLORFUL CELEBS, page 239

1. Jack Black
2. Al Green
3. Pink
4. Joel Grey
5. Amy Tan
6. James Brown
7. Ron White
8. Blue Man Group
9. Ultraviolet
10. Red Skelton

POOR LITTLE RICH KIDS, page 240

1. Peter I
2. China
3. Corey Feldman
4. "Poor Little Rich Girl"
5. Louis XVII of France
6. Franklin Delano Roosevelt
7. His nephews
8. Epilepsy
9. *Mommie Dearest*
10. Judy Garland
11. Queen Christina

ROBBING THE CRADLE, page 241

1. *How Stella Got Her Groove Back*
2. *Atlantic City*
3. "Bagel boy"
4. *Sabrina*
5. Bo and John Derek
6. Joan Collins
7. Tony Randall
8. Clint Eastwood
9. Charlie Chaplin and Oona O'Neill
10. Cary Grant

WHO SAID IT?, page 242

1. Alfred Hitchcock
2. Henry Kissinger
3. Franklin Delano Roosevelt
4. Thomas Edison
5. Mark Twain
6. Oscar Wilde
7. Yogi Berra
8. Sir Winston Churchill
9. Alexander Pope
10. Samuel F. B. Morse
11. Henry David Thoreau
12. Thomas Jefferson

FIRST IMPRESSIONS, page 243

1. The first African-American woman in space
2. Isabel Peron (president of Argentina)
3. Augustus (ca. 27 BC)
4. Swim the English Channel, in 1926
5. Nelson Mandela
6. He was first to climb Mount Everest, with Sir Edmund Hillary, in 1953.
7. Virginia Dare (Roanoke Island, Virginia)
8. *Sputnik 1*, in 1957
9. William Henry Harrison, the 9th president, in 1841
10. John Jay (1789)
11. *Life on the Mississippi* (1883), by Mark Twain
12. Edith Wharton, for *The Age of Innocence*
13. John Fitzgerald Kennedy
14. The United States of America

SILVER-SPOON SWEETIES, page 244

1. *The Simple Life*
2. The Symbionese Liberation Army
3. Camilla Parker Bowes
4. Romanov
5. Ivanka Trump
6. Richard Branson
7. Princess Stephanie
8. Grace Kelly
9. Wal-Mart
10. Christina Onassis

MR. MOMS, page 245

1. Jon Voight
2. Martin Sheen
3. Bruce Dern
4. John Drew Barrymore, Jr.
5. Tony Curtis
6. Kirk Douglas
7. Eddie Fisher
8. John Carradine
9. Francis Ford Coppola
10. Danny Thomas
11. Will Smith

LADIES FIRST, page 246

1. Dolley Madison
2. Abigail Adams
3. Florence Kling Harding
4. An insane asylum
5. Jacqueline Kennedy
6. Eleanor Roosevelt
7. Beautification of America
8. The Betty Ford Center
9. "A Tour of the White House with Mrs. John F. Kennedy"
10. *Hellcats of the Navy*
11. *Millie's Book*
12. "Just Say No"

BIG-CITY FOLK, page 247

1. "Stone Cold" Steve Austin (Texas)
2. Johnny Knoxville (Tennessee)
3. Charlotte Rae (North Carolina)
4. Whitney Houston (Texas)
5. Cleveland Brown (Ohio)
6. Janet Reno (Nevada)
7. Nathan Detroit (Michigan)
8. John Denver (Colorado)
9. River Phoenix (Arizona)
10. Donna Fargo (North Dakota)
11. Eugene Levy (Oregon)

DYNAMIC DUOS, page 248

1. Cain and Abel
2. Rodgers and Hammerstein
3. Sonny and Cher
4. Siskel and Ebert
5. Abbott and Costello. (The skit: "Who's on First?")
6. "Love and Marriage"
7. Penn and Teller
8. Sacco and Vanzetti
9. Bert and Ernie
10. *Amos & Andy*

KIDNAPPED!, page 249

1. John Paul Getty III
2. Robert Louis Stevenson
3. Aimee Semple McPherson
4. Patty Hearst; Tania
5. Bruno Hauptmann
6. Eyeglasses
7. Aldo Moro
8. John Walsh
9. *The Runaway Bride*

SEEING DOUBLE, page 250

1. Brett Butler
2. Dave Thomas
3. Bob Smith
4. Winston Churchill
5. John Madden
6. Paul Simon
7. Tiny Tim
8. David Copperfield
9. Francis Bacon
10. Tom Jones

ZZ TOPICS, page 251

1. Pizza
2. Chazz Palminteri
3. Hazzard County
4. Fizzies
5. Ozzie and Harriet
6. The Gas Guzzler Tax
7. Eddie Izzard
8. "Jazzman"
9. Tin Lizzie
10. Swizzle stick
11. Mezzanine

BOYS WILL BE BOYS, page 252

1. Chef Boyardee
2. *The Blue Boy*
3. Big Boy
4. Boy George
5. Little Boy
6. Pretty Boy Floyd
7. The Hardy Boys
8. *The Boys from Brazil*
9. *Boyz n the Hood*
10. Boy, girl, boy, girl
11. Poor boy, or po'boy

INITIAL IDEAS, page 253

1. Break dancing
2. Alex Rodriguez
3. Government
4. Kathy Griffin
5. Eat them
6. Orange
7. V-chip
8. *The X-Files*
9. O-ring
10. T-shirt
11. Harvard

LET'S DO "UNCH", page 254

1. Brunch
2. *The Wild Bunch*
3. Edvard Munch
4. Hawaiian Punch
5. Nestlé Crunch
6. *The Brady Bunch*
7. Truncheon
8. Cowpuncher
9. Ralph Bunche
10. Baron Munchausen
11. Cap'n Crunch
12. *Play Your Hunch*

CAN I GET BACK TO U?, page 255

1. Kathmandu
2. Cordon Bleu
3. Honolulu
4. Malibu
5. Emu
6. "Nanu-nanu!"
7. Bayou
8. Tiramisu
9. Haiku
10. Machu Picchu
11. Shamu

"X" MARKS THE SPOT, page 256

1. An anticlimax
2. Babe the Blue Ox
3. Redd Foxx
4. Brer Fox
5. Chatterbox
6. Saint Croix
7. Beeswax
8. Unorthodox
9. Coccyx
10. Castor and Pollux
11. Matthew Fox (*Lost*)
12. Jack-in-the-Box

LEND ME YOUR "EAR"S, page 257

1. Amelia Earhart
2. In arrears
3. Beverly Cleary
4. Bluebeard
5. *Fear Factor*
6. King Lear
7. Britney Spears
8. Beardless
9. Dearborn, Michigan
10. Mrs. O'Leary's cow
11. Calendar year
12. *Terms of Endearment*

FROM C TO SHINING C, page 258

1. Cadillac
2. Cambric
3. Cenozoic
4. Celtic
5. Chic
6. Chauvinistic
7. *Cyrano de Bergerac*
8. Czech Republic
9. Cognac
10. Cajun music
11. Cul-de-sac
12. Choleric

THE FIRST AND "L"AST, page 259

1. *License to Kill*
2. "Last call!"
3. Lemon peel
4. Lovin' Spoonful
5. "Let's get physical."
6. Lincoln Memorial
7. *Life Is Beautiful*
8. "Love conquers all"
9. Lackadaisical
10. Liverpool
11. Lauren Bacall
12. Lewis Carroll

GONE TO "POT", page 260

1. Mr. Potato Head
2. Sweet spot
3. Truman Capote
4. Potpourri
5. Apothecary
6. Beatrix Potter
7. Hippopotamus
8. Despot or potentate
9. Mesopotamia
10. Hypotenuse
11. Potemkin village

PEEKABOO! I-C-U-!, page 261

1. Cur<u>ricu</u>lum
2. Man<u>icu</u>re or ped<u>icu</u>re
3. Curl<u>icue</u>
4. Copern<u>icus</u>
5. Ep<u>icure</u>
6. Fist<u>icu</u>ffs
7. Part<u>icu</u>lars
8. Rid<u>icu</u>le
9. Mod<u>icu</u>m
10. Met<u>icu</u>lous
11. Hort<u>icu</u>lture
12. F<u>icu</u>s

LAND HO!, page 262

1. "Land of Lincoln"
2. Grover Cleveland
3. Edwin H. Land (Polaroid Land camera)
4. Landmark
5. Disneyland
6. Hinterland(s)
7. Jill Ireland
8. Legoland
9. Landscape (art)
10. Eland
11. "The Waste Land"
12. Judy Garland

M'M! M'M! GOOD!, page 263

1. Magnum
2. Marryin' Sam
3. Mayhem
4. Magnesium
5. Macrocosm
6. Mia Hamm
7. Malapropism
8. My Maidenform
9. The Magic Kingdom
10. Machiavellianism
11. Meerschaum

"SIT"TING PRETTY, page 264

1. <u>Sit</u>com
2. Curio<u>sit</u>y
3. <u>Sit</u>ting duck
4. In tran<u>sit</u>
5. A fence-<u>sit</u>ter
6. Propen<u>sit</u>y
7. <u>Sit</u>ka
8. Edith <u>Sit</u>well
9. Til<u>sit</u>
10. He<u>sit</u>ate
11. Prepo<u>sit</u>ional
12. <u>Sit</u>z

WORDS THAT DON'T MEAN WHAT THEY SAY, page 265

1. Rodent—a large ground squirrel
2. Sheep or goats
3. November
4. 116 years
5. Ecuador
6. Marsupial
7. The head
8. Gray
9. Baleen, a keratinous (horny) substance
10. They're cephalopods (or mollusks), related to squids and octopuses.
11. Dogs. The Latin word for dog, or canine, is *canus*.
12. Bright orange, to help make it easier to locate in wreckage.

DOUBLE DOT, page 266

1. Hawaii
2. Jigsaw (jigsaw)
3. Shiitake
4. Skiing
5. Fajita
6. Mt. Fuji
7. Demijohn
8. Basenji
9. Thingamajig

TO COIN A PHRASE, PAGE 267

1. George Orwell
2. Black hole
3. Lewis Carroll
4. Gelett Burgess
5. Samuel Taylor Coleridge
6. "The Jazz Age"
7. *R.U.R.* (for "Rossum's Universal Robots")
8. Vaccine
9. The Grand Slam
10. Theodore Roosevelt

R & R, page 268

1. Roman ruins
2. Road rage
3. Rat race
4. Rough Riders
5. Russian roulette
6. Robert Redford
7. Ruff and Reddy
8. Round robin
9. Relay race
10. Ray Romano
11. *Reading Rainbow*

ROYAL FLUSH, page 269

1. Dairy Queen
2. Jack-of-all-trades
3. "Dancing Queen"
4. "King of the Road"
5. A king's ransom
6. *Queen for a Day*

7. The *African Queen*
8. King salmon
9. Jack Russell terrier
10. Jack Tripper
11. King Kong

SON OF ALPHABET SOUP, page 270

1. "Fouled" Up Beyond All Repair
2. Not in My Back Yard
3. White Anglo-Saxon Protestant
4. Rolling On (the) Floor Laughing My Ass Off
5. Ordered a Quarter Pounder with Cheese, a McDonald's trademark, at Kentucky Fried Chicken
6. Uniform Resource Locator—basically, an Internet address
7. Standing Room Only

8. *Répondez s'il-vous-plaît* (reply, please)
9. Hybrid Electric Vehicle (such as a Toyota Prius)
10. (National Aeronautics and Space) Administration
11. It's redundant—ATM means Automated Teller Machine.
12. Bathroom Readers' Institute—hey, that's us!

TAKE A LETTER, page 271

1. Employees
2. Stock
3. Normal
4. Indigo
5. Breathing
6. Programming

7. Tactics
8. Exporting
9. Mining
10. Home
11. Emission
12. Camshafts

"EX" MARKS THE SPOT, PAGE 272

1. Extrovert
2. Extravaganza
3. Cineplex or multiplex
4. Playtex
5. Excalibur
6. Alex Haley

7. Pyrex
8. *Oedipus Rex*
9. Inflexible
10. The Orient Express
11. Exodus
12. Expressionism

IT'S HIGH TIME, page 273

1. *Hang 'Em High*
2. High fashion
3. High Point
4. High-rise
5. "High on the hog"
6. High rollers
7. Highboy
8. *High Fidelity*
9. High tea
10. High and dry
11. High jump

DO I HAVE TO S-P-E-L-L IT OUT?, page 274

1. 4 = Quarts in a Gallon
2. *101 Dalmations*
3. 13 = Original Colonies
4. 1 Day at a Time
5. 4 Wheels on a Car
6. 7 Deadly Sins
7. 1 Singular Sensation
8. 8 = Sides on a Stop Sign
9. 18 = Holes on a Golf Course
10. 6 = Wives of Henry the Eighth
11. 9 = Lives of a Cat
12. 5 = Digits in a Zip Code

MY FAVORITE MARTIN, page 275

1. "It makes me spill my martini."
2. Martinique
3. Martinmas
4. Steve Martin
5. Martina Navratilova
6. Martin Van Buren, the 8th president of the U.S.
7. A three-martini lunch
8. Dr. Martin Luther King (35 years old)
9. The Aston Martin DB5
10. The Martin Guitar Company
11. Dean Martin, who boxed under the name "Kid Crocett"
12. Martin Scorsese, for *The Departed*

TAKE MY LEAVE, page 276

1. Tea leaves
2. Gold leaf foil
3. *Leaves of Grass*
4. The Family and Medical Leave Act of 1993
5. "Leaves of three, let them be."
6. *Leave It to Beaver*
7. Toronto Maple Leafs (NHL)
8. Shore leave
9. *Leave Her to Heaven*
10. Fig leaves (Adam and Eve)
11. Leaf Phoenix

BELOW SEE LEVEL, page 277

1. Rabbit
2. H. G. Wells
3. An invisibility cloak
4. Fantastic Four
5. Ralph Ellison
6. *Pete's Dragon*
7. Genesis
8. Chevy Chase
9. Robert Cormier
10. Wonder Woman
11. The invisible hand

BIG RED, page 278

1. Red Buttons
2. Red Ryder
3. The Red Hat Society
4. Red velvet cake
5. "Red River Valley"
6. Red Skelton
7. Red-letter day
8. Red Rock Canyon
9. "Red Rubber Ball"
10. Red dwarf
11. Red Card

WHAT'S THE WORD FOR THAT?, page 279

1. A cranny is a crack or slit; a nook is a corner.
2. The weft is the yarn that is threaded over and under the parallel warp strands.
3. Oxymoron
4. A wino is a drunk; an oenophile is a wine connoisseur.
5. A bibliophile collects rare books; a bibliopole sells them.
6. Brunch; motel
7. Oprah (Winfrey)
8. Homonyms
9. Antonyms
10. Palindrome
11. Anagram
12. Simile

WHAT'S IN A (NICK)NAME?, page 280

1. Foggy Bottom
2. Genghis Khan
3. Pelé
4. The Ragin' Cajun
5. The Little Corporal
6. The Bambino
7. The Oomph Girl
8. The Velvet Fog
9. The Critic You Love to Hate
10. The Boop-Boop-A-Doop Girl
11. Minnesota Fats
12. The Tennessee Plowboy

THERE'S A WORD FOR IT, page 281

1. A Bowie knife
2. Coors beer
3. Not very wet; it's a sandstorm.
4. No—that's oil.
5. That would be chewing tobacco.
6. Maybe—it's grits.
7. An outfit of matching white belt and shoes, perhaps worn with a powder-blue leisure suit, per the *New York Times*.
8. A chestful of medals
9. An armadillo
10. Yes. It's a rich dessert with gooey chocolate filling on top of a graham-cracker crust, and usually served with ice cream.
11. Possibly—it's cheap wine or beer in a brown paper bag.
12. No. Camp Cupcake is the name for Alderson Federal Prison Camp in West Virginia, where Martha Stewart did time.
13. Broadway, New York, New York
14. The New York Yankees
15. Boston, Massachusetts

YOU DON'T KNOW "JACK", page 282

1. *Jackass*
2. Cracker Jack
3. Applejack
4. Blackjack
5. Jackrabbit
6. Steeplejack
7. Jackknife
8. Jackhammer
9. Skipjacks
10. Flapjack
11. Jackpot

DEM BONES, page 283

1. The neck bone
2. Tyrannosaurus rex
3. Bonie Moronie
4. Jolly Roger
5. Smithsonian Institute
6. Kneecap
7. Yale University
8. *The Lovely Bones*
9. Boneyard
10. Satellite
11. Leonard McCoy
12. Ossuary

NEVER TICKLE A SLEEPING DRAGON, page 284

1. Draco Malfoy
2. Spanish
3. Saint George
4. Jackie Paper
5. 2012

6. Dungeons & Dragons
7. *The Hobbit*
8. Komodo dragon
9. *Beowulf*
10. Dragon lady

B & W, page 285

1. Black
2. Oreos
3. Cream
4. Milton Berle
5. Deng Xiaoping
6. Police cruisers

7. "Ebony and Ivory"
8. All four hooves
9. The *New York Times*
10. M. C. Escher
11. Black and White Whiskey

TO SUM THINGS UP . . . , page 286

1. Escalator
2. Necktie
3. Light bulb
4. Key
5. Shovel

6. Bagpipe
7. Snowshoe
8. Hurdle
9. Fire hydrant
10. Stapler

GAME, SET, MATCH, page 287

1. Set
2. *Paris Match*
3. Set
4. War Game
5. Game
6. Match.com
7. Set

8. *The Little Match Girl*
9. A set
10. "The Match King"
11. *The Match Game*
12. An outdoor treasure-hunting game using GPS (global positioning system) devices

GET OUTTA HERE, page 288

1. Dwight D. Eisenhower
2. Candy Cane
3. *Explorer*
4. Ventricle
5. Earthquake
6. Buffalo Jill

7. Arequipa
8. Bear
9. Italian
10. Buffalo Bills
11. Aruba
12. Music for the ceremony

SQUARESVILLE, page 289

1. Times Square
2. *Hollywood Squares*
3. Brown
4. Square dancing
5. Square one
6. 12 is the square root of 144

7. Tiananmen Square
8. San Francisco 49ers
9. *Square Pegs*
10. Trafalgar Square
11. Madison Square Garden
12. Harvard Square

SOME FOURS, page 290

1. Four Corners
2. Four bits
3. The Fab Four
4. Four-leaf clover
5. Petits fours
6. Four-star general

7. The Gang of Four
8. *1984*
9. Two-by-four
10. Four-flusher
11. 4-H (Club)
12. The Final Four (basketball)

A "LITTLE" THIS & THAT, page 291

1. Little Rock, Arkansas
2. "The Little Drummer Boy"
3. Our Gang
4. *Little Men*
5. Lakota, Sioux, Arapaho, and Cheyenne

6. Little Deuce Coupe
7. Copenhagen, Denmark
8. *The Little Shop of Horrors*
9. Little Richard
10. Bette Davis
11. Little Caesars

APPLES & ORANGES, page 292

1. Gwyneth Paltrow
2. Isaac Newton
3. The College of William & Mary
4. Snapple
5. A knock-knock joke
6. *1984*
7. Disneyland
8. Cartilage
9. Agent Orange
10. *A Clockwork Orange*
11. Johnny Appleseed

TIME TRAVELERS, page 293

1. Donnie Darko
2. *Quantum Leap*
3. *Slaughterhouse-Five*
4. H. G. Wells
5. Mark Twain (The book is *A Connecticut Yankee in King Arthur's Court*.)
6. *Dr. Who*
7. *Groundhog Day*
8. *Time Bandits*
9. *The Time Traveler's Wife*
10. *Voyagers*

HAIR APPARENT, page 294

1. He is a barber.
2. The witch or sorceress who had imprisoned her.
3. Melanin
4. A queue
5. 30 days
6. Hurons
7. Two of the four: Roosevelt (mustached) and Lincoln (beard); Washington and Jefferson are clean-shaven.
8. The pompadour
9. Men
10. Filming a Pepsi commercial
11. Diane Keaton
12. Blondes, followed by brunettes

HATS OFF!, page 295

1. A tricorn hat
2. A boater
3. A derby
4. A deerstalker cap
5. The Homburg, after the town of Bad Homburg
6. The cloche
7. A top hat
8. The ten-gallon hat
9. The zucchetto
10. A milliner
11. Jacqueline Kennedy
12. A beret

IT'S BIBLICAL, KIND OF, page 296

1. Genesis
2. Jeremiah
3. Judges
4. *Exodus*
5. *Amos n' Andy*
6. Daniel
7. Ruth's Chris Steak House
8. Esther Williams
9. James
10. Mark Spitz
11. Luke McCoy

IT'LL REALLY MOVE YOU, page 297

1. Paul Bunyan's Babe, the Blue Ox
2. HMS *Beagle*
3. The USS *Caine*, in Wouk's *The Caine Mutiny*
4. "The General Lee"
5. *Moonraker*
6. Pecos Bill
7. The magic carpet
8. The *Flying Dutchman*
9. Calypso or *Calypso*
10. High Street

A LITTLE OF EVERYTHING, page 298

1. Benjamin Franklin. Richard Saunders was the "Poor Richard" of *Poor Richard's Almanack.*
2. "People's car"
3. The colors of the optical spectrum—red, orange, yellow, green, blue, indigo, violet
4. Grover's Corners
5. Christmas
6. Aeronautics [National Aeronautics and Space Administration]
7. Fear of peanut butter sticking to the roof of the mouth
8. Explorer-1
9. January 20th
10. David Letterman's
11. A giant baseball bat, leaning against the Louisville Slugger Museum
12. Dinah Washington
13. The owner before Elvis, Ruth Brown, named it for her aunt, Grace Toof.

ON THE STREET WHERE YOU LIVE, page 299

1. Backstreet Boys
2. Sesame Street
3. The Baker Street Irregulars
4. Della Street
5. Easy Street
6. Sydney Greenstreet
7. Elizabeth Barrett and Robert Browning
8. *Main Street*
9. *Mean Streets*
10. Picabo Street

"FRANK"LY, MY DEAR, page 300

1. Frank Sinatra
2. Frank Lloyd Wright
3. The New Deal
4. Mary Shelley's *Frankenstein*
5. The frankfurter
6. Attilla the Hun
7. Franking privilege
8. Frank L. Baum
9. The Franklin stove
10. The Franklin Mint
11. *The Diary of a Young Girl* by Anne Frank

LIVING IN THE MATERIAL WORLD, page 301

1. Velour
2. Nylon
3. Burlap
4. Flannel
5. Calico
6. Felt
7. Cashmere
8. Spandex
9. Mohair
10. Silk

IF THE SHOE FITS . . . , page 302

1. Stiletto
2. Flip-flops or thongs
3. Loafers
4. Espadrilles
5. Sneakers, or tennis shoes
6. Galoshes
7. Platform shoes
8. Rubber soles
9. Ferragamo, Gucci, and Prada
10. A dime

OOH! THAT STINGS!, page 303

1. *The Sting*
2. *The Grifters*
3. Leonardo DiCaprio
4. *Law and Order: Criminal Intent*
5. James "Sawyer" Ford is a con artist, as are Paulo and his girlfriend Nikki.
6. Tom Ripley (e.g., in *The Talented Mr. Ripley*)
7. *Sgt. Bilko*
8. *Pinocchio.* They're the ones who tempt Pinocchio into trouble.
9. George C. Scott
10. Mr. Haney

FLOWERY WRITING, page 304

1. Rosemary
2. Robert Burns
3. Hemlock
4. A Venus flytrap
5. "The Daffodils"
6. A pink carnation
7. Katherine Hepburn
8. Poppies
9. Daisy
10. Tiger Lily
11. A sled
12. *Steel Magnolias*

WHEELS OF FORTUNE, page 305

1. Mercedes-Benz
2. Rolls Royce
3. Aston Martin
4. BMW
5. Corvette
6. Volkswagen
7. Lamborghini
8. Cadillac
9. Bugatti
10. Sweden
11. Lexus (Toyota)

CLOSE ENOUGH, page 306

1. 210 (160–260 OK)
2. 142 (92–192 OK)
3. 436 (386–486 OK)
4. $150 ($100–$200 OK)
5. 160 (110–210 OK)
6. 167 (117–217 OK)
7. $225 ($175–$275 OK)
8. 370 (320–420 OK)
9. 168 (118–218 OK)
10. 342 (292–392 OK)
11. 1902 (1852–1952 OK)
12. 1,028 (978–1,078 OK)

SOUNDS A BIT LIKE BOWLING TO ME, page 307

1. Pocket veto
2. Captain Hook
3. Nathan Lane
4. Tin Pan Alley
5. "Brother, Can You Spare a Dime?"
6. Turkey Trot
7. "Strike while the iron is hot."
8. Brooklyn Dodgers
9. Picture frame
10. Lofts
11. Guttermouth

AS GOOD AS GOLD, page 308

1. Fool's gold
2. The Gold Coast
3. The Golden Bear
4. Goldeneye
5. The Golden Jet
6. The Golden Knights
7. J. C. Penney
8. The Goldfish Club
9. Paul Hornung
10. *Father Murphy*
11. Barry Goldwater (AuH_2O)

FOR CRYING OUT LOUD!, page 309

1. Crocodile tears
2. "Jesus wept."
3. Lacrimal gland
4. William Shakespeare, in *King Henry the Sixth*
5. Niobe
6. "My Old Kentucky Home"
7. Edmund S. Muskie
8. The Mock Turtle
9. Holden Caulfield, in *The Catcher in the Rye*
10. *The Crying of Lot 49*
11. Silver

WE'RE NUMBER TWO!, page 310

1. K2
2. The albatross
3. The Amazon
4. *West Side Story*
5. Saturn
6. Missouri
7. Elvis Presley
8. Argentina
9. India
10. Michigan

IT'S GREEK TO ME, page 311

1. Hades
2. Mount Olympus
3. Ambrosia
4. Atlas
5. Athena
6. Poseidon
7. Eros
8. Apollo
9. Gaia
10. A fennel plant
11. The Parthenon
12. Hera

IT'S NOT EASY BEING GREEN, page 312

1. A "green thumb"
2. *Green Eggs and Ham* by Dr. Seuss
3. The Green Bay Packers
4. The start or resumption of the race
5. Kentucky, famous for its smooth meadowgrass called "bluegrass"
6. Greenpeace
7. Jealousy or envy
8. The offstage waiting room for actors
9. Greenhouse gases
10. Greenhorn
11. Libya
12. Collard greens

ANIMALS ON THE ROAD, page 313

1. Jaguar
2. Hawk
3. Impala
4. Mustangs
5. Ram
6. Road Runner
7. Pinto
8. Rabbit
9. The Fiat Panda
10. Cobra
11. Marlin

IT'S LIKE POULTRY IN MOTION, page 314

1. Chicken Little
2. Hans Christian Andersen
3. Capons
4. *The Wild Duck*
5. Goose egg
6. Chicken, of course! (And frogs' legs.)
7. *Father Goose*
8. The Chinese calendar
9. The Spruce Goose
10. "Chickie run"
11. Mother Goose
12. A roast turkey

SMELLS GOOD, page 315

1. Perfume
2. Chow mein
3. Lemons
4. Doughnuts
5. Garlic
6. Flowers
7. Pie
8. Italian restaurant
9. The mint family
10. An herbal tea
11. Ginger

BOX IT, page 316

1. The soapbox
2. Boxcar Willie
3. Boxing Day
4. "Life is like a box of chocolates." (*Forrest Gump*)
5. Home Box Office (HBO)
6. The black box on an airplane
7. Box office
8. A boombox
9. A box spring
10. A batter's box
11. "Music Box Dancer"

IT'S A NUMBERS GAME, page 317

1. "Billions and billions"
2. 6
3. 0, 1, 8, 11, 69, 88, 96
4. 42
5. Catch-22
6. 867-5309
7. 15
8. 87
9. 14
10. 555 (it's used exclusively in movies and TV shows)
11. 144 (a dozen dozen)
12. 4

TUNNEL VISION, page 318

1. *The Great Escape*
2. The Tunnel of Love
3. Princess Diana, Dode Al-Fayed, and driver Henri Paul were killed when their car crashed into it.
4. *The Time Tunnel*
5. The Chunnel
6. The Shanghai Tunnels
7. A wind tunnel
8. The Lincoln Tunnel and the Holland Tunnel
9. Boston
10. Chesapeake Bay Bridge Tunnel

Happy Birthday, Uncle John!

It's our 20th Anniversary edition— jam-packed with **600 pages** of all-new, absorbing material!

You'll find all your favorites: obscure trivia, strange lawsuits, dumb crooks, origins of everyday things, forgotten history, wordplay, and more. Come celebrate two decades of great throne-room reading with the talented folks at the Bathroom Readers' Institute! Read about...

- The Origin of the Golden Rule
- The Death of the Pay Phone
- How Your Taste Buds Work
- The Real-Life Zorro
- Viewmaster and the 3-D Revolution
- Space Needles, Ferris Wheels, and the Weirdest Structures of All Time
- And much, much more!

On Sale Now!

THE LAST PAGE

FELLOW BATHROOM READERS:
The fight for good bathroom reading should never be taken loosely—we must do our duty and sit firmly for what we believe in, even while the rest of the world is taking pot shots at us.

In brief, now that we've proven we're not simply a flush-in-the-pan, we invite you to take the plunge: Sit Down and Be Counted! Become a member of the Bathroom Readers' Institute. Log on to *www.bathroomreader.com*, or send a self-addressed, stamped, business-sized envelope to: BRI, PO Box 1117, Ashland, Oregon 97520. You'll receive your free membership card, get discounts when ordering directly through the BRI, and earn a permanent spot on the BRI honor roll!

If you like reading our books...
VISIT THE BRI'S WEB SITE!
www.bathroomreader.com

- Visit "The Throne Room"—a great place to read!
  - Receive our irregular newsletters via e-mail
    - Order additional *Bathroom Readers*
      - Become a BRI member

Go with the Flow...

Well, we're out of space, and when you've gotta go, you've gotta go. Tanks for all your support. Hope to hear from you soon.

Keep on flushin'!